IRREVERENT PILGRIMS

The Pilgrim's Vision

IRREVERENT PILGRIMS

Melville, Browne, and
Mark Twain in the Holy Land

BY FRANKLIN WALKER

UNIVERSITY OF WASHINGTON PRESS

SEATTLE AND LONDON

Library of Congress Cataloging in Publication Data

Walker, Franklin Dickerson, 1900–
Irreverent pilgrims.

Includes bibliographical references.
1. Palestine—Description and travel. 2. Browne,
John Ross, 1821–1875. Yusef. 3. Melville, Herman,
1819–1891. Clarel. 4. Clemens, Samuel Langhorne,
1835–1910. The innocents abroad. I. Title.
DS107.W16   811'.3'09   74-10644
ISBN 0-295-95344-6

To my daughter, Susan

Acknowledgments

I SHOULD like to thank the staffs of the University of California at Berkeley Library, the Mills College Library, and the British Museum for aid in producing this study. Among specialized collections, the Mark Twain Papers at the Bancroft Library, University of California, under the generous direction of Frederick Anderson, and the John Ross Browne Papers in the care of Mrs. Lina Fergusson Browne of Berkeley, California, have been most helpful. For advice and aid in writing the book I am indebted to James D. Hart, Imogene Bishop Walker, and James Mitchell Clarke, who suggested the title after I had given up finding anything better than "Three Yanks in the Holy Land."

I should also like to thank the following publishers for permission to quote from copyrighted material: Hendricks House, Inc. for quotations and the use of the map "Jerusalem and Environs" from their edition of Melville's *Clarel*, edited by Walter E. Bezanson (copyright © 1960 by Hendricks House, Inc.); the University of New Mexico Press for quotations on pages 35, 39, 40, 50, 55, 56, 57, 80, and 106 from *J. Ross Browne: His Letters, Journals and Writings*, edited by Lina Fergusson Browne (copyright © 1969 by the University of New Mexico Press); Princeton University Press for quotations from Herman Melville's *Journal of a Visit to Europe and the Levant, October 11, 1856–May 6, 1857*, edited by Howard C.

[viii] *Acknowledgments*

Horsford (copyright © 1955 by Princeton University Press); and the University of Oklahoma Press for quotations from *Traveling with the Innocents Abroad* by Samuel Langhorne Clemens, edited by Daniel Morley McKeithan (copyright © 1958 by the University of Oklahoma Press).

I also gratefully acknowledge permission from Lina Fergusson Browne to use two previously unpublished quotations from Ross Browne and to reproduce six of his sketches (see pages 61, 89, 97, 98, 102, and 104) from *Yusef; or, the Journey of the Frangi* (New York: Harper and Brothers, 1853); and permission from James Chamberlain, President of the Mark Twain Company, to quote an excerpt of approximately 250 words of previously unpublished Mark Twain material copyrighted in the name of the Trustees under the Will of Clara Clemens Samossoud for this purpose.

The frontispiece and illustrations on pages 170, 173, 180, 188, 201, and 215 are reproduced from Samuel L. Clemens *The Innocents Abroad* (Hartford, Conn.: The American Publishing Company, 1901).

FRANKLIN WALKER

Mills College
Oakland, California

Contents

Illustrations

Maps

IRREVERENT PILGRIMS

ONE

Travel in Syria in the Victorian Age

O N 23 November 1851 John Ross Browne arrived by Austrian steamer in Beirut, the principal port of Syria, eager to visit the Holy Land, a long-sought goal in his restless wanderings. Born in Ireland, he had spent his boyhood in Kentucky and his young manhood in Gold Rush California and in Washington, D.C. Early developing a pattern of alternating desk work with wandering, he had already seen much adventure as a beachcomber on the island of Zanzibar and had followed Robinson Crusoe (or Alexander Selkirk) to the island of Juan Fernandez in a cockleshell. In 1846 he had published *Etchings of a Whaling Cruise*, an account of his life before the mast on an American whaler, which was used extensively by Herman Melville while writing *Moby-Dick*, published the year Browne reached the Holy Land.

The thirty-year-old Browne, carrying his flute and his sketchbook with him, was rowed ashore in Beirut and immediately turned his attentions to obtaining a good dragoman to guide himself and his two companions on an overland trek to Jerusalem by way of Damascus. He soon hired Yusef Simon Badra, who turned out to be an unusual character if only an indifferent guide. Browne and his companions, provided with the wretched horses reserved for travelers in the land

[3]

of the Arabian steed, made their way across the Lebanon ranges, on to Damascus, and down to Jerusalem by way of the Sea of Galilee and Nazareth. From Jerusalem they made a side trip to the desert convent Mar Saba, the Dead Sea, the Jordan River, and Jericho. Later, Browne joined other pilgrims in making the trek from Jerusalem to Bethlehem for the Christmas Eve ceremonies. He then returned to the seacoast at Jaffa (now a suburb of Tel Aviv) and there traveled north along the Mediterranean past Mt. Carmel, through the ancient Phoenician seaports, Acre, Tyre, and Sidon, and back to his starting point at Beirut. After completing his circuit of the Holy Land in some forty days (a good biblical time span), Ross Browne sailed for Egypt. Two years later he published *Yusef; or, the Journey of the Frangi: A Crusade in the East*, based on his Syrian experiences.

On 6 January 1857, almost exactly five years to the day after Browne had left Beirut for Egypt, Herman Melville landed at Jaffa, having come as a second-class passenger from Alexandria on another Austrian coastal steamer. (Both Browne and Melville were really roughing it by putting up with second-class accommodations on a Mediterranean steamer of those early days of steam navigation.) The thirty-seven year old Melville had long ago lived with the cannibals on one of the Marquesan Islands in the mid-Pacific and had served as a hand on a Yankee whaler and as an ordinary seaman on the frigate *United States*. After an initial success with such adventure tales as *Typee*, *Omoo*, and *White-Jacket*, he had lived through the ordeal of a cool reception for *Moby-Dick* and a condemnation and rejection of *Pierre* by his formerly faithful reading public. When he left, dejected and ill, for a vacation in Europe and the Levant, he carried with him the manuscript of *The Confidence Man*—the last prose fiction to be published during his lifetime—hoping to place it with a London publisher. Alexander William Kinglake's remark in *Eōthen* concerning Lady Hester Stanhope seems particularly applicable to Melville: "I can hardly tell why it should be, but there is a longing for the East, very commonly felt by proud-hearted people, when goaded by sorrow." [1] Herman Melville, unlike Ross Browne before him and Mark Twain after him, was alone in a land where one did not ordinarily travel alone. Like Browne, he came in the dead of winter but, unlike Browne, he was too late for Christmas in Bethlehem. He at least did not have to put up with the desiccating heat and desert conditions which Mark Twain was to face in late summer a decade later. Melville's diary tells us that he spent only nineteen days in Palestine. His visit did not take him north of ancient Judea; he traveled the rocky trail from Jaffa to Jerusalem in both directions, wandered both inside and outside the walls of the Holy City for several days, and made the circuit to Jericho, the Jordan, the Dead Sea, and Bethlehem in the company of a companion, Frederick Cunningham, with whom he had struck up an acquaintanceship in Jerusalem. On 24 January, once more alone and feeling as lost as Jonah, one of his predecessors in Jaffa—or ancient Joppa—he boarded a steamer for Beirut. If during his short stay in Beirut he visited the Cedars of Lebanon or the impressive ruins of Baalbek, he left no record of it. His contact with the biblical lands was indeed limited. He did not walk the Street called Straight in Damascus, nor watch the women draw water from Mary's Well at Nazareth, nor ponder over the ruins of the palace in Samaria where King Ahab had been confronted by Elijah. Unlike Browne and Mark Twain he sent no travel letters home to the newspapers. But in 1876 he published a narrative poem longer than *Paradise Lost* which he called *Clarel: A Poem and Pilgrimage in the Holy Land.* The poem drew upon his Holy Land visit in great detail, thus supplying a striking background to a verse counterpart of his great whaling novel. Though *Clarel* attracted few readers when it appeared, it has of late come into its own as a remarkable verse narrative.

On 10 September 1867 Mark Twain sailed in style into the harbor of Beirut aboard the nineteen-hundred-ton, side-wheel steamship the *Quaker City*, which was carrying the first floating tour of Americans visiting Europe and the Near East that had ever taken place. Though he was thirty-one years old, Mark Twain still looked upon himself as a journalist rather than an author, for the only book publication to his credit was a collection of frontier stories and burlesques titled *The*

Celebrated Jumping Frog of Calaveras County and Other Sketches.
He was the latecomer among the three travelers under discussion.
While Browne was visiting the Holy Land, "Mark Twain" was still a
boy named Sam Clemens, developed past the Tom Sawyer stage, but
he was not yet the journeyman printer and itinerant journalist who
wandered to St. Louis, Cincinnati, and New York. However, he had
already quit school in Hannibal, Missouri and was contributing
juvenilia to his brother's newspaper. By the time that Melville made
his trip to Jerusalem, Clemens was working as a cub pilot on a
Mississippi River steamboat. By the time Mark Twain turned up in
the Levant as one of "the innocents abroad," he had already
migrated to the Far West. It was in Virginia City, Nevada, and later
in San Francisco that he had earned a nom-de-plume and a lively
reputation as a journalist. He was, in fact, making the trip on the
Quaker City as a correspondent of the West's most prominent daily,
the *San Francisco Alta California.*

With seven companions, accompanied by a dragoman and muleteers, Mark Twain covered in three weeks the same itinerary that
Browne had followed during his forty-day journey, with the exception that Mark Twain rejoined the *Quaker City* at Jaffa and
proceeded to Egypt aboard her, rather than returning along the coast
to Beirut as Browne had done. In many ways his experiences echoed
Browne's, but the sixteen-year period that had elapsed between the
two journeys had brought a considerable change to Syria, although
not nearly so much as the Civil War had brought to America. Ross
Browne had come as one of the last adventurers in Palestine. In a
way he could expect the unexpected as had the Englishman, William
Kinglake of *Eōthen* fame and the impetuous Irishman, Eliot Warburton, of *The Crescent and the Cross*, a few years before him. In 1851
an American traveler in Syria was still something of a rare bird. To
some extent, this was true of Melville six years later, as evidenced by
the fact that he apparently met only one other American traveler in
Jerusalem. But by the time Mark Twain disembarked from the
Quaker City, which carried seventy-odd passengers who were all to
see something of Palestine, conducted tours were soon to be

introduced by Thomas Cook and the "Cookie" with his white-draped hat would soon be a common sight in the land. If one were to indulge in somewhat oversimplified categorizing, one could call Browne the adventurer, Melville the pilgrim, and Mark Twain the tourist. The last, however, was a tourist doing a job. By 1869, two years after his visit, Mark Twain had reworked his newspaper letters into a book: *The Innocents Abroad, or the New Pilgrim's Progress*. It was a great success, initiating Mark Twain's reputation as one of America's leading authors and becoming America's most famous travel book.

John Ross Browne, Herman Melville, and Mark Twain were, of course, far from unique as literary pilgrims to the birthplace of Christianity in the nineteenth century. By the time the first arrived, a good number of European writers, particularly French and English, ranging from Chateaubriand to Harriet Martineau, had left records of their reactions to the Bible Lands during the early 1800s. Nor was Ross Browne the first writer from the United States to tell of a visit to Palestine. Preeminent among his precursors was John Lloyd Stephens, who published his popular *Incidents of Travels in Egypt, Arabia Petraea, and the Holy Land* in 1837. However, Ross Browne's *Yusef* was early enough to establish itself as a pioneer account. It does not seem arbitrary to assert that Browne's *Yusef*, Melville's *Clarel*, and Mark Twain's *The Innocents Abroad* are the three most important literary works to result from American visits to the Holy Land during the nineteenth century or, for that matter, up to the present time.

Though pilgrims had been visiting the Holy Land for some fifteen centuries before the Americans arrived, many of them making the pilgrimage the principal journey of their lives as the Muslims did their journeys to Mecca, it cannot truthfully be said that they sought Palestine for scenic beauty or cultural stimulation. And when the tourists began coming in the nineteenth century they rarely antici-pated beauty or comfort. Rather, they knew that the principal attractions of this small strip of littoral at the eastern end of the Mediterranean were its historical and religious associations. They

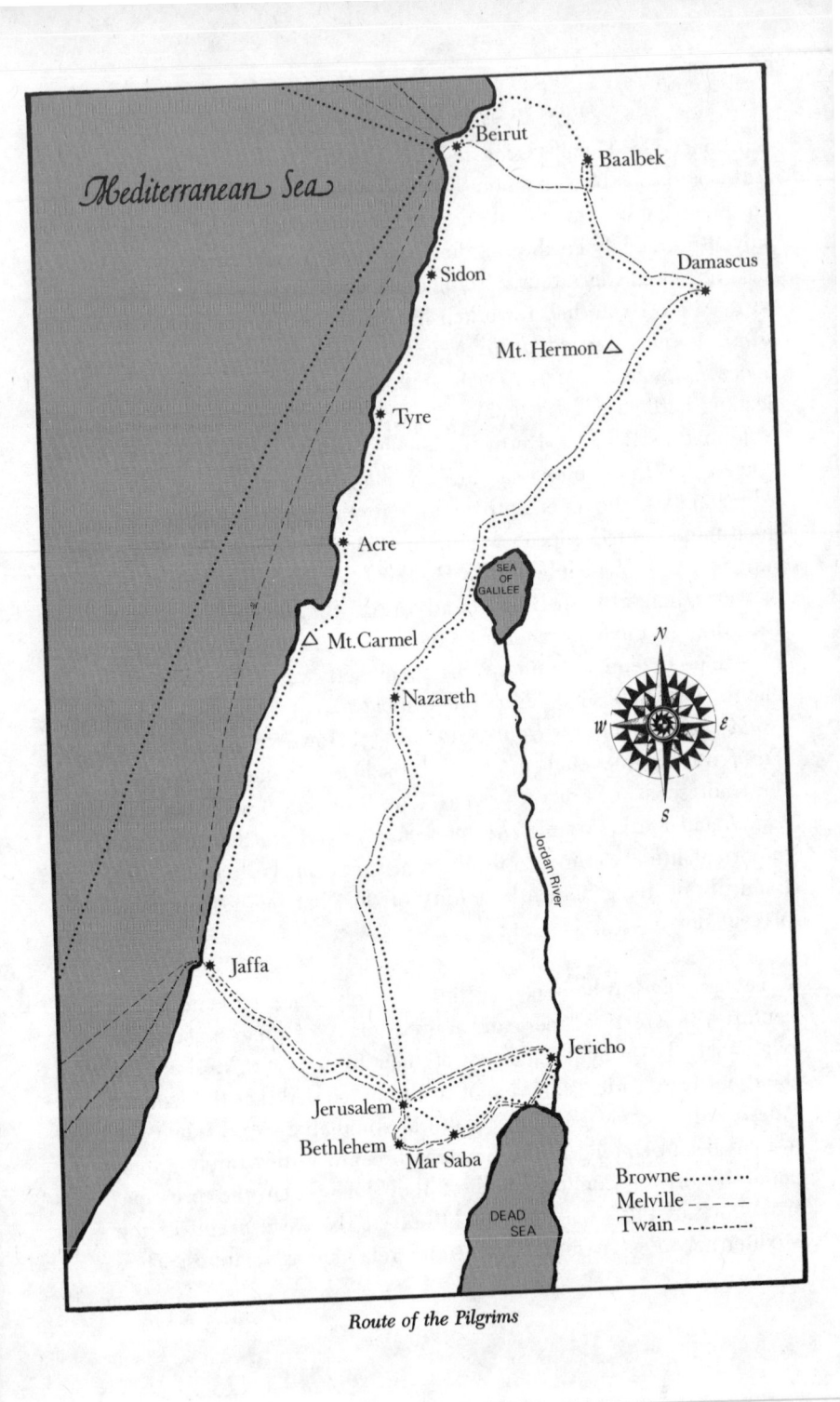

Route of the Pilgrims

were willing, as pilgrims disguised as tourists, to put up with many discomforts so that they might visit spots which they had been hearing about since they were children. The accounts of a score of western travelers such as Kinglake, Warburton, Martineau, Thackeray, and Flaubert from Europe, and John Lloyd Stephens, Bayard Taylor, John William DeForest, George W. Curtis, and William Cullen Bryant from America testify to the typical attitudes of Protestant visitors to the Holy Land during the period under discussion and form an effective background to a portrayal of the experiences and reactions of Ross Browne, Herman Melville, and Mark Twain.

At the beginning of the nineteenth century the portions of Syria which were later to become Lebanon, Israel, and Jordan were backward outposts of the Ottoman Empire, which had had loose control over them for four centuries, but had not developed them. As a result the Palestine hills were bare and rocky, and the valley of the Jordan River and the plains of Esdraelon and Sharon were almost wholly uncultivated and unattractive except for a short while in the spring, when the rains brought green grass and a profusion of flowers. The Arab towns were sprawling clusters of mud huts, and the chief ports, Beirut and Jaffa, offered little protection for either sailing vessels or the newly favored steamships. Haifa, which in time was to become the principal port on the sandy coast, was wholly undeveloped, although Acre, a few miles above it, was used infrequently as a landing place. The only spots where the traveler could anticipate any of the amenities of life were Beirut, Damascus, and Jerusalem. Anytime that he ventured a few miles from these centers, the traveler was subject to the depredations of the Bedouins, the Druses, or even the Turks.

Though Palestine had been a strategic crossroads in earlier times and had even prospered from the movement of caravans between Mesopotamia and Egypt, it had little such traffic during the centuries of Turkish control. What had been once a main highway had become a back trail, not overgrown with weeds but obliterated by rocks. There had been a stir of life when Napoleon, after his conquest of

Egypt, brought his armies as far north as Acre but after the British stopped his advance the life soon died out. The challenge to the Ottoman Empire by the Egyptians under the command of the aggressive Mohammed Ali who, with his son Ibrahim Pasha carried his revolt in 1831 from Turkish control as far north as Damascus, petered out in less than a decade, with the capitulation of the Egyptians to British and French intervention in support of Turkey in 1840. Mohammed Ali's activities had seemed for a moment to bring hope of improvement in the area, but the heavy taxes and conscriptions levied by the intruder had soon put an end to those hopes. The trouble was compounded in 1837 when a disastrous earthquake did much damage to Galilee and nearly destroyed Safed and Tiberias, communities which had long been centers of learning for the Jews.

The 1840s saw a slight improvement in economic conditions in Palestine, with renewed Turkish rule, which proved somewhat more enlightened than earlier, holding back the importunities of the local sheiks to some extent. Little was done, however, to curb the constant hostility between Christian sects over prerogatives at the Holy Shrines; indeed, a long, bitter feud between the Greek Orthodox and Roman Catholic ecclesiastics in the Church of the Nativity at Bethlehem actually became one of the causes of the Crimean War. Wishing to extend its influence, Russia declared itself protector of all Orthodox Christians *in partibus infidelium,* and in particular throughout the Ottoman Empire. The Turks naturally resented this, and expanded Russian hegemony in the Near East was by no means favored either by the British, who saw their passage to India threatened, or by the French, who were now eager for adventure under Napoleon III. The resulting Crimean War was fought entirely on Russian soil on the coast of the Black Sea, far from Palestine, but the renewed concern with the Levant brought better times and a loosening of Turkish restrictions after the peace treaty was signed in 1856. With tourism growing rapidly in Europe, aided particularly by the growth of travel by steam on land and sea, Syria, from Beirut and Damascus in the north to Jerusalem in the south, began to harvest its handful of casual local tourists. However, the Christian massacres of 1860, when fourteen thousand Christians, most of them local Maronites, were slaughtered in Damascus and in the Lebanon, demonstrated that the Muslim world was still no place to hold a relaxed picnic.

The heart of the Holy Land, at various times in history called Canaan, Palestine, and Israel, is a narrow strip of Mediterranean littoral which has been described as the "buckled and foundered western edge of the ancient plateau of Arabia." Some 250 miles long, it lies between a sandy and sometimes cliff-lined coast and the Great Rift, an unusual geological depression which starts near the headwaters of the Jordan River at the foot of Mt. Hermon and continues, slicing deeper and deeper, past the Sea of Galilee until it reaches the Dead Sea, some twelve hundred feet below sea level, and continues to the Gulf of Aqaba. Rarely more than fifty miles wide between the sea and the Jordan Valley, Palestine is made up principally of a spine of rocky hills averaging some two thousand feet in elevation and broken only once—by the valley called the Plain of Esdraelon, extending roughly from a few miles south of the Sea of Galilee (Lake Kinnerat) to the Mediterranean just north of Mt. Carmel. The two main sections of Palestine, Galilee in the north and Judea in the south (with Samaria holding a precarious position in the middle), rest upon a geological arch with precipitous sides toward the Great Rift and more gentle slopes on the west toward the sea. The principal cities famous in biblical stories lie along the spine, from Nazareth in the north past Nablus (Shechem) in the heart of Samaria to Jerusalem, Bethlehem, and Hebron in Judea. These towns experience scattered snow flurries in the winter and drought in the summer. Below them and to the east, the subtropical Jordan Valley experiences summer temperatures as high as 130°. Toward the coast a more temperate Mediterranean climate is to be found.

In the north, Palestine was bordered by Lebanon, with its Phoenician coast where Tyre and Sidon and Byblos had flourished, and its well-wooded, parallel mountain ranges, the Lebanon and Anti-Lebanon. Upon the ranges had once grown the famous cedars, now reduced to a small grove far above Tripoli; in the valley between the ranges lay Baalbek, or ancient Heliopolis, the most famous of ancient ruins of the Syrian area where not only Baal but Apollo had once been worshiped; and across these ranges lay the famous route from Beirut to Damascus on the far side of Mt. Hermon.

To the east of the Jordan River the formidable heights of Golan, Ammon, and Moab rose sharply from the Rift. Down towards Jerusalem they stood like a blue wall which one felt he could almost touch in clear weather. Somewhere on their heights was Mt. Pisgah, from which Moses had seen the Holy Land; hidden in their deep valleys to the south of the Dead Sea was the ancient city of Petra, carved out of the red walls of the canyon by the descendants of Esau. Southern Palestine flattened into the steppes and deserts of the Negev, which was bordered on its western side by the Sinai peninsula with its wild mountains and formidable desert.

From Jaffa south through Ascalon and Gaza and along the curving coast to the Nile, a distance of some two hundred miles, ran the ancient caravan trail linking Syria and Egypt. During the early years of the nineteenth century, an occasional traveler made his way to Palestine by this route and late in the century the newly built railroad made it a principal means of access to the Holy Land. During the days when Browne and Melville and Mark Twain visited the area, however, the most common approach from Egypt was by paddle-wheel steamer from Alexandria to Jaffa. These were mostly Austrian—small, low-pressured boats that hugged the coast and pitched and rocked their ways through fairly frequent squalls. If, on the other hand, the traveler reached Palestine from the north, he usually disembarked at Beirut, crossed the Lebanon ranges to Damascus, and then trekked across the volcanic country at the eastern base of Mt. Hermon to the upper reaches of the Jordan. This approach involved considerable effort and expense and was taken usually only by those who wished to visit Galilee and Samaria as well as Judea.

Whether arriving from the north or from the south, the first task facing a traveler to Palestine was to hire a dragoman to take him through Syria. The dragoman, called by a term which was an adaptation of the Arabic *targuman* meaning "interpreter," and frequently pluralized as "dragomen" by false analogy with "man," was a feature peculiar to the Levant. In Constantinople, as interpreters for foreign ambassadors to the Sublime Porte, dragomen often exerted considerable influence because of their knowledge of the notoriously devious ways of the Ottoman court. Concomitantly, they were sometimes feared as masters of intrigue, an attitude giving rise among the Italians of Pera, the foreign section of Constantinople, to a quip which grouped dragomen with fire and plague as misfortunes frequently encountered:

> *In Pera sonna tre malinni—*
> *Fuoco, peste, dragomanni.*

Throughout the reaches of the Ottoman Empire, dragomen flourished not only as interpreters for consuls but as combined interpreters, guides, and agents for travelers. They were quite indispensable, except for skilled linguists and adventurers like Sir Richard Burton. There was little English or French spoken in Lebanon and Palestine; and, although Italian was the most common European tongue of the area, even it was heard rarely outside of Beirut or Jerusalem. The typical dragoman knew Arabic and Italian, and sometimes Greek. Some were remarkable linguists: for example, William Cullen Bryant's dragoman Emanual Bathas, an Athenian who knew Ancient Greek as well as Aramaic, was fluent in Italian, Turkish, and Arabic, intelligible in French, and was beginning to learn English.

Acting as interpreter was only part of the dragoman's job, however. For travelers going any distance overland, he organized the party, hired horses, mules, donkeys and muleteers, and provided camping equipment, sometimes of the most elaborate nature. He planned the itinerary, bought the provisions, and made arrangements with the local authorities. In addition, he tendered his services as an armed guard, although this function was sometimes more of a gesture than a threat to the Bedouin marauders who were known to bother tourists.

Because of the absence of any public transport, travelers customarily banded together in twos or threes or larger groups, hired a dragoman at what seems today to be a reasonable per capita charge—approximately $5.00 a day—and left it up to him to make all arrangements for transportation, housing, food, protection, and entertainment en route. Most of the travelers in the first half of the century were appreciative of the services provided by their dragomen; they usually spoke well of them in their writings, and, as we have seen, Ross Browne named his book about the Levant after his dragoman, Yusef, and made him the principal character in his narrative. By the time Mark Twain reached Palestine, the dragoman was beginning to lose his indispensability; John Franklin Swift, another San Francisco correspondent who arrived in Jerusalem the same year as Mark Twain, complained in his *Going to Jericho* of the necessity of hiring a dragoman at $7.50 a day per person to accompany his party on a trail to Jerusalem which was already bordered by telegraph poles.

The routes which led down the coast or across the mountains in Syria, sometimes referred to as "roads," were rarely more than rough trails or constantly shifting caravan paths. Even the well-traveled route from Beirut to Damascus was not traversed by a wheeled vehicle until 1861, when a French company established a diligence service over the mountains. Not only were there no wheeled vehicles in Syria before that time, but the horse and camel trails were not systematically maintained and it is doubtful whether travelers found better footing for themselves or their horses than had Marco Polo in the thirteenth century. Though the indefatigable American adventurer John Lloyd Stephens discovered in the mid-1830s that the American consular agent at Jaffa had taken on the responsibility of constructing a road from Jaffa to Jerusalem, Stephens found it to be nothing but a mule path. Thirty years later John Franklin Swift was complaining that he found this same "road" more difficult to travel than any pack trail in California and was sure that no one had cleared away a stone since the times of Abraham and Lot.

Commenting on the route from Bethlehem to Hebron, sites of famous shrines, the Irishman Eliot Warburton wrote:

We pushed forward at a gallop over a wild and rocky tract, where the pathway was scarcely visible among the fragments with which it was thickly strewn: yet this has been a highway from the days of Abraham, and we read of the constant use of chariots along these roads. Now, the way lay over a smooth and slippery rocky surface; now, narrowed between blocks of stone, it was covered with tangled roots, or seamed by wide fissures. All the same to my bold Arab courser seemed smooth turf or rugged rock: eagerly she swept along over hill and hollow, as if it were a pastime; bounding from rock to rock with the ease of a gazelle and the mettle of a bloodhound. The evening was sultry warm, but no stain darkened her silken skin, not a pant escaped from her deep chest, not a spot of foam flecked the Mameluke bit.[2]

However, few dragomen even thought of providing their customers with an Arab steed; these were priceless possessions owned only by wealthy sheiks or provided occasionally for well-heeled sportsmen like Warburton. Most of the trail animals were trustworthy but they plodded along at a tedious pace. The mood of the usual traveler is better caught in a description by John William DeForest, who, in 1846 during a visit to his brother who was serving as a medical missionary in Beirut, set off to reach Jerusalem by the coastal route. "Thus we set out for the holy city. 'God preserve your eyes!' shouted beggars with sore optics or none at all, as we rode by them. 'God help your children!' screamed women, holding out disgusting babies to attract our pecuniary commiseration. 'God give you' roared the unlucky ones who had no ostensible title to pity except their dirt and tatters. 'O God!' shouted the servants, as they urged each other to hasten. 'God!' yelled the muleteers to their stumbling donkeys!" [3]

DeForest, who had the advantage of learning from his brother and his other acquaintances in the Beirut area that the dangers of travel in the Levant were often exaggerated, boasted that he went from Jerusalem to Jericho without any firearms, "not even the jawbone of an ass." His attitude, however, was not typical, and almost all European travelers in the area bore arms, even if they knew little about using them. The frame of mind of the novice is well illustrated by the behavior of a lone Englishman, who had presumably wandered from his party, whom Bayard Taylor met on the coast road to Jaffa. Bayard Taylor, like Warburton, wore Arabian clothes, since they were best suited to the climate and thus he looked like an Arab to the startled Englishman.

Towards evening, as Mr. H. and myself, with François [the dragoman], were riding in advance of the baggage mules, the former with his gun in his hand, I with a pair of pistols thrust through the folds of my shawl, and François with his long Turkish sabre, we came suddenly upon a lonely Englishman, whose companions were somewhere in the rear. He appeared to be struck with terror on seeing us making towards him, and, turning his horse's head, made an attempt to fly. The animal, however, was restive, and, after a few plunges, refused to move. The traveler gave himself up for lost; his arms dropped by his side; he stared wildly at us, with pale face and eyes opened wide with a look of helpless fright. Restraining with difficulty a shout of laughter, I said to him: "Did you leave Jaffa today?" but so completely was his ear the fool of his imagination, that he thought I was speaking Arabic, and made a faint attempt to get out the only word or two of that language which he knew. I then repeated, with as much distinctness as I could command: "Did-you-leave-Jaffa-today?" He stammered mechanically, through his chattering teeth, "Y-y-yes!" and we immediately dashed off at a gallop through the bushes. When we last saw him, he was standing as we left him, apparently not yet recovered from the shock.[4]

This Englishman was surely of a different breed than Alexander William Kinglake, who tells in *Eōthen* of his remarkable behavior on meeting a camel-borne Arab while crossing the desert between Cairo and Suez on his way to Palestine in 1835. Mounted on a swift dromedary, Kinglake had impatiently pushed ahead of his caravan and soon found himself lost, "alone and unprovisioned in the midst of the arid waste." Realizing that his best move was to trek eastward as rapidly as possible on the assumption that he would eventually reach the Red Sea, he continued unperturbed except for his growing thirst.

For several hours I urged forward my beast at a rapid though steady pace, but now the pangs of thirst began to torment me. I did not relax my pace, however, and I had not suffered long, when a moving object appeared in the distance before me. The intervening space was soon traversed, and I found myself approaching a Bedouin Arab mounted on a camel, attended by another Bedouin on foot. They stopped. I saw that, as usual, there hung from the pack-saddle of the camel a large skin water flask which seemed well filled; I steered my dromedary close up alongside of the mounted Bedouin,

caused my beast to kneel down, then alighted, and keeping the end of the
halter in my hand, went up to the mounted Bedouin without speaking, took
hold of his water flask, opened it, and drank long and deep from its leathern
lips. Both of the Bedouins stood fast in amazement and mute horror, and
really if they had never happened to see a European before, the apparition
was enough to startle them. To see for the first time a coat and a waistcoat
with the pale semblance of a human head at the top, and for this ghastly
figure to come swiftly out of the horizon, upon a fleet dromedary—approach
them silently, and with a demoniacal smile, and drink a deep draft from their
water flask—this was enough to make the Bedouins stare a little: they, in
fact, stared a great deal—not as Europeans stare, with a restless and puzzled
expression of countenance, but with features all fixed, and rigid, and with
still, glassy eyes; before they had time to get decomposed from their state of
petrifaction, I had remounted my dromedary, and was darting away toward
the east.[5]

Kinglake, however, was a real daredevil adventurer, and he even
tried to get an Egyptian magician to raise the devil for him so that he
could hold a conversation with him. The travelers who came a few
years later were more inclined to follow the local rules—with the
possible exception, that is, of William C. Prime, author of *Tent Life
in the Holy Land,* whom Mark Twain was to delight in satirizing.
Prime prided himself on being a crack shot and boasted of shooting
at both Bedouins and Druses when he felt they had threatened him.
After all, had not the Druses chanted *"Ma hala, Ma hala, Kothen
Nasara!"* ("How sweet, how sweet, to kill the Christians") during the
massacres of 1860? It is to be noted, however, that they did not
attack the European missionaries.

Most of the Franks who visited Palestine in the 1850s and 1860s,
however, carried their guns rather sheepishly, if they did not discard
them entirely, and trusted to their dragomen and luck to pull them
through any trouble. Most of that trouble was found either in the
Lebanon mountains or on the trail from Damascus to the Sea of
Galilee where the Druse tribesmen sometimes attacked travelers, as
they did the party of a Mr. Degen of New York near Tiberias in 1852.
This attack was possibly motivated by banditry rather than hostility
toward Christians; even as late as 1867 John Franklin Swift wrote
about the killing, shortly before his arrival, of a notorious bandit on

the route from Jaffa to Jerusalem. Bedouin danger was specially marked in the Jordan Valley below Jerusalem, in the Jericho and Dead Sea areas: W. H. Bartlett spoke of the road to Jericho as being more dangerous than in the time of the Good Samaritan. However, Europeans bought protection by paying regular fees to local sheiks to guard them on their trips to the Jordan Valley. As to Muslim hostility, it was sensed most in areas like the Mt. Moriah section in Jerusalem, and in the Samaritan country, particularly at Nablus. Until the mid-1860s no nonbeliever was allowed in the sacred precincts of Mt. Moriah, and rumor had it that any who slipped into the area surreptitiously would be stoned to death. Hostility in the Nablus area, as recorded by both Harriet Martineau and William Cullen Bryant consisted principally of thrusting out tongues and spitting at visiting Christians. Sometimes boys threw stones as well, but, as both the boys and the stones were small, little damage was done.

Danger from rocks and bullets may have been largely imaginary, but discomfort from fleas, mosquitoes, lice, and even scorpions was very much in evidence. Particularly, fleas were almost everywhere, and travelers to Syria rarely failed to complain about them. A local folk saying had it that the King of Fleas lived in Tiberias, but that he had innumerable followers in every town and village. As DeForest put it: "The annoyance caused by these vivacious animals to the Eastern traveller is almost insupportable. . . . How can a man think about Joshua or the valley of Jehoshaphat, when fifty indefatigable little bores are sharply reminding him of the actual and suffering present." [6] Mosquitoes were particularly abundant in the swamps of the Lake Huleh area of the upper Jordan but they also bred in almost every open cistern in Palestine—and open cisterns were to be found almost everywhere. The presence of flies and vermin was inevitable in the towns, for not a settlement in Syria boasted a sewer. Of all the towns and cities, however, Jerusalem impressed the Franks most adversely on this score. Typical was Bayard Taylor's remark: "The filthy condition of the city [Jerusalem] exceeds anything I have seen, even in the Orient." [7] Gustave Flaubert was repelled at the offal from butcher shops that he stumbled over in the Holy City, and even the enthusiastic William C. Prime was discouraged at the filth he saw in Jerusalem. John Franklin Swift pointed out that the city was unhealthy because its streets were so narrow that the sun's rays rarely reached the ground.

Thus, particularly during the rainy season, the visitors, even when they escaped cholera (which had been greatly cut down by the enforcement of quarantine), were exposed to smallpox, typhoid, and severe diarrhea and dysentery. Most of them carried their own favorite remedies, which usually worked; but when home remedies failed and they sought medical care, there was little to be found. If they could locate a physician at all he would more likely than not be of the type described by John Lloyd Stephens in his account of one who ministered to him when he was sick in Beirut: "After lying ten days under the attendance of an old Italian quack, with a blue frock coat and great frog buttons, who frightened me to death every time he approached my bedside, I got aboard the first vessel bound for sea, and sailed for Alexandria." [8]

It is not surprising, then, that usually the most satisfactory way to meet the accommodation problem was to camp out. Almost every visitor who hired a good dragoman was delighted to find how comfortable the tents were, how quickly they were raised at the end of the day's journey, how marvelously they disappeared in the morning. They were also delighted to find that the tents were furnished with bedsteads, mattresses, clean bedding, tables, china, cutlery, etc. Actually, by 1850 Frank travelers wisely arrived with little luggage, depending instead on the dragomen and the inns to supply them with most of their housing needs. This situation was a far cry from that described in the delightful *Spring Voyage* by R. J. Mitchell, which tells of the coming of pilgrims from Venice to the Holy Land in 1458. Then it was necessary to provide oneself before boarding a galley with mattress, featherbed, pillow, and sheets, which could usually be resold at half-price when one returned to Venice (if he survived the trip). It is true that some travelers in the 1800s moved with elaborate outfits; William C. Prime prided himself on his fine soup tureen, delicate wine glasses, and a handy gimlet, and Eliot Warburton, who regularly took his afternoon tea even if it meant a stop in the hostile desert, carried with him what amounted to an explorer's outfit. Describing the loading of his effects onto the boat going from Alexandria to Beirut, he noted, after commenting on the absence of hotels in the Levant that

an Englishman, therefore, with any regard to cleanliness or comfort, is obliged to travel with an assortment of goods like those of an upholsterer, comprising every article his various exigencies may require, from a tent to a toasting-fork. He must have bed, bedding, and dressing-room; a pantry, scullery, kitchen, and bakehouse, dangling on his camels: saddle, bridle, and water-bottles, arms of all kinds, carpets, mats, and lanterns; besides a wardrobe that would serve for a green-room, containing all sorts of garments, from the British uniform to the Syrian turban, the Arab's kefieh, and the Greek capote.[9]

No one needed all of this paraphernalia if he came only for a short time and was lucky enough to get a dragoman who could put together a good outfit. After all, the Arabs had been living in tents for centuries and knew well the procedures for supplying and moving them. Still, tenting was tenting; as John Franklin Swift put it, "the first night of tent life is the best night of tent life." [10] By the time travelers reached a town where there was anything resembling an adequate inn, they usually moved indoors for awhile.

Good inns were to be found only in Beirut, Damascus, Jerusalem, and Jaffa, however. Of the two or three at Beirut, the Demetrie seems to have been the best. Damascus had at least one hotel, which had once been the residence of a rich merchant, that was noted for its comfort and inner garden courts. Jerusalem had three or four modest inns, all within the walls, for the Old City, together with Mt. Zion, constituted the entire settled area in those days. Harriet Martineau and George William Curtis both stayed at the Salvador, on the Via Dolorosa. William Cullen Bryant was housed at the Melita, near the Church of the Holy Sepulchre. Later arrivals mention the Mediterranean and the Damascus, both run by Germans. The hotels were small, with cell-like rooms and barely passable cuisines. They were all run by non-Syrians—usually Greeks, Maltese, or Germans.

At other spots in the Holy Land, if one did not wish to camp out, he could often find accommodations in a convent. Most of those frequented by Franks were "Latin" (that is, Roman Catholic) with the signal exception of Mar Saba, the famous Greek Orthodox convent in the Judean wilderness between the Dead Sea and Bethlehem. There were Latin convents in Jaffa, Ramla (twelve miles from Jaffa on the road to Jerusalem), Jerusalem itself of course, Bethlehem, Nazareth, and several other places. These were built principally to shelter pilgrims of the several Catholic faiths represented in the Holy Land, but they were said never to turn away a stranger. Protestants also frequently used them as havens, customarily leaving "a grateful tribute to the convent and its charities," usually about equivalent to the fee at a hotel. Most travelers spoke kindly of their treatment at the convents. For instance, Eliot Warburton, who spent several pleasant days with the Carmelites on Mt. Carmel, found the company stimulating and the accommodations very clean and comfortable. (There was even one room prepared for visiting married couples, he reported.) He warned others, however, about the simplicity of the food: "The diet is simple, perhaps too much so, for those who have not become accustomed to Eastern habits. Meat, except pigeons, is unknown, and even in that form is very rare; soups made of vegetables; bread, eggs, coffee, and milk are the principal diet; there was also to be had a refreshing cordial (in which brandy figured advantageously) prepared by Fra' Clementi's own attenuated hands." [11]

Not all western travelers were as pleased as Warburton with convent hospitality. One such traveler found the Palestinian Franciscans a dull lot—mostly Spaniards and Italians not interesting or enterprising enough to be assigned elsewhere. William Cullen Bryant found the Terra Santa at Ramla both spacious and dirty, with only three monks in residence. And Charles Dudley Warner, who was clearly irritated by most Roman Catholic institutions he encountered in Palestine, spoke disparagingly of the Latin Convent in Bethlehem:

The Latin convent opens its doors to tourists; it is a hospitable house, and the monks are very civil; they let us sit in a *salle-à-manger*, while waiting for dinner, that was as damp and chill as a dungeon, and they gave us a well-intended but uneatable meal, and the most peculiar wine, all at a good price. The wine, white and red, was made by the monks, they said with some pride; we tried both kinds, and I can recommend it to the American Temperance Union: if it can be introduced to the public, the public will embrace total abstinence with enthusiasm.[12]

Occasionally an American traveler, such as John Lloyd Stephens, found hospitality in the home of an American consul or consular agent. This was not as common a practice in the Near East, however, as in some other parts of the world. In the first place the Porte was slow to welcome diplomatic representation within the Ottoman Empire, and it was not until 1831 that Commodore David Porter was received at Constantinople as U. S. Minister. In addition, the United States Government was slow in establishing a home-supported and home-supplied consular system. After Porter reached Turkey various "consulates" were opened up in Syria, in places like Beirut, Jaffa, and Ramla, but these were manned by Levantines who were called consular agents by everyone except Stephens, who referred to them as "petty vagabonds" because they were eager to attract American aid in improving their businesses. Even these were cut down in number in 1840, when the Porte reduced the spots in the Levant at which foreign consulates could be maintained to Constantinople, Smyrna, and Alexandria. The Turks had become more receptive to foreign representation within their empire, however, by 1852, when the U. S. Congress provided that all consuls be American citizens and receive regular salaries. Even at that, the first American consul to be established in Jerusalem, John William Gorham, arrived in 1856.[13]

Travelers looking for accommodations in the Holy Land could always resort to the Arab caravansaries or khans and even to native huts for shelter. Most of the visitors had been warned that this was a step to be taken only in dire emergency but the practice was fairly widespread, nevertheless. The big caravansaries of Egypt, built to take care of whole caravans crossing the desert, were not found widely in Palestine, although Bryant described one with a paved court 150 feet square which he had seen not far from Gaza. The caravansary was displaced by the khan in the area between Beersheba and the Lebanon; the khan was smaller but it still managed to house both men and animals. Here one could obtain barley for the horses and mules, and tobacco pipes, coffee, sour milk, and watermelons for their riders. Such places were scattered along most routes about one-half day's travel, or fifteen miles, apart. As late as 1867 John Franklin Swift attempted to stay in one such khan near Ramla on the road to Jerusalem. He reported that it consisted of a large enclosure where Arabs sat for hours by a blazing fire, smoking chibouks (pipes with long stems), drinking coffee, and listening to a professional storyteller. The human inhabitants took up about one-quarter of the area, the rest of which was devoted to horses and mules, "moored head and stern." Swift tried to get some sleep, but the noise and vermin were too much for him; shortly after midnight he went on his way alone, hoping to get a glimpse of Jerusalem in the dawn. Both khâns and Arab houses were noted for their fleas, sometimes with bedbugs and cockroaches thrown in. Most western-ers found them intolerable.

The condition of the roads, the virtues and faults of dragomen, the hospitality of convents and the filth of khans were all fairly well-known to travelers coming to the Holy Land in the middle of the nineteenth century. Over the centuries much lore had been collected by pilgrims about pilgrimages. Now that the tourist era was about to open, there was no shortage of books about the area which had cradled three of the world's great religions. The Bible was a first source of information among most Christian visitors. Some of them had also read Josephus and perhaps Marco Polo and Mandeville, as well as reports of travelers who had made their way to the Levant with difficulty during the time of the Grand Tour. The standard tourist literature was not yet available in 1850, however; the first Murray guide to Syria and Palestine did not come out until 1858 (too late for Browne and Melville), and the first Baedeker guide (in German) even later, in 1875. Three books by travelers to the Levant had been very popular, however; they are already familiar to readers of this study. John Lloyd Stephens' *Incidents of Travel in Egypt,*

Arabia and the Holy Land had appeared in America in 1837 and had
almost immediately won a wide audience. Seven years later Kinglake's classic *Eōthen* and Warburton's *The Crescent and the Cross*
came out in England and were soon republished elsewhere. For more
detailed knowledge of the relation of the Holy Land to the Bible
story, one could turn to the definitive work of that remarkable
American scholar, Edward Robinson, *Biblical Researches* (1841).
William H. Bartlett's very detailed *Walks About the City and
Environs of Jerusalem* appeared three years after Robinson's scientific treatise; it was geared more toward the average traveler but it
was confined strictly to Jerusalem and its immediate environs, going
as far as Bethany but not as far as Bethlehem. William M. Thomson,
still working with the American Mission in Beirut, did not publish his
enormously popular *The Land and the Book* until 1859. Thus, though
midcentury travelers did not have the convenient facts and statistics
and prices compiled in a Murray or a Baedeker, they had plenty of
good reading material to guide them on their way. If they wished to
read further than the books listed above, they could turn to such
sources as Alphonse de Lamartine's account of his visit to the area as
a poet and statesman, contained in his *A Pilgrimage to the Holy
Land*, or Harriet Martineau's treatise stressing moral philosophy
published as *Eastern Life, Present and Past.*

Though one or two books would not weigh down an outfit—for
the visitor of a century ago was not arriving by air, or sightseeing
from a tourist bus—it was evident that the modest traveler had to
limit himself fairly severely, particularly in taking the long route from
Beirut to Jerusalem by way of Damascus. Not everyone traveled as
lightly as Ross Browne, however, who prided himself on getting
along with what he could carry in a knapsack. The more common
practice is suggested in a letter to the States from Henry H. Jessup,
American missionary in Beirut who, after fifty-three years in Syria
helped to found the American University of Beirut. Shortly after he
reached Lebanon he made a journey up to the Cedars and
commented thus concerning his duffle: "He is not a wise traveller
who neglects his overcoat, white umbrella, drinking cup, straps,

strings, papers, drawing paper (if he can sketch), geological hammer (if he be given to scientific research), mariner's compass, spy-glass, pamphlets for pressing flowers, and a full supply of clothing." [14]

Obviously the clothing varied according to the taste and experience of the individual, ranging frmm the "backwoodsman's garb" of Ross Browne to the English gentleman's outfit, including vest and tie, worn by Kinglake. As we have seen, some of the pilgrims, like Eliot Warburton, Bayard Taylor, and William C. Prime, adopted Arab dress, including turban, finding that it was better suited to the heat of the desert. Warburton, in fact, even made a point of keeping his turban on when he swam in the Dead Sea. With westerners, the use of huge white or blue umbrellas to ward off the sunshine was a common practice, even though these were undoubtedly difficult to manage when aboard a horse or a camel. Overcoats were sometimes left behind in the summer, though they were frequently included as a precaution against chilly nights in the Lebanon Mountains or in Jerusalem.

As to geological hammer, mariner's compass, and pamphlet for pressing flowers, they could well be omitted unless one intended to loiter. The sketching pad however was obviously a forerunner of the ever-present camera of today, and unfortunately required greater skill than do the creation of transparencies and home movies. Cameras were in use by the mid-1850s, but they were hardly equipment for the usual tourist. Thus, William Cullen Bryant found a French woman taking photographs of Egyptian temples in 1853, but he apparently had no impulse to get a camera and follow suit. After all, the Eastman Company did not develop the Kodak until 1880. Its appearance as well as that of travelers checks, first put out by the American Express Company in 1891, were two features which greatly encouraged the tourist boom. In the meantime, "Frangi"—a term used indiscriminately for all western Europeans since the crusades—in the Levant carried letters of credit or money belts stuffed with Turkish and Italian coins which varied in value according to the towns visited.

The two main purposes for carrying cameras to distant places—to bring home the far away, and to prove that one had been there—were achieved in other ways. The best way to bring back a picture of what one saw was to draw it oneself, but few travelers had the skill to make this possible. David H. Finnie in his excellent *Pioneers East: The Early American Experience in the Middle East* has written that Francis Schroeder's *Shores of the Mediterranean* "seems to be the first Eastern travel book by an American containing the author's own pictures of what he saw." [15] This book, published in 1846, was one of several accounts resulting from American naval visits to the Levant; perhaps the best known of these was Nathaniel Parker Willis' unillustrated *Pencillings by the Way* (1835), which reflected the experiences of Willis as guest of the Navy on board the famous frigate the *United States* during her visit to the eastern Mediterranean in 1833. Willis, whose book helped to encourage Browne to try his hand at travel writing, was one of the first Americans to write about the Levant, but he got no nearer to Palestine than Smyrna. Among writers who traveled overland in the Holy Land, the two who were most successful in illustrating their journeys from their sketchbooks were Ross Browne and Bayard Taylor.

Another, though less commendable, way of capturing something of the Near East was to return with souvenirs, obtained legitimately or illegitimately. Quantities of these could be obtained from the many vendors selling olive-wood and mother-of-pearl momentoes, just as they still do today. Perhaps the only difference in such souvenir hawking that has come about through the ages is the banishing of vendors from the courtyard in front of the entrance to the Church of the Holy Sepulchre. The second type of souvenir, taken surreptitiously rather than purchased openly, has always been popular with pilgrims and tourists, who possibly act unconsciously on the age-old practice of bringing relics from Palestine. Not infrequently this continuous vandalism took the form of breaking off bits of rocks from sacred spots. Thus, William Wey, Fellow of Exeter College, Oxford, and author of *Itineraries*, a medieval guide for pilgrims, not only helped himself generously but left a record of the relics that he himself, perhaps a typical pilgrim, brought home in 1458:

> a stone of the Mownte of Calvery
> a stone of Sepulkyr
> a stone of the hyl of Tabor
> a stone of the pyler that ovre Lord was stowryched too
> a stone of the plas wher the crorse was hyd and funde
> also a stone of the holy cave of Bethlem.[16]

Miss R. J. Mitchell, who includes an inventory of Wey's relics in her *Spring Voyage* comments: "Had all pilgrims been as acquisitive as Wey it is easy to see that there would soon have been no Holy Places left to visit." [17] Only the eventual covering over of most of the sacred shrines with slabs of marble—as with the Stone of Ointment, the shelf of Christ's Tomb, and the top of Mt. Calvary (all in the Church of the Holy Sepulchre)—has prevented visitors from taking a good portion of sacred Palestine home in their pockets.

In the nineteenth century nearly every Protestant visitor to the Holy Land, from the conscientious Harriet Martineau to the skeptical Mark Twain, at least brought home bottles of water from the Jordan River. Also, there was much picking at the wood of the olive trees in Gethsemane. One of the favorite places to scrape off a good souvenir was at the Milk Grotto in Bethlehem, where a drop of the Virgin's milk is said to have turned the rock walls white, rendering a stone particularly helpful in overcoming barrenness. If one is to take at face value Mark Twain's accounts of the vandalism perpetrated by his fellow travelers, he may conclude that John Lloyd Stephens' snitching of bits of the tombs of both Aaron and Saul was common behavior, which he euphemistically called getting "a pilgrim's share." William C. Prime was more ambitious than Stephens: he failed in his attempt to buy one of the paintings in the Grotto of the Nativity but openly hired stonecutters to provide him souvenirs chipped from the Golden Gate, the gate in the wall around Jerusalem through which, according to tradition, Christ made his triumphal entry on Palm Sunday and which, perhaps because of the Christians' veneration for it, was sealed forever by the Turks in 1530.

As with photographs, the bringing back of souvenirs helped to prove that one "had been there" and thus enhanced one's *amour propre*. There was another, more reprehensible, way of doing this—that was, to carve one's name where later travelers could see it. This most annoying form of man's passion for graffiti was possibly even more common in the nineteenth century than it is today. When Lord Byron set a bad example by carving his name on the inner side of a column in the Erectheion on the Acropolis, he used discreetly small letters and put his name where it could not easily be seen, but the visitor to Sounion today cannot miss the bold B Y R O N carved on the dramatically located temple to Hephaestus. Perhaps the practice had some utilitarian value, however. John Lloyd Stephens tells of how he traced the wanderings of one of his former companions, a man named Bradford, "by the places where he had scratched his name on antiquities."

The tendency to take home relics or to carve one's initials on an ancient tomb were but feeble gestures of faith from travelers who were almost always skeptical about holy shrines; if they expected these shrines to evoke a religious response in their hearts, they were almost always disappointed. Long gone was the day when Marco Polo journeyed all the way to Jerusalem to obtain some of the oil from the lamp which burned over the Holy Sepulchre so that he might take some of the precious drops to the Great Khan in Tartary. In the Middle Ages pilgrims truly believed that the lamp was miraculous and did not doubt the story that its flame died out every Good Friday and sprang up by divine intervention on Easter. By the middle of the nineteenth century, there were forty-three lamps hanging above the tomb, and the only miracle seemed to be the fact that the Armenians and Greeks and Latins did not kill each other in filling them. When the author of Sir John Mandeville's Travels visited Jerusalem a century later than Marco Polo, he did not for a moment doubt the fallibility of St. Helena's judgment in firmly locating most of the exact spots associated with Christ's life and death. During the fourteenth century, the genuineness and efficacy of holy relics was strongly believed in, and the putative Mandeville was able to write without a skeptical quiver: "And in this Temple was Charlemagne when that the Angel brought him the Prepuce of our Lord Jesus Christ of his Circumcision; and after, King Charles had it brought to Paris in his Chapel, and after that he had it brought to Peyteres [Poitiers] and after that he had it brought to Chartres." [18] There, like relics from the True Cross, it was to bring many benefits to true believers.

In the nineteenth century, however, most of the British and Americans who visited the Holy Land and wrote books about their reactions were Protestants whose ancestors had long ago spurned the truth and efficacy of relics and who were by temperament inclined to question the authenticity of shrines. In *Eōthen*, Kinglake sets the tone which was to be repeated time after time.

The Church of the Holy Sepulcher comprises very compendiously almost all the spots associated with the closing career of our Lord. Just there, on your right, he stood and wept; by the pillar on your left he was scourged; on the spot just before you he was crowned with the crown of thorns; up there he was crucified, and down here he was buried. A locality is assigned to every, the minutest, event connected with the recorded history of our Savior; even the spot where the cock crew, when Peter denied his Master, is ascertained and surrounded by the walls of an Armenian convent. Many Protestants are wont to treat these traditions contemptuously, and those who distinguish themselves from their brethren by the appelation of "Bible Christians" are almost fierce in their denunciation of these supposed errors.[19]

Thus it was that a person as religious at heart as Harriet Martineau would, through her knowledge of Near Eastern mythologies and comparative religion, find the visiting of holy places crass idolatry. A young idealist like George William Curtis could feel the presence of Christ in the Holy Land but would take no stock in the shrines, quoting the cynical Arabian proverb "the worst Muslims are those of Mecca, and the worst Christians those of Jerusalem." Though he had run the last few miles to catch an early glimpse of Jerusalem, he left the city with the remark: "The Christianity peculiar to Jerusalem is unmitigatedly repulsive." [20] Charles Dudley Warner found the Christian shrines "puerile inventions of monkly credulity," and J. W. DeForest summed up the impressions of many of his fellow travelers when he wrote: "There is such an air of absurdity about most of the sacred localities and traditions which abound in Jerusalem, that they excite unbelief and irreverence rather than faith and devotion." [21] Bret Harte, in his review of Swift's *Going to Jericho* in the *Overland Monthly*, summed up the attitude particularly of American "pilgrims" when he called them "exuberant image-breakers": "A race of good-humored, engaging iconoclasts seem to have precipitated themselves upon the old altars of mankind, and like their predecessors of the Eighth Century, have paid particular attention to the holy church." [22]

There were exceptions, of course, to the customary reactions of disappointment with the shrines which had drawn pilgrims ever since the days of Empress Helena, that busy mother of Emperor Constantine. In the early thirties Alphonse de Lamartine discovered that his journey became one continuous prayer as he approached Nazareth. As he said, he traveled with the heart and soul rather than just the eyes and mind. But he was a Catholic and a Great Romantic; the dry iconclasm of a Gustave Flaubert is more the French counterpart to the mood of the American travelers of the period.

Above everything else, one's reaction to the first glimpse of Jerusalem, usually gained after the long climb on the hot dusty trail leading up from Jaffa, was a key to the modern pilgrim's reactions to the Holy Land. Here was a sight, an experience, which each pilgrim had dreamed of since he started reading the Bible. The reactions ranged widely. Eliot Warburton and his companions knelt at their first sight of El Khuds. William C. Prime prostrated himself upon the ground and wept. The much-traveled Bayard Taylor felt a moment of ecstasy and fulfilment—"my sight grew weak, and all objects trembled and wavered in a watery film"—but admitted that he could not summon up his spiritual excitement again when once within the city. Even Harriet Martineau, with the many doubts brought to her by a scientific approach to Bible stories, chose to separate from her party so that she might receive her first impression of Jerusalem in silence—"we all felt that it was such a moment as we should never know again." On the other hand, W. H. Bartlett, who was to write a guidebook to Jerusalem, admitted that although he gained his first view of the Holy City at dawn, he found nothing striking in the view: "Her mournful aspect well suits with the train of recollections she awakens . . . . Within, the city is as dull as without. . . ." John William DeForest's comment was typical of his reactions to Palestine: "Seated on a rocky hill, and surrounded by a wilderness of other hills, stands Jerusalem the fallen." But it remained to Gustave Flaubert in his journal kept during his visit to the Holy Land in 1850 to complete the range of reactions. His comment (and action) was reserved until he actually rode on his horse through the gate of the city: "Nous entrons par la porte de Jaffa et je lâche dessus un pet en franchissant le seuil, très involontairement; j'ai même au fond été fâché de ce voltairianisme de mon anus." [23] He may have been really annoyed with his anus for betraying him on reaching Jerusalem, but he was still expressing the spirit of Voltaire when he found the open latrines as noteworthy as the Church of the Nativity which they flanked when he finally arrived at Bethlehem.

It was not merely that the nineteenth century fostered skepticism in religious matters, although that was certainly a strong element in the reactions of the writers we are following. Most of the Protestants who came to the Holy Land were hardly in the mood of traditional pilgrims, who still came by thousands, particularly from Eastern Europe, to prostrate themselves on first sight of Jerusalem, kiss the marble slab over the Holy Sepulchre, or risk their lives in emersing themselves in the swift waters of the Jordan River. The American Protestants came partly out of curiosity and love for travel, and partly because they felt, in spite of everything, that a visit to this land which they had heard so much about might answer some of their questions of faith or lack of faith. They certainly did not express this latter motive with the vigor of Lord Montecute, Disraeli's protagonist in *Tancred*, who went to the Holy Land for a spiritual purging: "I, too, surrounded by the holy hills and sacred groves of Jerusalem, would relieve my spirit from the bale that bows it down; would lift up my voice to heaven, and ask, What is DUTY, and what is FAITH? What ought I to DO, and what ought I to BELIEVE?" [24] But it is safe to say that there was hardly even a nominal Christian who voyaged to Palestine without hoping that he might in some way gain a step toward clarifying his religious attitudes and strengthening his ideals.

The questioning habits of the visitors, however, merely fortified the impressions of a wretched country, at its lowest social ebb, which nearly always failed to evoke the emotions they had hoped to experience. Many of them went away feeling that Jerusalem and Nazareth and Bethlehem and the Sea of Galilee were the last places in the world to strengthen one's faith in Christianity; they were far from the dreams about them nourished since childhood. The landscape disappointed and the inhabitants irritated the onlooker; the natives often seemed the dirtiest, the most backward of peoples. The climax, however, came in discovering the superstition, the tawdriness, and the constant conflict among the sects of believers at the holy shrines. Traveler after traveler found the Arabs who guarded the Church of the Holy Sepulchre more temperate and reasonable in their attitudes than the monks and pilgrims whose traditional jealousies were evident wherever one turned.

For the nineteenth-century Protestant a visit to the Holy Land produced, more than travel to any other place, a constant battle between the real and the ideal, between fact and imagination. During such an experience, the individual reflects his cultural heritage but, more to the point, he reveals his own personality. As Eliot Warburton put it: "It is not what a country is, but what we are, that renders it rich in interest, or pregnant with enjoyment." Their reactions to visits to the Holy Land shed considerable light on the personalities of Ross Browne, Herman Melville, and Mark Twain; their use of those experiences in their writing also tells much of the nature of the creative process as it operated in each of the men concerned.

TWO

John Ross Browne

THE lives of Herman Melville and Mark Twain have been explored and exploited for three generations. As a result, some acquaintance with their personalities together with their experiences in other places than the Holy Land can be assumed. Such is not the case, however, with Ross Browne. Though he has his coterie of enthusiastic supporters and has been the subject of biographical studies dealing with particular aspects of his colorful career, he is not well known to the general reading public. Accordingly, it seems fitting to devote a chapter to his life before the publication of *Yusef* so that the reader can get acquainted with him.

John Ross Browne was born near Dublin early in 1821, the son of an Irish protestant who was exiled from Ireland when Ross was twelve years old. His father, Thomas Egerton Browne, originally from Queen's county where he had been a farmer and a miller, emerged into public view in Dublin in the early 1830s as a journalist prominently involved in the widespread agitation against the paying of tithes to support the Church of Ireland, for all intents and purposes the Irish branch of the Anglican Church. As its membership included only a small minority of the Irish population, there was widespread resentment, particularly among farmers, against a law requiring them to turn over a tenth of their earnings to the government for church support. Much disorder resulted. For instance, during a riot in June 1831, eighteen men were killed and many more wounded; the next year saw at least nine thousand agrarian "outrages," of which more than two hundred were homicides.

It was in this tense atmosphere that thirty-nine-year-old Tom Browne and eighteen-year-old John Sheehan organized the Comet Literary Club made up of a dozen Protestants and Catholics determined to attack the iniquitous tithing system. From their office in Dublin they issued a number of anonymous satires; a typical one was titled *The Parson's Horn-book*. With such slurs as: "It is notorious that Mrs. C—— has been living with Mr. S——, as his acknowledged concubine, for a very considerable period, to the great scandal of the real friends of both parties," [1] accompanied by caricatures of Mrs. Church and Mr. State, the pamphlet was a great success overnight and went into several printings. Browne and Sheehan also published a weekly journal called *The Comet*, which eventually annoyed the government so much that the two journalists were haled before the King's Bench under charges of seditious libel and enticing to riot. The trial, which opened late in November 1832, became a political *cause célèbre*, with the famous Daniel O'Connell devoting his considerable gifts as an orator to the defense. Though modification of the tithe law was not far in the offing, the judge ruled against the pair of rebellious writers, giving them one-year sentences and stiff fines. Neither Browne nor Sheehan ever paid their fines, however; after the two were incarcerated for a few months in the Dublin version of Newgate Prison, friends of Browne not only obtained his release on the condition that he leave the country, but in addition raised enough money to allow him to establish himself and his family, including several children, in America. Sheehan, in turn, went to England where he became a friend of Thackeray (who pictured him as Captain Shandon in *Pendennis*) and eventually became known as "the Irish Whiskey Drinker," a dubious distinction indeed.

It is tempting to assume that Ross Browne's twelve years spent as a boy in Ireland left an indelible mark on his personality, and no doubt they did, but it is difficult to ascertain just what form it took. It has been suggested that his life-long wanderlust was encouraged by the youthful practice of watching the ships in Dublin harbor but he made no mention of such activity in his later writings. He may have carried in him the seeds of rebellion against tyranny, nurtured by the bitter days of the tithe war, but he showed little tendency toward espousal of political causes in his later life, although he was always devoted to honesty in government and spent much time trying to further it. His sense of humor may have owed something to his Irish origins but it is easier to identify it with the humor of the frontier in America. There is nothing to indicate that he did not enjoy his childhood in Ireland but he never mentions it. Though he later traveled thousands of miles in Europe, he made no attempt to visit the country of his birth. Apparently only once (when he was in his forties), returning from Iceland to his family which he had left in Germany, did he for a moment think of such a visit. "We reached Leith last night. I am greatly tempted to pay a flying visit to Ireland. It would only cost me for passage to Dublin and back about $10. I could visit my old home at Ballykilkaran for a few dollars more; and a trip to Giant's Causeway would be but a trifle." [2] He did not, however, make the effort and we can assume that Dublin held no such appeal for Ross Browne as Hannibal did for Mark Twain.

Ross Browne's next eight years, from 1833 to 1841, were spent mostly in Louisville, Kentucky, where his father had settled after short tries at running a sawmill and operating a ferry on the Ohio River, not far below Cincinnati. His youthful environment, thus, was not unlike that of Sam Clemens a decade later; he came to know intimately a small river town, he picked up on the way something of a desultory education which apparently ended when he was sixteen, he played on a sandbar, dreamed of adventure, took to the river on a flatboat, saw something of the world as far away as Texas, and went to work for a newspaper. Meanwhile, his father, eager to establish himself and support his family of five boys and two girls, offered a choice between instruction in "the true Italian handwriting" and training in several types of shorthand to interested citizens of

Louisville. At the same time, Ross's mother and sister hired themselves out as visiting governesses. Their talents were soon combined to create a Young Ladies Seminary where the English curriculum was supplemented by offerings in French and music. Although the school did not flourish, it did survive for a number of years. Meanwhile, Thomas Egerton Browne put another iron in the fire by returning to journalism, first buying a local paper, then taking a position as associate editor of the well-established *Louisville Daily Reporter*. It is said that Ross's father was industrious, informal, humorous, and an excellent family man. However, he shocked some of the pious folks around town when he published some verses titled "Hymns of the Soul" in which he spoke of his dislike for religious creeds and revealed his faith in a nonpersonal God who was present in Nature. Though some called him an atheist, he might better be called a Romantic Deist.

It is assumed that such further schooling as Ross Browne achieved after his elementary school days in Ireland was obtained at his parents' female seminary, which welcomed a few boys to its classes. Here he doubtless learned something about the major English writers and he may have picked up a bit of French and possibly a smattering of Latin; later, deploring his lack of linguistic training, he admitted that he had got no further than *Quousque tandem*. As a boy he also developed a taste for music, manifested by learning to play the piano, violin, and flute well enough to entertain himself and some of the people he met in his wandering. His practice of sketching appears to have been self-initiated, although he doubtless had encouragement from his parents. His directed reading surely ended by his sixteenth year, when he left school, but he continued to pounce upon the books he liked. His taste is made evident in a comment in *Yusef* in which he disclaims an interest in "the classics." "In my younger days that sort of reading was forced upon me as physic for the mind; and having no taste for extravagant scenes of bloodshed and disgusting exhibitions of sensuality and folly, the result was that I took to *Don Quixote, Gil Blas, Robinson Crusoe,* and other authentic histories in which I could believe, without doing violence to common sense." [3]

Of these "authentic histories", undoubtedly the most influential on the growing boy was *Robinson Crusoe*. When he was a lad in Ireland, young enough to be versed only in fairy stories, his father had given him a copy of Defoe's novel bound in cream-colored muslin and fresh from the press. It captured him as no other book was to do. He read and reread it, spent hours making knife cases and shot pouches out of rabbit skins, and prayed God each night that he "might some day or other be cast upon a desolate island, and live to become as wonderful a man as Robinson Crusoe." After he crossed the ocean and went to Kentucky, a secluded spot on the bank of the Ohio River came to serve as a little bit of a Crusoe world. "I gathered up drift-wood, and built a hut among the rocks, whole days I lay there thinking of that island in the far-off seas. A piece of tarred plank from some steam-boat had a sweeter scent to me than the most odorous flower. . . ." Naturally, he let a "favored few" into his secret—"we went every afternoon to a sand-bar, and called it Crusoe's Island; . . . I was Robinson Crusoe, and the friend of my heart Friday, whom I caused to be painted from head to foot with black mud, as also the rest of my friends; and then the battles we had; the devouring of the dead men; the horrible dances, and chasing into the water; and, above all, the rescue of my beloved Friday—" [4]

Perhaps it was the "friend of his heart," appropriately cleaned of mud, who accompanied him when Ross Browne finally broke away from school and town and found a job as a deckhand on a flatboat which floated down the river to New Orleans. During his seventeenth year he worked on the river, going up and down the Mississippi as well as the Ohio, covering a total of sixteen hundred miles. An additional six hundred he covered by hiking into the country beyond the Mississippi, "bushwhacking," as he liked to call it, getting all the joy he could out of breathing the fresh air, cooking over a campfire, and playing a flute under the stars.

The jobs he took when he returned to Louisville hardly continued the excitement of river and prairie and desert. Running errands for a tailor and clerking in a store were not stirring occupations. It was inevitable, with his family background, that he should take to scribbling. A job at eighteen as "police reporter" for Louisville's leading newspaper might at the moment have lent excitement, but would certainly in time prove to be dull routine. Perhaps it was at this time, however, that he learned from his father the techniques of shorthand—"Gurney's, Taylor's and Gould's Hieroglyphics"—so that he could keep notes on a homicide or, better still, maintain a diary in secret script. As he moved rapidly toward his majority, he began to sense that writing might make it possible to roam beyond the horizon. He is said to have done some free-lancing for Louisville, Cincinnati, and Columbus papers. In time, items in *The Louisville Literary Newsletter* gave way to sketches and stories in *The Southern Literary Messenger* of Richmond and *Graham's Magazine* of Phildelphia. He also, about this time, wrote two slight items which later were to be classified by the Library of Congress as books.

An incomplete novel, *Confessions of a Quack; or the Autobiography of a Modern Esculapian* was a by-product of Browne's short exposure to a medical training in the Louisville Medical Institute, which opened in the fall of 1838. Years later Browne wrote that he once studied medicine in Louisville, Kentucky, with Dr. Gunn, author of "Gunn's Domestic Medicine," as well as anatomist Flint, and pathologist Bullitt. He wrote some of the episodes of *Confessions of a Quack* when he was seventeen or eighteen, planning to add to it later, and eventually to extend it to four volumes. A picaresque satire on doctors and their patients, the fragment reveals Browne's first concern with fraud and charlatans. Like *The Confidence Man*, it was doomed to stop in mid-passage, appearing in April 1841, as thirty-two pages of almost unreadable type printed in double columns on what is clearly paper for proofs; these were bound, were reviewed by the prestigious *Knickerbocker Magazine*, and a copy eventually found its way to the Library of Congress.

The Great Steam Duck, or a Concise Description of a Most Useful and Extraordinary Invention for Aerial Navigation, with two drawings by the anonymous author, identified only as a member of the "L.L.B.B.," also appeared in the spring of 1841. *The Great Duck* was a satire on a proposal put forward in a pamphlet by one R. O. Davidson of St. Louis in which he suggested building a flying machine resembling an American eagle with a flag in its beak, which was to be flown by a mechanic who would move the wings by riding a bicycle within the bird's bosom. In his booklet Ross Browne matched the eagle with a huge mallard duck with rotating wings to be driven by a steam engine housed within the bird. A lively and slightly scatalogical touch was added when Browne suggested that the escape pipe for the steam engine be "conducted out a small hole under the tail or rudder, and thus give an additional impetus to the Aerostat, every puff." Thus he anticipated the jet airplane, and his squib has been rather widely republished in this century on that account.

After the booklet was published, Browne explained its attribution to "a member of the L.L.B.B." in a letter to Charles Peterson of *Graham's Magazine*. The initials stood for the Louisville Literary Brass Band, a group made up of fourteen amateurs who actually once appeared in a concert together. To be eligible for membership in the band a man was required to perform on an instrument of brass, to write epigrams with a brass pen, to deliver lectures with a brazen face, and to have enough brass to write a book, kiss a pretty girl, or pop the question without blushing. Browne was definitely of an age to write a book and kiss a pretty girl. In fact, the evidence suggests he was busy kissing quite a number of them. As to the book, he had indicated in an earlier letter to Peterson that he was already on the trail that was to lead to several notable volumes. He wrote on 14 March 1840 that he hoped soon to start a tour to Europe and added: "I am anxious to effect some engagement with the editors of a few prominent periodicals, for the publication of Letters or Sketches, to be written during the tour, descriptive of the scenery through which we shall pass, and of the manners and customs of our foreign neighbors—somewhat in the style of Brooks Letters, or Willis's Pencillings." [5]

By the fall of 1841 he had developed a scheme which he thought would make this trip actually a possibility. He would go to Washington, D.C. with his father, who was planning to use his knowledge of shorthand to provide verbatim accounts of congressional debates for his audience back in Louisville. As Ross was by now also very adept at shorthand, he would be able to help and could doubtless make enough money during the winter session to pay his way to Europe. In the meantime he could spend all his evenings at the congressional library studying up on the countries he would visit. He might even have the "brass" to pop the question to some pretty girl in the nation's capital—but marriage must wait until he got back from a very extensive trip.

Soon after reaching Washington he obtained a job as reporter for the *Congressional Globe*, the precursor of the *Congressional Record*. As his task was to report the debates in the Senate word for word, his rapid overexposure to Washington oratory and intrigue soon brought the inevitable reaction. "The profession I had chosen enabled me to see behind the scenes and study well the great machinery of government, and I can not say that I saw a great deal to admire," he wrote; "I became thoroughly disgusted with so much hypocrisy and bombast." [6] He decided, however, to stick through the session and use his savings to go to Europe and the Near East. He found a young man from Ohio named Henry Wilson who was equally eager to leave Washington and see the world; the two decided, in the pleasant spring evenings, to make a fortune during their wanderings and marry Arabian princesses. However, when they pooled their savings by the end of the session, they found they had only forty dollars. Ross Browne had planned on accumulating from six to eight hundred dollars but he could contribute only fifteen when the time of departure came. On the Fourth of July he kissed his current pretty girl goodbye ("the sweetest parting kiss I ever had in my life") and set out with Wilson's companionship, his father's blessings, his sweetheart's love token ("in the shape of some lines from Byron, enclosed in a note, containing also a piece of cedar"), and a sublime confidence in his own energy and the favor of Providence.[7]

In his preface to *Yusef* Browne summarized the adventure that followed:

Ten years ago, . . . I set out from Washington with fifteen dollars, to make a tour of the East. I got as far east as New York, where the last dollar and the prospect of reaching Jerusalem came to a conclusion at the same time. Sooner than return home, after having made so good a beginning, I shipped before the mast in a whaler, and did some service, during a voyage in the Indian Ocean, in way of scrubbing decks and catching whales. A mutiny occurred at the island of Zanzibar, where I sold myself out of the vessel for thirty dollars and a chest of old clothes; and spent three months very pleasantly at the consular residence, in the vicinity of his Highness the Imaum of Muscat.[8]

Further details that Browne might have added include the facts that his whaler was called the *Bruce* (in his *Etchings of a Whaling Cruise* he renamed it the *Styx*); that it sailed from New Bedford and was a small clumsy barque (it registered at 147 tons, whereas the brig *Pilgrim* on which the nineteen-year-old Richard Henry Dana of *Two Years before the Mast* had sailed from Boston eight years before was 181 tons in burthen, and the brand-new *Acushnet* on which the twenty-one-year-old Melville had sailed from Fairhaven some eighteen months before was a 358 ton ship); that the *Bruce* took a route more nearly resembling that of the fictional *Pequod* of *Moby-Dick* than that of Melville's *Acushnet*, crossing the Atlantic to the Azores and the Canaries, and then sailing around the Cape of Good Hope toward the whaling grounds in the Indian Ocean and the Pacific; and that Browne had a thoroughly wretched time during most of the voyage, finding neither officers nor crew compatible and quickly learning to dislike both sailing and whaling. Like Dana on his merchant ship, he tried to relieve the tedium of physical labor by ferreting out any reading matter he could locate on the ship. This included a grubby item by Lady Dacre titled *The Diary of a Chaperon* and some old newspapers which Browne read over and over. Also he kept his shorthand journal, played his flute, drew sketches of the more friendly of the sailors, and tried to learn navigation from the second mate in return for lessons in writing, while he put up with the dirt of forecastle life and the food, which featured salt junk, and cockroaches in molasses.

That Ross Browne's treatment on the *Bruce* was any more unpleasant than that accorded to most young novices who took to the sea is doubtful; but his resentment against conditions aboard ship and particularly against the arrogant behavior of the skipper was compounded by the fact that his friend Wilson became very ill under the harsh conditions and was left ashore in the Azores to either recuperate or die. Though Browne was probably more rugged, he thought of himself as "light-bodied rather than heavy-bodied" and he certainly did not have the brute strength of the old Portuguese hands who constituted most of the crew. Standing at 5′ 11″ and weighing 145 pounds, and unaccustomed to any harder labor than hiking and swimming, it is surprising he held his own as well as he did.

His three months on Zanzibar, that equatorial island off the coast of Africa where all nations met, gave him his first glimpse of truly foreign life; and his reactions, particularly to the Muslims who abounded in this section of Africa, have some bearing on his attitudes in Palestine at a later date. He made no criticism of the religious convictions of the Muslim Arabs, having long ago come to tolerate all religions as basically good. He even admired one Arab for praying to Mecca in the midst of the forest, thus acknowledging the appeal of Browne's beloved Nature. But he condemned the Arabs for their laziness—"second to no people in the art of loafing", their inveterate gambling, and their licentiousness—"of all the shameless libertines I ever saw, the Arabs are preeminent." [9] He contended that the women were ugly—even the greasy concubines belonging to the Sultan seemed to him less attractive than the quadroons he had seen in New Orleans—and "the females, from the age of twelve, are at the service of the public." [10]

He said little about the slave trade, partly because it was going through a period of "supression" while he was there. But he knew that Zanzibar was one of the principal and most notorious slave markets of the world. He maintained he found slaves on the interior of the island who were treated better than those he had seen in Mississippi. But they were subject (as everyone else was) to the incredible conditions of filth and disease in Zanzibar. In town, he was shocked by "the gaunt forms of men rotting with fever, leprosy, and ulcers, . . . seen staggering from street to street, begging a morsel of food to prolong their sufferings; slaves crawling about on their knees and hands, in the condition, and bearing the appearance, of brutes; half-naked skeletons tottering about with sunken eyes, maimed by the cruelty of their owners, and unsightly from disease." [11] He did not see, or at least he did not mention, the horrible sight observed by Sir Richard Burton a few years later of dogs on the beach chewing the flesh and gnawing the bones of "the washed-up bodies of sick slaves, thrown overboard by slavers just before landing to avoid paying the Sultan's head tax on poor or valueless merchandise." [12]

Three months in Zanzibar were more than enough, and Browne was grateful when an American merchantman arrived which afforded an opportunity to work his way home. After a quiet trip, made principally eventful by a pleasant flirtation with the daughters of the American consul in St. Helena, he arrived on the *Rolla* in Salem harbor on 19 November 1843.

A penniless Ross Browne returned to Washington, where he spent the next five years doing routine work which he detested. For awhile he continued reporting speeches in Congress for the *Globe*; later, after learning something about bookkeeping, he became a clerk in the Treasury Department, where he spent much of his time compiling bank statistics. Eventually Robert J. Walker, the Secretary of the Treasury under President Polk, became impressed with Browne's talents and made him his private secretary. Though this position allowed for more variety in his tasks as well as occasional trips to Philadelphia and New York, it did not remove him from what he called "the debasing and pestilential atmosphere of political life." However, for these five long years he curbed his wanderlust, fought against the nervous depressions which frequently accompanied his desk work, and put up with what he termed "a life of servitude" and "employment which I loathe." In the meantime he had married and started a family and he had published a book, even while he was adjusting himself to routine tasks.

His bride was Lucy Anna Mitchell, the daughter of a prominent

Washington physician, Spencer Cochrane Mitchell. When he looked back upon his courtship it seemed to him that he had spent years persuading Lucy's family to accept him—his ordeals sound something like Mark Twain's difficulties with Livy Langdon's family—but actually he was married in November 1844, less than a year after he returned from Zanzibar. The many letters which have been preserved that he wrote to his wife, recently published by Lina Fergusson Browne, indicate that the marriage was very happy and that Lucy Mitchell almost won out over wanderlust in making a good husband and father out of the genial, gregarious, and temperamental Browne. By the time he could no longer resist the temptation to travel and broke away from home in the year of the Gold Rush, he was the father of two children and was anticipating the arrival of a third.

While working in Washington, Browne felt certain that he was "wasting God's best gifts." One of these gifts, he was sure, was an ability to write, and he had ready at hand material which he felt cried for expression. A few years before, Richard Henry Dana, a young Harvard student, had written a book, *Two Years Before the Mast*, about his experiences working on a merchant ship in the California trade, and had seen his book become one of the successes of the hour. Why couldn't Browne do the same with whaling, a subject which remained comparatively untouched, at least as seen by the novice?

During the two years following his return to Washington Browne had published six articles about life aboard a whaler, most of them in Ohio River journals and one in *Ned Buntline's Magazine*. During a trip back to Kentucky and Ohio, he had met Ned Buntline in Cincinnati and the latter had offered him a job as editor of his newly founded journal. However, Browne was not so foolish as to tie himself up with a job at editing nor even to provide Buntline with ideas for another dime novel. He went on to Columbus, where his whaling companion, Wilson, was living after having been brought home from the Azores. The latter was still enduring dizzy spells from the sunstroke he had suffered on the *Bruce*, and at that time Browne was tempted to accept his friend's offer to set the type for a book the two would publish privately. Apparently Browne even considered making a novel from his whaling experiences. Over a year later, he worked his material into a book-length factual account and Harper and Brothers, a firm which was to publish most of his later books, accepted it for publication. According to Perry Miller in *The Raven and the Whale*, Evert Duyckinck edited the manuscript, finding the writing crude but the treatment forcibly "truthful," even though he thought that Browne had introduced too much roughness and profanity to suit the reader's taste. Though Browne protested: "If you think sailors are a refined class of men, or that I have at all exaggerated their profanity, you are much mistaken," [13] he gave in and submitted to the expurgations. Dana's manuscript for *Two Years Before The Mast* indicates that he had run into a similar problem with that book. It is unfortunate that Browne's manuscript has not survived for it would be interesting to see how outspoken he was, in this his first book, for in later works he was meticulously proper in his handling of sensitive subjects.

Etchings of a Whaling Cruise, with Notes of a Sojourn on the Isle of Zanzibar appeared late in 1846, the same year that Melville published his first book, *Typee*, telling of his adventures after jumping a whaler at about the same time Browne bought his release from the *Bruce* in Zanzibar. Apologizing for dealing principally with the darker side of whaling, Browne, who admitted that he preferred the sunny aspects of life, told his audience that he wrote in order to accomplish for sailors in the whaling industry, whom he felt were much abused, what Dana had attempted to do for merchant seaman. This meant stressing the wretchedness of the forecastle, the bad quality of the food, and, above all, the bondage of the sailor, the tyranny of the captain, and the use of such punishments as solitary confinement and flogging in order to maintain discipline. Naturally, there was not much room in such a program to indulge in humor or to treat the beauty of sunsets at sea or to tell of the excitement of pursuing and killing whales. Concerning the latter occupation, Browne asserted that he could conceive of nothing "more strikingly

awful than the butchery of this tremendous leviathan of the deep."
However, as the narrative was handled in journal fashion, there were
light moments, even happy ones, and the indignant attacks on the
captain and the "slimy Portuguese" were balanced with fairly
well-developed portraits of such shipmates as the black-whiskered,
grumbling Bill Mann; the storyteller Taber; the talented English liar
and thief, Jack Smith; and the typical Yankee tar, Charley Clifford,
Browne's favorite.

Etchings of a Whaling Cruise was basically factual, even containing an appendix with encyclopedic comments on the history of
whaling and surprisingly, a five page vocabulary of "Sowhelian"
(Swahilian) words which Browne had picked up in Zanzibar. Rarely
does the book suggest any of the metaphysical overtones found so
frequently in Melville's *Moby-Dick*; however, such a passage as
Browne's account of turning the grindstone rises above the customary pedestrian pace of the book:

There I turned that grindstone, and turned on hour after hour, and turned
the palm of my right hand into a great blister, and turned the palm of my left
into another; turned both my arms into a personified pain; turned every
remnant of romance out of my head; turned and turned till my grand tour
seemed to have turned into a grindstone; round and round I turned that
stone till I began to think I was a piece of the handle, and turned with it; and
my head appeared to turn, and the ship to turn, and the sea and whale, and
the sharks and the clouds, and all creation seemed to be turning with myself
and that grindstone.[14]

Etchings of a Whaling Cruise was well received by the critics, who
frequently compared Browne to Dana, in one case, at least, in
Browne's favor. The book was even noticed in Great Britain, with
kind words from *The Edinburgh Review*. Unlike *Typee*, it did not sell
very well, the many illustrations being expensive and the book,
according to Browne, being priced too high for the public. It
eventually achieved some fame, and was recently revived through
republication in the prestigious John Harvard Library, probably
because of its obvious influence on Melville. As a matter of fact,
Melville's first published review was a generous essay about *Etchings*
written for *The Literary World* in which he pronounced it "a faithful

picture of the life led by twenty thousand seamen employed in the seven hundred whaling vessels which now pursue their game under the American fleet." [15] And three years later, when Melville wrote his masterpiece, he drew upon *Etchings* extensively for both facts and quotations. It has even been suggested that Melville's Ahab owes something to Browne's Captain A——.

Though Browne gained some reputation through his first book, he soon hit a fallow period as far as writing was concerned, contributing nothing to the journals for the four years following its appearance. By the time the excitement in 1848 following the discovery of gold in California had grown to stampede proportions, he was in a fit of depression over his tedious desk work in Washington, a depression which seems even to have made him physically ill. Eager to change his surroundings and mode of livelihood, he was torn between his love for Lucy and his children, and his desire to get away on a new adventure. Like many another married man during the Gold Rush, he took the second course, assuring his family that it was for their good that he was going to El Dorado. He would not be away long and he would return with a fortune. Paradoxically, though he found no gold, the trip to California was one of the most fortunate ventures that Ross Browne ever embarked on.

Secretary of Treasury Walker did what he could to make it possible for the still improvident Browne to reach the West Coast. He made him a third lieutenant in the U. S. Revenue Marine and provided him with two rather ridiculous assignments. One was to try to determine why seamen deserted their ships on arrival in San Francisco Bay, and the other was to carry a vague message to a revenue cutter to be stationed in Oregon. The suspicion that the assignment was the result of a bit of finagling on the part of Secretary Walker, a Democrat who was due to lose his position in a couple of months with the inauguration of the Whig president Zachary Taylor, is borne out by the fact that one of the first bits of news that Browne heard after his six months voyage around the Horn was that his appointment had been cancelled by the new administration. The maneuver, however, did pay for his passage and his salary until he reached the West Coast, which was probably all that he had expected from it. He sailed, prepared to maintain himself in other ways: he had his photo taken by Brady for publicity purposes, he carried his flute and newly purchased guitar and violin for pleasure and to aid in making acquaintances, he stocked up on drawing paper so that he could execute portraits at twenty dollars a head, and he kept a journal aboard the *Pacific* so that he would have materials to write a book about his adventure. Curiously, although the voyage was by no means without incident (the passengers revolted and put the captain ashore in Rio de Janeiro), the principal incident on which Browne capitalized was a harebrained expedition made to Juan Fernandez Island, "Crusoe's Island," which appeared as "a light blue spot, scarce bigger than a handspike" [16] from the *Pacific* as it lay becalmed seventy miles away.

Browne and ten companions set off in a quarter boat owned by one of the passengers, sure that they could row the distance during a day and then the *Pacific* could pick them up later when it reached the island. Against the captain's advice, they embarked in the sheet-metal boat with the gunwales only ten inches out of water. It was built for six and was carrying eleven. They found themselves at nightfall miles from their goal, equipped only with a lantern and a pocket compass, and aware that a squall was blowing up. Juan Fernandez Island was somewhere ahead and Chile was five hundred miles to starboard. But Robinson Crusoe's Divine Providence saw them through their ordeal and they landed on the island the next morning. Though it was already occupied by fifteen Chileans plus one American, and was being visited at the moment by a shipload of Mormons, black-bearded, tobacco drooling, and armed to the teeth, whom Sam Brannan was bringing from Brooklyn to California in hopes of setting up a Mormon republic in the Far West, Browne and his friends found that the island more than measured up to their most romantic imaginings. It was rugged and wild and even supported goats, which they felt surely were descendants of the ones domesticated by Alexander Selkirk when he had lived alone on Juan Fernandez for four years more than a century earlier, before he was rescued and carried to England to be immortalized by Daniel Defoe as Robinson Crusoe.

Browne found romance and reality to be in conflict on Crusoe's island; in his account of his visit he even invented a Doubter who, like Mark Twain's Mr. Brown, was a constant thorn in the flesh of the romantics. The adventurers slept in "Crusoe's cave" in spite of the dampness of the ground and the prevalence of fleas. They discovered a pot which they hauled away, as well as a skull, which they presumed was human but which turned out to have belonged to a dog. They learned that since Selkirk's day the island had been used to house convicts for a time and at a later period it had seen a nasty murder, such a one as Melville had heard about in the Galapagos, another Pacific paradise where men turned brutal, as Melville was to point out in "The Encantadas." However, convicts and murders did little to darken Browne's enthusiasm for the lush island; he took a fearful climb up a cliff, coming as close to slipping to destruction as Tomo had done in *Typee*; he discovered a wilderness on the other side of the Nipple which he was sure was as lovely as Rasselas' happy valley, and he spent hours in a cave in the jungle, almost sure that he was lost. Like Dana before him, who had declared Juan Fernandez "the most romantic spot of earth," Browne left, when the disgruntled captain of the *Pacific* picked up the adventurers, convinced that "all the gold in California was not worth the ecstatic bliss of that moment." He wrote at once to Lucy directing that their third child, now due to arrive, should be called Robinson Crusoe Browne. Something happened to keep her from carrying out his wishes, but years later he acquired an Indian servant whom he cherished under the name of Yuba Friday.

Ross Browne's first few hours in San Francisco were not very happy ones. He was appalled at the brownness of the hills, at the dust, at the crowds of people, and at the ramshackle buildings; "As for San Francisco, it is about the most miserable spot I have seen in all my travels." He soon learned that the prices for food and lodgings were incredibly steep, and, furthermore, he was broke. And worst of all, he had arrived on Sunday and the post office was closed, meaning there was no chance of hearing from Lucy to find out whether she had by then forgiven him for leaving on this harebrained venture. (His letters indicate he had felt very remorseful at times even though he had escaped "the living death I endured in the Treasure Department for the last four years.") But suddenly his luck changed. Hardly three steps from the closed post office he ran into none other than Dr. William M. Gwin, whom he had known in Washington as a close friend of Secretary Walker. Gwin exclaimed: "Browne, you are the very man I want in California. Come along, we'll talk it over. Consider yourself the luckiest man in existence."

Soon fortune's cornucopia poured forth its bounties. Gwin arranged to have Browne's mail released from the closed post office; he also invited him to live in his house as his guest. Gwin confided to him that he had come to California to form a convention and get himself elected senator from California. The new area, which had been ceded by a defeated Mexico eighteen months before, was still operating under a military government, as it had not been granted either the status of a territory or a state. The plan was to have General Riley call for the meeting of a convention, whereupon a state constitution would be drawn up, ready for use when Congress belatedly got around to acting. Browne arrived just at the propitious moment. To Lucy, Browne wrote in elation that Gwin had said he would be elected Stenographer to the Convention. In the meantime, during the month before the convention was to convene in Monterey, Browne, through Gwin's intercession, was given a temporary commission to set up post offices all the way to San Diego. "I am crazy with enthusiasm," he assured Lucy. "I look forward to my career in California as a series of triumphs. What will please you more than anything else is the wonderful improvement in my health. I am a new man altogether. I hope to pass through all dangers in safety. You must be perfectly easy on that score." [17]

The trip south through the pueblo of San Jose and the Salinas Valley particularly appealed to him. With the companionship of a friend he had made on the Pacific voyage and a handsome mule to ride, he was full of anticipation; "I have a *carte blanche* to do what I please, go where I please, and cost what I please. We are to sleep under trees, light a fire, cook our meat, and live in real Indian style." [18] The venture did not work out quite that way. When he wrote to Lucy from Monterey after making a six-day journey, during which he had had to turn back just short of San Luis Obispo, he revealed that the mule had been most refractory, the friend equally unsympathetic, the weather wretched, the fleas abundant, and his euphoria replaced by a wretched fever. Actually he did manage to establish one post office, in San Jose. Years later, writing of the trip in the delightful "A Dangerous Journey" he made it seem like a combination of a lark and a nightmare, including accounts of seeing a fight between a bear and a bull, watching the stabbing of a Mexican girl by a jealous rival, and stumbling upon a corpse in the hovel where he planned to spend the night. Perhaps all of these things really happened; or perhaps by 1862 he had learned to embroider his accounts in true California fashion.

Back at Monterey, Browne set about making sure that he would in fact have the position of reporting the constitutional convention, which was to start on 3 September. Although there were two other candidates for the position, he succeeded in obtaining it, presumably principally through the efforts of the future Senator Gwin. It proved to be a real bonanza. He was paid ten thousand dollars in gold for the job; this sum was to include provision for the costs of publishing 1000 copies of the report in English and another 300 in Spanish. However, Browne was free to keep all of the returns on the book and, when it appeared in 1850 in Washington, the debate on granting of statehood to California was in full swing and the demand for it far exceeded the original planned issue. Browne turned to expert help for the Spanish translation, in spite of the fact that he had boasted to Lucy: "It would astonish you to hear me speak Spanish. I can spout it out like a native and manage to make all my wishes understood." He also confided to his wife that he hoped to translate the Spanish manuscript of the California memoirs of Señor Don Juan Bandini of San Diego into English and publish them.

During the six weeks that the constitutional convention met at

Colton Hall in Monterey, Browne was a very busy man. He acquainted himself with the delegates to the convention, including such California stalwarts as Captain Sutter, General Vallejo, and Robert Semple, and he took down all speeches faithfully in shorthand. He apparently did not have time to transpose his notes during the session; in doing so in Washington it is said he improved on the language of the speakers somewhat. Thirty years later a California newspaper reported a rumor that had become a tradition: "The manner in which the crude efforts of the early legislators of California were upon this occasion pruned down and dressed up by the enterprising shorthand writer was ever after a source of merriment to the initiated." [19] There were doubtless many moments of humor, as when one delegate objected violently to calling his confreres "peers," and even more of bitter controversy, such as that which nearly broke up the convention over the subject of whether Indians should be allowed to vote. But a viable and not unworthy constitution was finally adopted by the assembly on October 12, after which there was a great scurrying about to find clothes to wear to the celebration ball, where two violins and two guitars furnished the music late into the night.

There is no indication that Browne was much involved in the social life of Monterey, although he speaks of playing his flute for Mr. Ord's family and also of finding the Spanish ladies in Monterey much cooler than those he had met in Chile. He attributed their attitude to the fact that shortly before his arrival they had had to fend off the soldiers of Stevenson's Regiment. As he lodged in a room provided gratis by Captain Henry W. Halleck, a veteran of the Mexican war, and had found a place where he could eat for eleven dollars a week, his expenses did not run very high. His favorite recreation was taking walks around Monterey, and it was possibly through this practice that he became well acquainted with Bayard Taylor. In his *El Dorado* Taylor tells of going with Browne on a walk to Cypress Point, where the two barbecued beef and pried abalones off the rocks.[20]

Taylor was a fortunate acquaintance for Browne to make. Four years Browne's junior, he had already gained a wide reputation as a travel writer. At twenty-four, he had been sent by the *New York Tribune* to write about California and the Gold Rush, and the resultant *El Dorado* was to be one of the best books dealing with that most publicized event. Like Ross Browne, Taylor liked roughing it, and had walked from San Francisco to Monterey to observe the people on the trail. Five years earlier, when he was only nineteen, he had set out to establish a new pattern for Americans traveling in Europe. He had walked all over Europe, living for two years on the minuscule sum of five hundred dollars; his *Views-a-Foot* was a great success. His tastes in travel were very much like Browne's, except perhaps that he went in somewhat more for the exotic; like Browne, he had early learned to draw and paint, and was in the process of picturing California life for the world public. Like Browne, he preferred to carry his belongings, including pocket thermometer, barometer, compass, and spyglass, in a knapsack; but his clothes, "a complete suit of corduroy, with shirt of purple flannel," were in startling contrast to Browne's nondescript wear, and he carried a revolver, something which Browne never cared to do.

Taylor and Browne must have talked much of their dreams. Browne had taken notes for a book on his trip around South America and the life he saw in California but his most persistent ambition was still to visit the Near East. He even entertained ideas of crossing the Pacific and approaching the Levant through China and India. Shortly before Ross Browne was eventually to reach Jerusalem, Bayard Taylor started on a round-the-world trip which took him to North Africa, the Near East, and on through India and China to the Pacific, where he joined the squadron of Commodore Perry. While visiting the Holy Land, he was to take the same route that Browne did, except that he traveled in the opposite direction. This was just five months after Browne made the journey, and thus Taylor's *The Lands of the Saracen* provides an excellent companion piece to *Yusef*.

On 2 November Ross Browne set out on the journey home via the Isthmus. He had already sent the ten thousand dollars in gold ahead to await his arrival; he was determined that he would use part of it to stake him to that long delayed trip to the Holy Land. He returned home by Christmas 1849, and was delighted to see his family. It took him an additional fifteen months to manage the getaway. He finished and published the book on the convention; acted as consultant on California affairs with politicians like R. J. Walker, who were eager to take advantage of developing projects in the new state; and was even tempted to go back to California with the offer of free lots in the newly established capital, Benicia, and any one of various jobs when he got there. But now he was not to be diverted. Though his three months in California had caused him to look upon himself as a Californian, he was headed the other way. He felt that he had solved the family problem by his plan to take the whole household, including his sister-in-law Dart, to Italy. He would establish them in Florence and make that Renaissance city a base for his wanderings. The money earned in California would get him there, and he hoped articles for the Washington *National Intelligencer* would keep him and the family alive after they reached Europe. Someway or other he would manage eventually to get them home. On 19 March 1851 Browne sailed with his family from New York, with Bayard Taylor at the wharf to see him off, and a letter from Henry Clay in his pocket to aid him in foreign parts.

THREE

Honorary General of the Bobtailed Militia

IT SUITED the humor of Ross Browne to refer to himself while traveling in Europe and the Near East as an "Honorary General of the Bobtailed Militia." By this term he meant not only that he was a man of the people, but that he scorned all pretentiousness—particularly that attitude which caused people to go into ecstasy about ruins when history did not really mean much to them, and to wax enthusiastic about art when they really had no art background. Though he admitted in Rome that "it was quite easy to work yourself into a state of inspired credulity," he avoided that process as much as possible as not befitting Americans, who presumably were to get their joys out of living in the present. "We don't build pyramids and coliseums," he explained, "but we build railroads." In much the same spirit he admitted that he "felt no great interest in old daubs of paintings or in figures of saints." Even after viewing the treasures of the Vatican, including the Apollo Belvedere, the Laocoön, and the paintings of Raphael and Michelangelo, he wrote to his wife: "I must confess I saw nothing to change my views of ancient art." [1]

It is surprising that Ross Browne was such a philistine in his attacks on the Old Masters, for as soon as he established himself and family in the midst of the American art colony in Florence he set

[55]

about trying to improve his own sketching and painting. He was aided in this endeavor by a newly made friend named Kellogg, an artist who accompanied him to Rome on one of his visits and provided him with art instruction as well as travel companionship. The key to the paradox may be found in an article which Browne wrote from Rome for the *National Intelligencer* after he returned from the Holy Land.[2] It dealt with praise of American artists working in Florence and Rome, pointing out that art buyers should turn to them for canvasses and statues rather than buying copies of Old Masters or such "emasculate productions" as those of the popular Italian sculptor Canova. If he was a philistine, he at least was a patriotic one.

A fortnight after sailing from New York, Ross Browne had disembarked with his family in LeHavre; following three weeks in Paris and elsewhere in France they went by ship from Marseille to Leghorn, suffering from most miserable seas and cramped conditions on the steamer. Leaving his family in Florence, Ross set off to visit the Lombardy cities, as well as Venice and Austria. Once again his impulses were divided between staying at home and traveling, but, as his family's support depended on his going where he could find material for his travel letters, he felt he had no choice but to leave home. "I have all the love of home and domestic enjoyment that ever dwelt in the breast of a man; but destiny seems to make me a wanderer." From Venice he boasted that his expenses for nearly three weeks traveling in North Italy had come to only sixty-five dollars. He could not resist teasing Lucy about his enjoyment of gondola rides on the canal, "with ladies gliding by, and the guitar sounding its love-notes"; he was not wholly kind in adding, "How I wished you were here. But I knew you would not feel romantic with three babies on your lap and one in your—thoughts of the future." [3] By the first of September, he was back in Florence in time for the birth of his fourth child, this time a girl, christened Nina Florence in honor of her birthplace. Nine days later he was off on the long tour—spending some time in Rome and Naples, then passing over to Sicily and Malta, and finally going on to the Aegean and the Levant.

Thus, on his third attempt to reach the mysterious East, he was successful. As he wrote in the preface to *Yusef*, "I got there at last, having . . . visited the four continents, and traveled by sea and land a distance of a hundred thousand miles, or more than four times around the world, on the scanty earnings of my own head and hands." [4]

In Sicily, Browne most enjoyed the catacombs of Palermo, the climbing of Mt. Etna, and the view from Taormina; the ruins of Syracuse reminded him that he really had little interest in the wars of the Greeks and Romans. For of what consequence was it to a humble wanderer like himself to learn "how many were killed on certain occasions, or who were the best cut-throats of ancient times?" Now that the summer heat was slackening, he was eager to reach the Near East. Cheerfully he put up with the discomfort that went with the cheapest accommodations, "ranging from deck-passages to the second cabin" on the French and Austrian steamers that plied the area; cheerfully he set about living on four francs (eighty cents) a day when he was ashore—this amount covering both hotel and food in Greece, where he was satisfied with bread and grapes three times a day. He carried no baggage except a knapsack, "principally filled with leaves and small pieces of various ruins for my friends at home." In a letter to Lucy from Athens he explained his philosophy of traveling:

My traveling companions wherever I go are always complaining of the heat or the cold or the hardship of walking half a mile, or the terrible evils of a bad hotel or a bad dinner. Now walking is a luxury to me; a bad dinner is a godsend because it takes but little time to eat it; a broiling sun just makes me feel comfortable; and as to the thousand and one other evils of which I hear them complain they form the spice of travel.[5]

In Athens he found the Acropolis "a very respectable mass of ruins" from which one could get a good, detached view of the modern town of seventeen thousand inhabitants, principally "degenerate" Greeks. He looked in vain for the Maid of Athens but found instead King Otho's queen on display—"in Washington City, which I have the honor to represent, she might pass for the daughter of a neighboring farmer, more accustomed to jumping fences and hunting up the cows than to the atmosphere of royalty." [6] His Austrian steamer stopped at Syros in the Cyclades, a crossroads port which he was to see three times before leaving the Eastern Mediterranean, and then proceeded to Smyrna, where he found he could put foot on Asia only by going into quarantine and allowing his ship to sail without him. Never daunted, he went ashore and spent eight days smoking long-stemmed chibouks, sipping muddy Greek coffee, and watching veiled Smyrniote women to see if they were as beautiful as they were reputed to be. "They certainly deserve their reputation for dark flashing eyes and classical features; and that being the only flattering reputation they do deserve, from all I could learn on reliable authority, as well as my own limited observation, it affords me great pleasure to accord it to them." [7] Eventually he found a steamer which would take him to Constantinople.

Like many another traveler, Ross Browne arose before dawn to see the minarets and domes of Stamboul from the vantage point of his steamer anchored in the Bosphorus. The sight thrilled him as nothing had done since his arrival in Europe. Also, like many another Frank, he was disappointed when he went ashore and established himself in a modest hotel in Pera. An "enchantment beyond all the dreams of fancy" had in the light of harsh reality been completely dispelled: "To see, is bliss; to smell, is reality; to touch, is misery in the last degree." But he spent three weeks in the gateway to the Near East, nevertheless.

In Turkey there was nothing left but to admit that he was a tourist, there by virtue of steam and dependent upon a guidebook. The language barrier kept him from getting acquainted with the inhabitants; the roaming dogs and lawless thugs prevented his strolling at night. He found that the novelty of picturesque costumes and strange customs soon wore away. Yet he did the things he was expected to do.

No traveler considers himself completely initiated into the mysteries of Oriental life till he has suffered scalding and strangulation in a Turkish bath, purchased a fez, and smoked himself sick at a narguilla [sic]. . . . I have

been thoroughly boiled out of my skin in a public bath; have suffered my
beard to grow till I can swear by it; smoked narguillas till I came within an
ace of getting the delirium tremens; and purchased a fez, which I wear two
hours every night before going to bed, in the hope of conquering a certain
bashfulness which yet prevents me from appearing with it in public.[8]

He also took a ride in a caïque, watched performances of both the
whirling and the howling dervishes, and bargained in the bazaar for a
piece of silk for Lucy only to find when he returned to his hotel that
he had paid too much and that his silk had been made in Paris. He
peered at the Turkish women, finding that their features were ugly
when he caught glimpses behind the *yashmacks* with which they
covered their faces; like other Frangi he was startled to find that they
readily bared their breasts while keeping their mouths and chins
concealed.

One morning he saw the Sultan, Abd-ul-Mejid, riding out from the
Seraglio, found him too pale and emaciated, and thus assumed he
was probably drugged and stupified as many had reported. The great
architectural monuments of Constantinople elicited little comment
from Browne. By joining a large group of tourists he was able to
enter many of the mosques of Stamboul, including the famous Santa
Sophia. His only comment on the latter structure involved a gibe at
Lamartine, whom he considered the prime offender among the
romantics who had written about the Levant. Though Lamartine had
called Santa Sophia "a grand Caravanseri of God," Browne wrote he
couldn't find a camel in sight but was sure that there had been "an
animal with very long ears about the premises."

Before leaving Rome Browne, doubtless with the aid of the letter
from Henry Clay, had persuaded the American minister, Cass, to
give him a commission as a bearer of dispatches to Constantinople,
thus saving him the trouble of going through customs and getting
visas from American consuls. Now, for his further journeys, through
the kindness of Mr. Brown, Secretary of the American Legation, he
obtained a firman, signed by the Sultan, recommending him to all
Pashas, Reis, and Sheiks throughout the Turkish dominions. He also
obtained a similar firman for "a most intelligent and agreeable young
gentleman from North Carolina" who was eager to share Browne's

adventures in the Holy Land. The two left Constantinople on an Austrian paddle-wheel steamer, rode out the Levanter which greeted them on reaching the Aegean, stopped briefly at Smyrna, Rhodes, and Lernica in Cyprus, in all of which places Browne made sketches, and on 23 November steamed into Beirut, which was the starting point for all pilgrimages to Jerusalem by way of Damascus and the Street called Straight.

In the hubbub that developed almost the moment his steamer dropped anchor in the wretched harbor at Beirut, Ross Browne had little time to enjoy the view of the beautiful Lebanon range which lay behind the small Syrian port. Most of the inhabitants of the village seemed to be on hand to sell boat transportation to shore, space in a hotel, or the services of a dragoman. Browne, in his backwoods clothes, accompanied by his tall, slender friend from the South named Baker, properly dressed with a red guide book in hand, were soon taken in tow by a handsomely mustached lady-killer in an Albanian costume who introduced himself as Demetrie, formerly a dragoman, now an innkeeper. Demetrie arranged for transportation ashore, after which he led his clients to the Demetrie Hotel, just outside the city walls, a hostelry which was to furnish the cleanest and most commodious lodgings Browne was to find in Syria. Also Demetrie introduced Browne and Baker to a dragoman named Yusef Simon Badra, who at once captivated them with his personality. The travelers were delighted to find that they had acquired a droll character to play a role which, according to Browne, included the guises of "tutor, lexicon, valet, cook, caterer, comforter, warrior." To help with expenses, they expanded their party to three, adding a young Englishman named Clark, the chief officer of a coastal steamer who had a vacation of two months which he planned to spend seeing the sights. Though the customary charge for the services of a dragoman and his equipment was five dollars a day per person, the three bargainers, stressing the lateness of the season, persuaded Yusef to take care of them for ninety-six Turkish piasters each, about four dollars, a day.

In retrospect, Browne felt that he could have made his way

Yusef

through Syria for half the price he paid Yusef, largely because he felt his dragoman carried more equipment than was necessary. Yet Browne would have been foolhardy to try to see Syria on foot, knapsack on back, as he had done in California. He was keenly aware, however, that he had started from Florence with some $230, had spent two-and-a-half months getting to Beirut, and that he still intended to pass a month or more in the Holy Land, and a couple of weeks in Egypt. Nevertheless he even lengthened the trip by spending three days following the Syrian coast north to Tripoli so that he might see the Cedars of Lebanon on his way to Damascus.

Yusef, for his part, provided not only his own services and all cooking and camping equipment necessary but four horses, three mules, a donkey, a boy, and food and muleteers to take care of the pack animals. The plan was to camp each night, and the first night out Yusef had the tent up in no time and served a meal on a table furnished with knives and forks, napkins, and "different courses of plate"; the bedsteads in the tent sported clean linen and warm blankets. However, the luxury was short-lived. The rain, which was a month overdue, arrived on that very night and drove the campers from the leaky tents to the shelter of a nearby khan, extremely filthy and inhabited by animals, fleas, and Arabs who seemed never to go to sleep. As the journey continued the party spent more nights in khans and native hovels than they did in tents. Browne, who was devoted to "Rough and Ready" traveling, bore the discomforts with little complaint, remarking wisely: "Whatever may be the inconveniences of living among mules, asses, fleas, and smoking Arabs, they are not so great as those of sickness in a foreign land, where no assistance can be had. Many a traveler has laid his bones in Syria in consequence of wet nights and sunshiny days." [9]

During the three days it took to reach the Cedars, Browne admired the industry of the Syrians in cultivating small patches of ground terraced out of the rocky hills, of growing enough mulberry trees to support a silk culture, and of building villages which clung to the sides of the steep hills and valleys, even though the houses looked like "mud boxes put out on the hills to dry" and proved on closer examination to be wretched, vermin-ridden huts. After struggling along trails worse than the ones he had encountered crossing the isthmus of Panama, and stopping to make sketches in Byblos (Djbel) and Tripoli, the party climbed up a precipitous but very picturesque valley half way to the top of the Lebanon range, where they found the Cedars of Lebanon, "a mere patch of green in the bare and desert hollow of the mountains." The impressive cedars seemed very old and Browne was persuaded that the twelve most ancient ones possibly had existed in Solomon's day. Also persuaded that the trees would benefit from pruning, he and his companions cut walking sticks for themselves and peeled off relics for the folks at home. Probably Browne did not carve his name, having seen among other names so carved that of Lamartine, "said to have been carved by an Arab while the great sentimentalist was going into ecstasies in his comfortable quarters below."

On over the summit the party plodded, finding the climb well worthwhile when they saw the late afternoon view not only back down the mountain to the Mediterranean but on the other side to the great valley which lies between the Lebanon and the Anti-Lebanon, the valley in which the famous Orontes runs north and the almost equally famous Leontes (Litani) runs south, both rising in the area where the ruins of Heliopolis or Baalbek glittered in the evening sun. It took nearly two more days to reach Baalbek, however, what with their getting lost once, sharing a cave with goats at another time, and coping with their recalcitrant mounts in between. When he reached the valley floor, Browne was reminded forcibly of the Salinas Valley in California, but he missed the "life, vigor, and spirit" he had found among the forty-niners. The Beka' Valley, which has proved so fertile in the twentieth century and had probably been so in the days when the original Baalbek was created, was now lying fallow, with only an occasional feeble attempt at cultivating to be seen.

The ruins of ancient Baalbek completely captured Browne and his friends. "The ruins of Baalbek are among the few sights one sees in the East that will bear the test of scrutiny; the more they are studied the greater is the admiration they excite; and if one can not go into the sentimentalities of Lamartine, he will see enough at least to afford both pleasure and wonder." [10] The origins of Baalbek were in Browne's day even more of a mystery than they are today, and goats and smoking Arabs camped among the magnificent ruins that archeologists have since made tidy. Browne was unwilling to accept the legend that the Palace of the Sun had been raised by genii, but he did assume that the vast ruins were the remnants of temples which had once been the pride of Assyria, the part Rome had played in their construction not then being generally known. Like all who look upon Baalbek, he marveled at the huge stones, huge like the stones in the Egyptian pyramids, which were used in the base of the temple; he was struck with the beauty of the bas-reliefs on cornice and pedestal; he was moved by the stark beauty of the few remaining tall pillars silhouetted against the sky by the afternoon sun. He poked his way through long subterranean passages where sunlight filtered through cracks and a strong smell of goats was pervasive. He sketched the ruins from every angle. He then decided paradoxically that a Baalbek in ruins was probably more impressive than it was at the height of its glory. He asserted that we are all prone "to false impressions by feeding the mind with the poetry of the past. . . . Strip the past of all its romance, and there is little left to write about."

But there remained the immediate problem of where to spend the night in the dirty little village of "modern" Baalbek. The weather discouraged camping; the Greek convent was about as tempting "as a comfortable pig-sty"; but Yusef found a private dwelling large enough for the whole party—not, this time, a hovel, but "a respectable little stone box covered over with mud." Once housed and fed, it was good to relax, to sip coffee, to smoke the chibouk, and to get acquainted with the congenial Arabs. Soon Browne thought of his flute, and assembled it while everyone waited eagerly. After all, he carried the flute "to relieve the lonely hours at night and excite a social feeling among the natives."

Ross Browne started entertaining the Arabs with his favorite melody, the feet-tingling "Old Zip Coon," which they delightfully accepted and referred to as "Ezepa Kouna," as they joined in the clapping, and then he grew sentimental and played, "Give me back my heart again; oh! give it back again!" The contrasting tones of the two songs reflected the incongruous mixture of realism and romanticism that was so deeply ingrained in his personality, the same contrast that is found between his satirical sketches and his love of dreamy landscapes. As to his taste in music, he pretended to no more complexity than he did in art; he liked simple tunes as he liked simple paintings. He frequently complained that he could not enjoy the music of operas, and to Lucy he confided that even Jenny Lind was too sophisticated for him: "I do not pretend . . . to know anything about music." He preferred the ballad style and it was well suited to his talent with the flute and the social uses to which he put it.

One or two more visits to the ruins the next morning, a call on the Greek Bishop (who asked amusing questions about California), and a perfunctory and skeptical look at the "tomb of Saladin" in the local mosque, and the party was on its way for the two-day trip to

Damascus. On the route out of town they, of course, stopped at the quarry from which the stones of Baalbek had been hewn and marveled at the block which had been cut but not carried to the temples, perhaps because it was bigger than any of the blocks that were used. Browne was delighted at the folk tale that the men being unable to carry it, a woman put it on her shoulders, trotted over to Baalbek with it, and, when the Sultan refused to pay her, kicked him into the ditch and returned the stone to the quarry.

In spite of the inclement weather, Browne enjoyed the trip over the ridge of the Anti-Lebanon and down into the fruitful valley. Here there was water in the stream bed, delightful to listen to even in the rain. Here was a primitive grain mill to contrast with the more modern one he had seen his father run in Kentucky; here were camels lying down waiting to be sketched; here was the legendary Tomb of Abel. But in the dusk the Arabs and the Christians became separated and Browne and his companions feared that they might be set upon by robbers. Browne felt that if the marauders attacked they could get little loot from him.

For my own part, I had made up my mind, if attacked by the robbers, to offer them my old coat, two shirts, a tooth-brush, a small pocket comb, some sketches of Baalbek, and a few shorthand notes from which these pages are written, together with a draft on my friend the Southerner, who was kindly paying my way to Alexandria, where I expected a remittance. I had likewise about me some small paper money, amounting to twenty kreutzers (sixteen cents), payable in Austria in the course of forty or fifty years; a letter of introduction to the Pasha of Egypt, two Seidlitz powders, and a pocket-compass.[11]

They met no robbers, but did find Yusef, drunk on arrack, when they finally reached Zebdene, which was so much of a garden town that it seemed a veritable Eden. On the next morning's trek the members of the party knew they were approaching traditionally hostile Damascus because they were abused for being Christian dogs by a living skeleton of an old woman. Not long after, they stood upon the rise overlooking Damascus, the spot where a famous sheik had preferred to die on the heights because he felt that he would never enjoy Paradise if he entered that fairy-like city. With its many green trees, its sparkling watercourses, and its striking domes and minarets, it looked like everything Browne had dreamed of the Orient since he was a boy. He soon found that, though Damascus looked fine from a distance, entering it was a mistake. "All travellers bound to Damascus, in search of the beautiful, should take a good look at it from the summit of Jebel-el-Nazir, and die as soon as possible, like the Sheik, but not go a step farther." [12]

Though Browne passed through rain as he neared the city, his principal impression of Damascus was the presence of a tremendous amount of dust—layers of dust on the trees and clouds of it in the air. On his approach to the center of the city he saw nothing but high mud walls, broken and dilapidated gateways, lazy dogs and lazier Arabs, basking by the roadside "showing mutually the luxuries of dust and flies." The farther he rode the more narrow became the streets, made dark by the mats which hung across them, the more prevalent became the lepers and beggars, the more harrowing were the caravans of camels, who crushed his legs against the wall in passing with their heavy loads. To cap the visitors' troubles, children threw stones and spat at them, yelling, "Frangi! Frangi!" to their Muslim elders' delight.

The contrast of the wretched streets with the Hotel de Palmyre was overwhelming. Here was a beautiful courtyard with orange trees and fountains. Here was a welcoming tavern keeper, resplendent in red fez and reeking of attar of roses, who led them to the special chamber, also equipped with a fountain and marble floors. Browne felt it was all quite "Lalla Rookish." After dinner and a pipe and coffee, Browne persuaded the entire staff to accompany his flute with "Ezepa Kouna." Then the party of three went to bed to the murmur of fountains, only to experience violent nightmares, and wake next morning with bad colds. The charcoal heaters supplied them barely served to warm their hands.

Though Browne did the routine things in Damascus, taking a Turkish bath, hiring a learned Jewish guide, and seeing "all in Damascus he was expected to see," he carried few pleasant memories away. In his account in *Yusef* he mentions St. Paul only once. Doubtless he visited the house of Ananias, who had sheltered Saul, saw the place on the wall from which Paul was lowered, and walked along the Street called Straight, although he does not mention them. As he pointed out to his readers, he intended to avoid "as far as practicable, everything that has given fame to those who have preceded me." He found few ruins and as a Christian dog he could not enter the Damascus mosques. It was well, as Bayard Taylor points out, that the oldest city in the world possessed few relics of antiquity worth visiting.

As for savoring contemporary life, Browne was more hesitant than Taylor about lounging in coffee shops and getting behind garden walls; certainly he did not try hashish—as Taylor did, much to his discomfort. Rather, he made a point of visiting American mission-aries as he had done in Athens and Beirut; in this latter place he had been struck with the talent of the Reverend Eli Smith, who was even then translating the Bible into Arabic. Browne, who admitted to having had a prejudice against missionaries before reaching the Levant, was struck with the success which they seemed to be having. He probably did not know that most of their converts were from other Christian sects, such as the Maronites, rather than from the Muslims, who faced the considerable likelihood of being beheaded if they turned Christian. He approved of the missionaries' intelligence, their candor, their industry; in fact the missionaries in the Levant, particularly in Beirut, were a most talented and devoted group of men, of which Eli Smith and William Thomson were outstanding examples.

It was characteristic of Ross Browne that he considered the task of spreading Christianity a fairly simple one, providing that the missionary stuck to the fundamentals of that religion as Browne conceived them—that is, the promulgating of "peace on earth and good will to men." "The Christian religion is simple and easily understood," he insisted. All who knew him well felt that Browne was deeply religious, with a simple faith but no creedal commit-ments. As for Catholics, both Greek and Roman, he accepted them and did not ridicule them; he made it clear, however, that he considered them superstitious. Of Judaism he said little and of Islam he was tolerant, for he truly respected other people's religious views and had much of the universalist in his beliefs.

From Damascus, Browne and his companions turned almost due south, climbed part way up the slope of Mt. Hermon, and dropped down, after three wretched days of rain, sleet, and snow, into the upper Jordan valley at Baniyas, site of the former Caesarea Philippi. He later wrote his wife that he had nearly died from cold and exposure on the road to Baniyas but said nothing about the fact that the spot was named after the god Pan or that this was the first soil he had reached upon which Jesus was said to have trod. In *Yusef* he wrote that during his life he had at various times agreed to meet friends and foes in Philippi. "The friends were not there: I was not disappointed in regard to the foes. We all had an abundance of them during the night, and in the morning had no cause to complain of having met nothing in Philippi." [13]

Browne's feelings about Baniyas were no doubt acerbated by the fact that he passed the night in a khan. The difficult ride the next day followed by another unpleasant night did little to raise his feelings. It is true that he was pleased to see the Bedouins north of Lake Huleh diligently working the soil with their buffalo and crude plowing sticks hoping to produce Indian corn, wheat, and rice. He even found these first Bedouins he was to meet attractive in feature and behavior, though he thought they lived more like beavers than humans. The land was swampy and the path difficult to follow. As the day wore on, the party was forced to thread its way along wretched trails, which sometimes followed the edge of the hills to avoid the swamps, and more than once he and his friends were crowded off the path by caravans of camels carrying produce to Damascus. Yusef had assured Browne that all discomforts would be forgotten when they reached a mill at Malaha, where they were to sleep, but conditions there were terrible and Browne spent a night which he turned into a great joke when he wrote *Yusef*.

The Sea of Galilee lay still another day's journey ahead, a day which took the party along the edge of the hills west of Lake Huleh and eventually up a ridge which acted almost as a natural dam separating the two bodies of water. Sometime about noon they caught their first glimpse of Kinneret, variously known as Lake Tiberias and the Sea of Galilee; there it glimmered, encircled by barren mountains, dim in the haze, and "still and desolate as it lay outspread before us in the noonday sun." It seemed part of a "dreary waste of whitish stones and sodless heights . . . yet rich beyond all that earth could yield in the history of Him who had stilled the tempest and walked upon the waters." [14]

At about the time they got their first glimpse of the Sea of Galilee, the party became aware that they were being stalked by armed Arabs, and, as they were hardly equipped to defend themselves, there was some apprehension. However, they soon learned that the Arabs were followers of the Sheik of Baalbek, who had revolted against the Turks and was hiding with his nineteen remaining followers in the old Khan called Jub Yusef. Browne and his companions stopped to visit him and were welcomed most graciously by the doomed leader. This was one of the few opportunities Browne had of meeting an Arab of stature; although he could not talk to him, knowing no Arabic and but imperfect French and Italian, he could admire him and did so. About thirty years old, the sheik was boldly handsome, with eyes at times brilliant, fiery and piercing, at other times "as gentle as a woman's." In contrast to most of the Arabs Browne had seen, he was dressed richly, with a handsome turban setting off his magnificent beard, embroidered trousers and costly vest, ornamented with braid and silver buttons, and over his shoulders a robe of beautiful colors. He was, of course, genteel and hospitable, but not hospitable enough to present his wife, a deliciously pretty creature whom Browne caught a glimpse of in the background. The Sheik did, however, show them his horse, a true-bred Arabian, which far excelled all the Arabian steeds Browne had seen in America, Zanzibar, and even Syria. For once, romance was wedded to reality, and the Orient was embodied in fitting colors, thus providing at least one exception to the "dreary, commonplace, comfortless reality" which Browne assigned to Arab life. He learned with a pang that the rebel sheik was sure to be slain in the not too distant future by Turkish soldiers.

The contact with the sheik, the glimpse of the distant lake, and the escape from rocky trail to cultivated valley may all have contributed to Browne's enthusiasm for the Sea of Galilee, which he reached just before sunset. He and his companions at once rode their horses into the clear water and sat long, admiring the mountains on the other side of the lake, suspended in air and blue in the fast vanishing twilight. The evening was warm and balmy, there were fig trees and olives, and the atmosphere hinted of green grass, wild herbs, and oleanders. The spell continued while they rode down the side of the lake and they reached Tiberias, late in the evening, ready for dinner and a pleasant rest.

Adequate accommodations were found at a hotel for Frank travelers run by a genial German Jew named Wiseman. After dinner it was suggested that the party take advantage of the moonlight and make a boatride on the lake, but perhaps the spirit of adventure was slipping away, for the travelers decided to write in their journals instead of braving the waters. In the morning they found Tiberias a sad disappointment. Once the arrogant Roman capital of Galilee under Herod Antipas, it was now a stagnant ruin, eroded by centuries of neglect and finally laid waste by a sizable earthquake fifteen years before their arrival. For centuries it had been the principal seat of Rabbinical learning in Palestine, but now, though it retained a predominantly Jewish population, it no longer played an important part in the intellectual world. Sick women and lethargic men played their lackluster roles against dilapidated walls through which threaded filthy streets, where hairless dogs served as scavengers and fetid pools of green water emitted foul odors. Only the beautiful, gaudily dressed Jewish children provided a touch of relief.

For their one day trip westward across the hills of Galilee to Nazareth the travelers were blessed with good weather which provided them a pleasant view of the Sea of Galilee from the heights. As they rode on, they saw to their left the truncated cone of Mt. Tabor, traditionally thought of as the site of the Transfiguration, and passed over the plain below the Horns of Hatin, where Saladin had butchered the Crusaders. At nearby Cana, Browne felt for once close to the Bible story as the ragged children came down to the well of sweet-tasting water which he had stopped to sketch. Early in the afternoon the party arrived at Nazareth, having successfully ignored the advice to take an armed guard with them through this dangerous area of Palestine, supposedly filled with bandits. Though they saw some scowling Bedouins, they were more impressed with the hard-working Arabs who were scratching the soil with rude wooden plows drawn by stunted oxen.

In spite of its attractive location at the head of a valley, Nazareth proved another disappointment, "one of the worst specimens of a Syrian town." Its square, flat-roofed houses and its convents were inhabited on the one side by a most villainous looking set of Arabs and on the other by monks who were eager to exploit the holy places. Nevertheless, Browne spent a pleasant night at the Latin convent, after which he found praise for the medical aid the monks provided the poor. Like many another visitor to Nazareth, he generalized on the beauty of the women on the basis of the few glimpses he got of them. He visited the reputed birthplace of the Virgin, a "catch-penny show" in one convent, and the home of the Holy Family in a cave below another convent. He apparently missed the place of the Annunciation and the charming Mary's Well. About the only spot in Nazareth which he felt could be accepted as genuinely established as a holy site was the village itself.

The trip south to Jerusalem, first across the plain of Esdraelon, then through Samaria, and finally along the central spine of Judea, took most of four days. The famous fertile Esdraelon and the mouth of the Jezreel Valley he found to be a wilderness of rich land covered with wild grass and weeds, brown like California in the late summer. The party, which had amused itself with a futile gazelle hunt during the day, approached its first night stop at Djenin with trepidation, for they had learned at Nazareth of the fate of an American traveler a few months before who had been left for dead by the Arabs who had attacked and robbed him just outside the village. He was traveling with only a dragoman as companion, and it was rumored that this dragoman had led him into ambush as maliciously as the dragoman had done to Conrad, the Holy Roman Emperor, during a Crusade in Cappadocia seven centuries before. True to their fears, the Arabs at Djenin proved hostile and it took some time for Yusef to obtain lodgings for the party with a Christian Arab; the fleas at this place were so terrible that Browne once more wished Lamartine were there to weep for him.

A more pleasant stay awaited them at Nablus (ancient Shechem), in the heart of the Samaritan country, after they had duly admired the ruins at Sebastia, where they were really excited at the glimpse of the Mediterranean they obtained from the most elevated site of ancient Samaria. Jacob's Well and Joseph's Tomb were passed without comment and they spent the third night in an old khan in the curious hillside village of Singel. The next day, after twenty-two days of constant travel, they gained their first glimpse of Jerusalem and were soon installed in Senior Stephano's Hotel, where Ross Browne wrote Lucy that he could hardly believe that he had arrived.

Though he went on to tell Lucy that he had been much impressed by his first view of Jerusalem from a rise on the Damascus Road, and elsewhere referred to this view as "strangely beautiful and impressive," he later said little about his first impressions of Jerusalem in *Yusef*. Actually, during the week that he spent there, he found the physical aspects of the city, then having some seventeen thousand inhabitants with an annual influx of perhaps as many more pilgrims, in better shape than he had expected. The houses and bazaars seemed to him as good as those of Beirut, and the walled city with its minarets, domes, and towers, appropriately picturesque. Though he did not describe them in *Yusef*, feeling that they had been written about by too many before him, he mentions that he visited the usual tourist spots outside of the walls, including the Tombs of the Judges, the Mount of Olives, the Garden of Gethsemane, the Grotto of Jeremiah, and the buildings on Mt. Zion. Inside the city, he of course went to the Church of the Holy Sepulchre but he saw nothing of the beautiful Dome of the Rock and the Mosque of El Aksa, for access to

Mt. Moriah, the former location of Solomon's Temple, was then forbidden to Christians on pain of death. Nor did he see anything of the Wailing Wall, although he was aware that there were many Jews still living in what had once been the capital of Judea.

Other than expressing mild amusement at the presence of holy relics and their vendors everywhere one turned (he even admitted to violating his conscience by absconding with some twigs from the remaining, closely guarded, eight olive trees in the Garden of Gethsemane), he concentrated his comments on two phenomena of Jerusalem which disturbed him profoundly. These were the constant feuds between Christian sects in the Church of the Holy Sepulchre and the wretched condition of the lepers outside the Zion Gate. To find that the nondescript church which presumably housed all the sacred spots where Christ was crucified and buried was but a ramshackle affair (rain leaked through the roof tiles and windows into its murky interior—a condition brought on by the feuds among the Roman and Greek Catholics, the Armenians, the Copts, and others) was very disturbing to him, even blotting out for the moment his reactions to the tastelessness of the decorations and the doubtful authenticity of the many sites shown to the visiting pilgrim. This hostility among Christians, a hostility which could only be controlled by the intercession of armed Turks, was what bothered him most; "to witness in their worst form envy, hatred and malice practiced in His name, and the outward worship of God where sin and wickedness reign triumphant" caused him to conclude that "perhaps upon the whole face of the globe there could not be found a spot less holy than modern Jerusalem." Not even the sight of the lepers who squatted outside her walls, begging for food as they exposed their sores, moved him as much as the failure of Christians to live and worship together.

Browne and his companion, the North Carolinian Baker, made a three day trip to Mar Saba, the Dead Sea, and the Jordan River without their friend, the English sea captain, who had returned to Beirut, but with a guard of Arabs to protect them from the notoriously hostile Bedouins of the Judean wilderness. The day before he started this journey, Browne confessed to Lucy: "Tomorrow, under the protection of the Sheik of the Bedouins and twelve Arab guards we go to the Dead Sea." [15] His statement that it was to the "Sheik of the Bedouins" that he was to owe his safety shows that he considered the charge for protection of one hundred piasters per person with another forty thrown in to provide a sheep to feed the guard when they reached the Jordan River (an imaginary sheep, Browne found later) to be a form of blackmail forced on travelers by the Bedouins themselves. At any rate, Browne and Baker spent considerable time dropping stones into "Job's Well" at the foot of Mt. Zion waiting for the guard to turn up. Browne declared that the first guard who arrived was "the most ferocious, unshaved, unwashed and delapidated looking vagabond" he had seen in all his travels. The five "guards" that eventually joined the party all carried terrifically long rifles and rusty pistols, and they handled their firearms so carelessly that Browne decided that if a fracas started with the Bedouins, he would at once join the enemy to be safe from the guards' bullets.

The distance from Jerusalem to the Dead Sea is only about fifteen miles as the crow flies (if a crow could survive the flight) but the trail that Browne and Baker took carried them through the harsh Judean wilderness down some four thousand feet in elevation. They broke the difficult journey by spending one night at the monastery of St. Saba [or St. Sabas], known uniformly by the Frangi as "Mar Saba." Browne chose to visit Mar Saba on his way to the Dead Sea rather than to follow the customary practice of going first to Jericho and the Jordan River. He could have omitted a visit to Mar Saba but his curiosity had been aroused concerning the famous monastery by the presence in Jerusalem of a constant stream of pilgrims, many of them in rags, who had come from Eastern Europe, particularly Russia, to visit this famous shrine of the Eastern Church. Accordingly, after some three hours of riding down the Valley of the Kedron, he and his friends, armed and otherwise, were waiting at the small door in the high wall that borders the upper side of the monastery—which hangs on the steep slopes of a gully named Wadi en Nar (valley of fire).

When a basket was lowered from a window near the top of the wall, Browne and Baker put into it a letter from the Patriarch of Jerusalem for which they had paid about a dollar, and, after the basket was raised and the letter examined, they were admitted to the monastery. Those elaborate precautions were taken to prevent the entrance of marauding Bedouins (who had frequently raided the place), and women, who were under no circumstances to be allowed inside. Thus Harriet Martineau, most earnest of feminists, had been forced to stay outside, much to her publicized indignation.

The monastery or *laura* (Greek for "narrow way") of St. Saba, perhaps the best known of the many cenobite establishments which had been founded by anchorites in the deserts of Palestine during the fourth and fifth century after Christ, was in fact a spectacular sight. Made up of terraces and caves some six hundred feet above the dry bed of the Wadi, it looked like a group of wasp nests, interspersed with chapels. It had developed from a number of caves inhabited by the followers of St. Saba in the fifth century; gradually it had become a monastery rather than a collection of anchorite cells. Famous monks like St. Saba, St. John Damascene, and Stephen the Thaumaturgist had lived there and taken part in the disputations and writings of the early church; a fine library had in time been developed. Though the members of the community were humble followers of St. Basilius, living on vegetables and cereals when not fasting, and feeding the birds when not contemplating or writing, they had periodically been subject to harassments by Persians, Turks, and Bedouins, and over the centuries many of them had been slaughtered. Just eleven years before Browne visited the monastery, it had been restored by the Russians and was now a very busy place. Today it is more inaccessible than it was in the nineteenth century and it housed only six monks when the present writer visited it in 1968. As if to compensate for its rundown condition, it now shelters the bones of St. Saba, returned recently from Venice after centuries of exile.

Browne made little comment on Mar Saba, allowing it no such prominent position in his writings as Melville was to do in *Clarel*, where it is used as a sort of landlocked *Pequod*. Browne was pleased to have clean lodgings and good fare (for which there was a gift of a custom-established amount); characteristically he enjoyed the gracious hospitality of the monks, who showed him the traditional spots of interest—the cave full of the skulls of martyred monks; the cell which St. Saba had lived in, with an accommodating lion as a companion; the palm tree which St. Saba had planted; and the chapel with the garish pictures of his most noted activities. Like other visitors to the *laura*, Browne enjoyed leaning over the parapets and peering at the caves across the Wadi. He regretted he could not spend several days in the monastery.

Early the next morning the Arab guides were waiting and the party set out for the dry, rough ride down to the Dead Sea through almost unbelievably wild and desolate country. A lone jackal licking his lips, and some skulking Arabs, were all the creatures the party saw en route. Once, like the characters in *Clarel*, they caught a view of Bahr el Lut (the Sea of Lot, as the Dead Sea is known) glistening below them, with the formidable Moab Mountains rising abruptly on the other side of the Great Rift. Fortunate in not being exposed to the heat of summer, as Mark Twain was to be, the pilgrims spent an hour or two by the brackish sea, noting the sultry mist which hung over it, the dwarfish shrubs, gnarled and leafless, on its edges, and the mud and slimy foam of its shores. They tasted the water and found it vile; they filled bottles to take samples to their friends; but they made no attempt to bathe in it.

The trip north to the Jordan River, a few miles above its entrance to the Dead Sea, was accomplished before lunch. There is no mention as to whether Browne's party reached it at the point where tradition says Jesus was baptized by John the Baptist—the place where thousands of pilgrims came each year to bathe in the dangerously rushing Jordan. Browne was surprised to find that the famous river was much smaller than he had expected; he estimated its width to be thirty yards, he found he could throw a stone across it, and he declared it no bigger "than what we call a creek in the back-woods of America." No one felt moved to immerse himself in its sacred waters. After a good lunch made up of a cold leg of mutton, provided by Yusef, and some brown bread which had been given to them by the monks of Mar Saba, they filled still more bottles with water for friends at home and set off westward to Jericho, at the base of the Mount of Quarantina, where Jesus had fasted forty days in the wilderness.

Three hours later they were at the site of the Jericho whose walls were said to have fallen down at a blast of Joshua's trumpets, but they found no ruins and correctly assumed that modern Jericho was not located on the same spot as the ancient city. The excavations which were to reveal the ancient ruins had not yet been started. For the Jericho of 1851 Browne had few kind words:

A ruinous old Khan, eight or ten wigwams built of mud and bushes; half a dozen lazy Arabs lying about on piles of rubbish, smoking their pipes; a few cows, sheep and goats, browsing on the stunted bushes; some mangy-looking dogs, engaged in devouring the carcass of a dead mule, and a few hungry crows waiting near by for a share in the feast, were all the signs of habitation and life that we could see about Jericho.[16]

It seemed a far cry from the garden spot which Mark Antony had given Cleopatra as a magnificent gift.

If the travelers were disappointed in the oasis, they were more than overjoyed with the purple sunset which so dramatically set off the mountains of Amman and Moab so that the latter "were admirably finished on top with cities of gold made out of naked rocks and sunshine." They could not pick out Mt. Pisgah but they doubtless thought of the thrill which came to Moses and the Israelites when they gazed out over Judea from that lofty height. In the meantime, they were due to suffer the hospitality of the Sheik of Jericho by attempting to sleep in his khan overnight. They had some trouble finding room for themselves among the chickens, goats, and asses (no camels) which were being housed indoors to prevent their capture by Bedouin marauders, who had made a raid across the river only four nights before. Warmed by the fresh manure in the bed from which the ass had been routed moments before, they all slept peacefully except Yusef, who feared that he might have to defend them against the Bedouins. The next morning they took the road up the wadies to Jerusalem, passing the place where the unfortunate victim of earlier bandits had been rescued by the Good Samaritan, and the town of Bethany, where Jesus had known Mary, Martha, and Lazarus.

On Christmas Eve, Browne joined a horde of pilgrims of many nationalities who were making their way over the few miles from Jerusalem to Bethlehem. He had looked forward to enjoying a very special Christmas at the spot of Christ's birth. Instead, he had a horrible time. All his accumulated objections to the worship of sacred sites and the rituals which were involved came to a head that night beside the Holy Manger. Pressed close by the crowds around him, he entered the awkwardly shaped church or convent which had been built over the two grottoes celebrated as being the places of Christ's birth and the manger in which he was laid. Though his authorities had told him that the authenticity of these sites was highly questionable, he was ready to suspend his disbelief in order to worship with others who felt differently than he. But pressure of the crowds, the sight of many sweating priests carrying candles and constantly chanting and prostrating themselves, the stifling effect of the thick incense and hot breaths all militated against his capturing any moment of spiritual exaltation. But for him the worst disappointment of all was to discover that the Christ child was represented by an ugly wax image or puppet which lay upon an altar in the crypt. The white dress with its beads and spangles and tawdry lace seemed to accentuate the horror of the image—"a strange, disgusting thing, with staring eyes of glass, tawny skin, and wrinkled neck; its cheeks puffed out, and its mouth slightly open as if it had been suffocated with thick incenses."

As the ceremony proceeded, with the waxen image being carried from the altar to the manger at midnight, Browne's disturbance grew more acute. He discovered that the priestly worshippers sported shaved heads, and beards that were covered with foamy sputum. The fat monks, dripping sweat, eyes rolling, seemed to him to be lustful as they stared at kneeling women pilgrims. It was "the most sickening exhibition of brutish superstition that the eye of man could behold." It was the most miserable Christmas of Browne's life and he was filled with pain and humiliation. Finally he made his way to the room which he had been fortunate to obtain in the dormitory part of the convent and lay for hours, shuddering at the noises coming from the celebrants, sweating in a waking nightmare of horrible pictures. He concluded that these pilgrims to Bethlehem were worshiping death, not life—paying homage to a pagan image, not a loving Christ. Finally, as he remembered a former Christmas at home with his loved ones, he found some relief: "And in the soothing of those happy memories and the hopefulness of better things to come, I committed myself to the keeping of Him who showeth the path of life, in whose presence is fullness of joy, at whose right hand are pleasures forevermore." [17]

Though Browne had left Beirut with some idea in his mind of making his way across the desert from Jerusalem to Cairo, he abandoned this plan after the Christmas season and decided to go out to the coast at Jaffa and return north along the littoral to Beirut. He wrote nothing of the trail down the mountains and across the Plain of Sharon to Jaffa, and he apparently left Jaffa as eagerly as Jonah had done before him. His party plodded their way over the sand dunes where Tel Aviv now stands and kept as close to the coast as possible north past the ruins of Caesarea Palestina, the headlands of Mt. Carmel, the bazaars and crusader fortresses of Acre, the ruins of Tyre and Sidon, back to their point of departure some forty days earlier. The heavy rains had swollen the streams, so that frequently their horses and mules mired down, their baggage was soaked, and they were carried piggyback by Arabs across the angry waters. At one such crossing, Browne was amused to meet the venerable Patriarch Maximilian being carried backward seated in a basket hung over the shoulders of an Arab. He could not resist sketching him just as he sketched the ruins of Caesarea Palestina, the erstwhile headquarters of Pontius Pilate, which seemed to him the most desolate place he had ever visited.

After an uneventful voyage from Beirut to Alexandria, Browne's hopes of seeing the pyramids, the sphinx, and other fabulous monuments in Egypt were dashed first by his being forced into four days of quarantine on reaching the Egyptian port, and then by the reception of bad news from his family. It is true he found no letter from Lucy awaiting him (he had not heard from her since he had left Florence), but instead he found a message from his artist friend Kellogg which the latter had written two months earlier, even before Browne had reached the Holy Land. In it Kellogg told Browne that Lucy's health was not good and that her husband's presence was requisite for her recovery. Though he did not actually state that Lucy was ill, Browne feared that she had become so during the time since the letter was written; these apprehensions coupled with his homesickness after the Christmas Eve in Bethlehem and his perennial bad conscience about wandering from his family threw him into a marked depression. On 7 January he wrote Lucy, "I am still in the miserable Lazzaretto and will not be released for three days yet. It is worse than a prison, and under existing circumstances a place of perfect torture to me. Yesterday on the receipt of Mr. Kellogg's letter I was well-nigh crazy." [18] He went on to say that, although Baker had urged him to delay long enough to spend a week visiting Cairo and the pyramids, he was determined to sail, as soon as he was released from quarantine, on an English steamer which would take him to Malta and then he hoped to get a boat straight to Leghorn, the nearest Italian port to Florence. In fact, his return, presumably as rapid as he could make it, took him more nearly a month than the twenty days in which he had hoped to cover the thousand miles. He actually had to go from Malta, where he was forced to spend three more days in quarantine, to Sicily and from there to Naples. When he got back to Florence he found Lucy and the children well. Doubtless Kellogg had sincerely meant to be of help and the fact that Kellogg himself was ill that winter, may have prompted his ill-advised interference in Browne's domestic life. But Ross Browne was never one to hold a grudge, and, though he regretted not including Egypt as a necessary component of the lands of the Bible, he at once set about altering his shorthand notes into articles for the Washington *Daily National Intelligencer.* And already he had hopes of making a book of them.

FOUR

"Yusef"

YUSEF; *or, the Journey of the Frangi: A Crusade in the East* was issued by Harper and Brothers in the early spring of 1853, approximately a year after Ross Browne returned to Florence from his trip to the Levant. According to Lina Fergusson Browne, who owns most of the Browne papers, his writing during his journey to Jerusalem had consisted only of rough notes in shorthand; these have not survived, but his letters to the *Daily National Intelligencer* of Washington, D.C., presumably all written after he reached Florence and printed in eight installments running from 4 March to 17 June 1852, are, of course, available to the scholar. Though they do not contain all the material which appeared in *Yusef*, the episodes which they do contain were used in the book with only an occasional minor alteration. In the preparation of his book for Harpers he spent little time revising his journalism—in contrast to Mark Twain's intensive revision of his *Alta California* letters in preparing *The Innocents Abroad.* Though it cannot be said that *Yusef* was entirely written "on the hoof," it came periously close to being so created.

Actually, in the preface to *Yusef* Browne explains that the informal tone of his book is to be attributed to the fact that it emerged from newspaper letters written "chiefly for the amusement of my friends in Washington." Thus he assumed an attitude "more familiar" than that adopted by other writers for the staid metropoli-

[82]

tan press. "That I considered it probable I might make use of the material at some future period, I frankly admit; but in looking over my notes and the mass of sketches thus brought together, the task of re-writing, and making any thing of them in the way of a serious work on Palestine, seemed too formidable to be undertaken by one who has scarcely yet commenced his travels" [1] he warned his readers. Accordingly, Browne declared that *Yusef* was planned to be more cheerful and less profound than the usual book on the Holy Land; "it will be seen that I have not felt it to be my duty to make a desponding pilgrimage through the Holy Land; for upon a careful perusal of the Scriptures, I can find nothing said against a cheerful frame of mind." Obviously he was not approaching his subject with the political interest of a Lamartine or the sociological, feminist weighing of a Harriet Martineau. He disclaimed any lofty didactic purpose; he would merely show that pleasure in travel did not depend on wealth, that the common man could enjoy himself without being a specialist, and that an honest writer could help develop a more liberal feeling "respecting the customs and prejudices of the uncivilized world" as well as a clearer sense of his own parochialism.

A summary such as has been offered of Browne's reactions to life in Palestine together with his keen disappointments with holy places in Jerusalem and Bethlehem hardly supports his contention that he was writing a cheerful account of the Holy Land. Yet *Yusef* does definitely strike the reader as a lighthearted book. This is partly because Ross Browne embellished his narrative with most of the techniques of the school of American humor variously labeled "frontier" and "humor of the Old Southwest." He also set about creating characters upon whom to hang the narrative, the most developed of which is his dragoman Yusef. These devices, fortified with several wildly exaggerated "episodes," such as a hilarious gazelle hunt on the Plain of Esdraelon, overshadow the occasional indignant attacks on Syrian life and even tend to obscure the frequent trite moralizing in the book, in which Browne tells us how much better are American ways than those found abroad.

Unlike many other visitors to the Levant, he confined his animadversions, diatribes, sermons, and eulogies to a few passages in his book. He could not resist generalizing on the inconsistency of human nature, particularly as displayed by vehemently republican Americans who were awed by royalty, even when as poorly represented as by the King and Queen of Greece or the Sultan of Turkey. Believing that harems encouraged sexual license and degraded the inmates, he was easily led into a homily on the virtue and good fortune of American women. When he wrote of Turkish tyranny he could hardly avoid an extensive praise of liberty in America, although as a former Kentuckian he revealed some discomfort over slavery in the United States. He was on surer ground when he urged tolerance for all religions, for this attitude was an inherent part of the lack of enthusiasm for Christian dogma. Fortunately, only once in *Yusef* did he posture with the *sic transit gloria mundi* stance, for he really was not interested very much in history or the ruins that reflected it. Beside the sea at Caesarea Palestina he found a desolation that impressed him more than that of Pompeii—not only had the people disappeared but all their artifacts were gone. It was marked by an appalling silence.

The silence of a ship upon the sea at night, when all are buried in sleep, . . . is without gloom. . . . Not such is the Desolate City; the city of the silent dead. Here is nothing to tell of them that dwelt there. The land is laid waste, and the earth mourneth and fadeth away. "The Lord hath done that which he had devised; he hath fulfilled his word that he had commanded in the days of old: he hath thrown down and hath not pitied." [2]

Probably part of the reason that Browne had little to say about the "monuments" of culture was because in his account of his visit to the Levant he had purposely avoided, "as far as is practicable, every thing that has given fame to those who have preceded me." This largely meant omitting the temples and playing down the history. However, when it came to describing the details of everyday life in the countries he visited, he was enthusiastically articulate. Thus he wrote pages about the sights in Constantinople, paying particular attention to the appearance of workers and passersby on the Galata

Bridge, occupants of the stalls in the bazaar, or those who rode in the multitude of boats that swarmed on the waters of the Golden Horn. It was a teeming world.

Boatmen are bawling madly for passengers, the *hamil* are running to and fro with heavy burdens, shouting *guarda!* as a matter of habit; crowds of bare-legged laborers are tugging at big timbers, and deafening one another with loud conversation; Greek sailors, piratical-looking Italians, Russian, French, and English men-of-war crews are lounging about the *cafés*, smoking, drinking, and quarreling; Turks and Arabs are bowing down to Mecca in the midst of the confusion; Jewish merchants are bartering their wares; native peddlers are crying the merits of their glittering trinkets; bakers are shouting from their bread stands; hucksters from their tables of figs, cheese, and sausages; fruiterers from out of baskets of grapes; coffee-carriers running about madly with large tin urns, heated by red-hot coals, shrieking the charms of muddy coffee; grave Persians and pale Armenians gliding silently and with ghostly solemnity through the crowd— all touched, you would say, on some point—a little cracked about the affairs of life, just like the rest of us.[3]

Even with such detailed descriptions as these, Browne apparently found when he came to write his book that his Levant experiences did not round out into a full volume, and accordingly he prefaced them with "A Gira in Sicily," which told of his approach to Athens by way of Palermo, Syracuse, and Mt. Etna. To create further variety in his narrative, he thrice passed from glowing pages of anticipation to hard facts of experience, in dealing with Constantinople, Damascus, and Jerusalem. This was a not unusual device for contrasting imagination and experience. For another contrast, he used Lamartine as a foil—the noted Romantic versus the homespun unknown frontiersman—just as Mark Twain was to do with William C. Prime in *The Innocents Abroad*. Browne also introduced special chapters dealing with such things as Syrian horses and Damascene baths, just as Bayard Taylor did in *The Lands of the Saracens* with chapters on "Bathing and Bodies," "Pipes and Coffee," and "The Visions of Hasheesh." Another standard device which Browne used sparingly was the citing of quotations and literary allusions; this practice stood him no better than his occasional introduction of an execrable pun.

The humor of exaggeration was another matter and in this field

Browne showed himself to be an old hand, like Mark Twain knowing not only the words but the tune. Sometimes the *reductio ad absurdum* technique faltered a bit, as in his description of watching the king and queen of Greece in Constitution Square, with much emphasis on the queen smiling and the king frowning at him with appropriate speculations on what they must be thinking. Much more in Browne's line is his introduction of the little old man in Syros who laid claim to a classical fountain of the nymphs, basing his ownership largely on his extensive acquaintance with "Mélor Beeron," that great English poet and supporter of the Greek cause who was so long his master—"a very kind master too; sat up rather late, but good pay."

Odd customs of the countries visited provided grist for exaggerated accounts which sometimes reached hilarious proportions. There was some guide baiting, although nowhere nearly so much as in *The Innocents Abroad*. Bargaining in the bazaars of Stamboul provided an excellent anecdote about a set-to with a grave old Turk, who woke only momentarily to haggle with Browne by the finger method, there being no other common language between them. The seller won by a half-knuckle. The baths of Damascus gave rise to a hilarious account of being stripped, boiled, and well-scrubbed by enigmatic Arabs who never got far from their chibouks and black coffee. A passage near the climax of the crescendo read:

The captain [Browne's companion] vanished in a white mist, leaving a parting impression on my mind of a man gasping for life in a sea of soap-suds. I saw no more of him for a quarter of an hour. Meantime I was jerked out of my winding sheet by the one-eyed monster, and thrust down into a sitting posture, close by the vase of hot water. "Hold, for God's sake! What——" It was too late. A perfect deluge of foaming lather came pouring down over my head and face, running into my eyes, ears, and nostrils, and stopping up my mouth beyond all hope of speech. I have an indistinct recollection of a confusion of agonies through which I went for the next five minutes, but can not depict them with anything like the force of reality.[4]

Nevertheless, he continued describing his agonies in outrageous terms.

The animals encountered were, of course, good subjects for

burlesque. Browne pretended to having developed a feud with all camels, a feud which had started in Zanzibar when three camels chased him into the quicksand where he would have died had not some friendly Arabs rescued him. In Syria he was always on the verge of being brushed off his horse by caravan camels led by Arabs who had little use for tourists. Once a camel forced him and his mount Saladin off a trail causing them to roll to the bottom of the hill. Browne asserted that the camel's reputation for being picturesque and gentle was entirely unwarranted; he was picturesque only when seen from a distance and never when viewed from the rear, and his gentleness was mere laziness. "As to his physical strength and powers of endurance: Can he jump as far as a flea? can he carry half as heavy a load on his back; can he endure half the amount of heat or cold? I mean in proportion to his size? . . . I would recommend all camels in future to keep clear of anybody that looks like a General in the Bobtail Militia." [5] Even the wild dogs of Constantinople were preferable to the camels. Traveling in packs, they were both effective scavengers and lethal threats to the lone pedestrian, particularly at night. Browne chose to treat them humorously, describing a battle between the "Byzantines," which lived in the area of the Byzant hotel, and the "Mohammedans," which lurked among the tombs not far down the hill. While Browne smoked his chibouk in safety on the balcony, the dogs put on a fracas that was presented in mock-heroic terms similar to those used by Henry Fielding in his description in *Tom Jones* of the battle between Molly Seagrim and her detractors in the graveyard beside the village church.

As might be expected, the animals who furnished the most constant subject for travesty were equine—horses, mules, and donkeys. Browne seemed to have had many of the same misfortunes with horseflesh that Mark Twain experienced on numerous occasions. Browne's Saladin is a distinct character in the story, sometimes reliable but more often involved in such reprehensible behavior as running away and biting Yusef's Syed Sulemin in the rump, thus starting a stampede. One chapter of *Yusef*, in fact, is given over to Syrian horses, a topic introduced by Browne's ecstasy over the genuine Arabian stallion which belonged to the rebel sheik who had fortified himself in the ruins of Khan Jub Yusef. Browne, who had already given a chapter over to the ancestors and characteristics of his own one-eyed horse, Saladin, described the clumsy mount with a shortened tendon in one leg ridden by the English captain and christened Waterloo (the switch was just as indispensable a part of the rider's machinery as the piston rod to a steam engine) and the little iron-grey ridden by the Southerner with a body "that tapered off toward the hind part without the slightest symptom of a stomach" so that the saddle inevitably slid backward and occupied the space directly over the tail. Also described were the pack mules, who were principally evident by being always hungry, their only fodder being what the muleteers could steal from the horses, and who panicked on several occasions, losing their luggage in the process.

Browne's favorite animal in the party was a little donkey named Tokina, who usually carried a load twice as big as himself and who struck Browne as being a transcendentalist—"there was no telling what he was about half the time, he maintained such an aspect of profound wisdom, and used such obscure and uncouth language to himself." Tokina could also bray very lustily for the benefit of others. Browne knew that he "had a soul very much above any common ass." "He was not much bigger than a Newfoundland dog, but he had an amount of ambition concealed beneath his shaggy little hide that would have done honor to any horse in Syria. If his ears were long, so was his head; he carried a good deal in it as well as on it." [6] Browne felt some of the affection for Tokina that Sancho Panza did for his "little gray" and his introduction of the donkey is but one of numerous reflections of his enthusiasm for *Don Quixote.*

His playing up of the party's mounts and pack animals led to several scenes in *Yusef* in which the zany activities of men and horses were magnified into a rout with all of the excesses of a scene in a Marx Brothers comedy. Such was the event when, on the outskirts of Beirut, Yusef introduced Browne to his new mount Saladin by putting the latter through some remarkable capers in a race with the dragoman's own illustrious steed, Syed Sulemin. Of like

Saladin in Action

texture was the description, near the end of the book, of the rout at Tantara when Yusef's horses were involved in a battle with another traveler's horses. In the resulting melee, which drew in the mules and Tokina, of course, the sheds of an ancient khan were completely reduced to shambles. But the most ambitious of these episodes was the gazelle hunt to which Browne devoted a chapter of cumulative burlesque. Tantalized by the glimpse of some lively gazelles on the great plain of Esdraelon, the whole party set out to hunt, led by the Southerner with Yusef's double-barrel gun, followed by the English Captain, who hoped to run a gazelle down with his horse, and Ross Browne, with his penknife in his pocket ready "to bleed somebody in case of a bruise or fracture." Most ebullient of all was the irrepressible Yusef who shot off his pistols at almost every onward leap of his horse. Naturally the mules succumbed to the infectious enthusiasm and began rearing and running around in circles so that the pack saddles soon slipped around and hung below their bellies. The most distracted of mules was the one carrying the chickens that

Yusef had "requisitioned" for the spread that night; the chickens, together with various pots and pans, slipped down between the mule's legs, creating a mighty and unholy racket.

The pans and kettles, sliding down on each side of the mule, remained hanging by the handles underneath, and banged away there against each other in the most terrific manner; and the chickens, having nothing to balance them on top, slipped over behind, and hung between his hind-legs, where they got up such a cackling and fluttering that the unfortunate animal, driven to distraction by the noise and other causes, went perfectly insane with fright, and ran all round in a circle for ten minutes, by which time every cord was broken, and our entire stock of provisions and implements of domestic economy deposited at intervals over nearly a hundred acres of ground. The other mules had knapsacks, mattresses, bundles of clothes, and a variety of other articles hanging over them and under them; but by dint of hard kicking, and an occasional fit of rolling, they got rid of them at last, and went their way at random.[7]

In the midst of the excitement, Tokina the ass, who had much the coolest head in the party, resolved to be direct and resolute, laid his ears back, started a prolonged braying, and lit out on a beeline for Nazareth, where the group had spent the previous night. Francesco, the lad who was responsible for his supervision, eventually brought him back. In the meantime, there remained nothing to do but calm the animals, pick up the duffle, and indulge in a boasting contest on how close each of the riders had come to getting a gazelle. The English captain had barely missed overtaking the largest of the gazelles when it had suddenly disappeared; the Southerner thought he had wounded one, "for he saw it leap more than thirty feet when he fired"; and Yusef, not to be outdone, told how he had wounded two or three. However, no gazelles, sound or wounded, were in sight, and the party resumed its journey, quite willing to abandon competitive boasting in favor of peace for the night.

Following a similar burlesque pattern, Browne made much of the discomforts his party faced at night, blowing up two particular incidents into hilarious slapstick comedies. One was his account of the "rest" spent at the mill of Malaha, just above Lake Huleh. He prefaced his scene with several references to promises made during the day by Yusef about the grand night's sleep which was ahead of him, sleep that would be particularly welcome after the wretched stop at Baniyas the night before. When the mill finally came in sight, Browne, who had been indulging in his "natural disposition to invest everything with the charms of romance" saw that the night's shelter was but a partially ruined stone box, with the usual assortment of camels and smoking Arabs at the door. "Every thought of the hospitable old gentleman and his accomplished daughters; the flower-gardens, the choice home-made bread and sparkling wines of Lebanon, vanished in a moment."

After the usual long palaver to determine the price of a night's lodging, a palaver conducted in the pouring rain, the party entered the mill, ducking their heads below the low roof and walking gingerly over a poorly-lit floor full of holes through which they could see the water rushing underneath. Browne felt that there was "every prospect of tumbling through during the night, and being carried down among the wheels, and afterwards deposited in the lake of El Huleh," eventually no doubt to be swept into the Sea of Galilee, then on down the sacred Jordan, until they found rest in the brackish waters of the Dead Sea. Continuing to feel their way around two huge whirling millstones, they were finally ushered onto a narrow shelf, covered with dust, chaff, and a very rich deposit of manure. There they ate their excellent dinner, prepared by the resourceful Yusef, smoked their ever-pleasant Latakia tobacco in their chibouks, and late at night lay down to sleep, or, as Browne puts it, to close their eyes to "see how ridiculous it would feel." "Stables I had slept in; caves, haystacks, trees, and the broad canopy of heaven had afforded me lodgings in cases of emergency; but I had seen nothing half so strange or curious in the way of accommodations for a night's rest as the mill of Malaha." [8] He had barely discovered that the fleas were, as his companions said, "as big as humblebees" and many times more active, when he was startled in the pitch dark by a snuffling nose, which proved to be part of a Syrian ass, who had arrived, not to eat him, as he first thought, but to share his bed. Protests did no good; the Arabs made it clear that either the Frangi put up with animals for bed companions or they got out into the storm. The night noises became a medley of the braying of asses, the rushing of water, the whirling of grindstones, and, as a bourdon under all, the buzz of Arab voices in perpetual discussion.

I will not undertake to describe how we spent the rest of that memorable night: how the grindstones came within an inch of grinding us to death every time we stretched our legs out; how in attempting to escape from the furious attacks of the fleas we got ourselves involved under the hoofs of the asses; how the old miller stopped smoking about midnight, and by the united assistance of all his Arabs succeeded in the course of two hours in getting his mill stopped; how every one of them talked all the rest of the night, and went to sleep about daylight; and how we got up at the same time and made a vow never again to stop at the Mill of Malaha. At sunrise we were mounted, and on our way toward the Sea of Galilee.[9]

But the night Browne asserted he would remember the longest was the one at Tantura, on the way home along the Mediterranean littoral, when he, the Honorary General of the Bobtailed Militia, was accused of stealing onions when all he was doing was attempting to find a comfortable place to sleep on a shelf in the Arab hovel where he was spending the night. Unfortunately, in trying to escape the fleas he had chosen to climb up onto the very place where the Arab stored his precious onions and the "host" had ordered him down precipitously.

It was enough; I got down from the top of the cupboard; mildly reproved my companions for making a laughing matter of so serious a charge; requested Yusef to light my chibouck and say no more; calmly seated myself upon a spare mat, and gave free indulgence to melancholy reflection. Oh destiny! had it come to this?—to this at last! That I, who had spent four precious years of my life in the Treasury Department of the United States; whose chief study was the study of the banking system; whose most earnest hope was, never, by any visitation of Providence, to be Secretary of the Treasury, president of a bank, or signer of a circulating note; that I, whose only ambition was to be thought an honest man as well as to be one in reality; that I, who had chased the mighty leviathan of the deep, slept in the veritable castle of the renowned Crusoe, dug the glittering ore out of the gold mines of California, explored the remotest corners of the earth for the benefit of mankind; that I, who had smiled at the Queen of Greece, and frowned at Otho, King of Greece; who had entered upon the grandest Crusade against the Mists of Fancy that ever was conceived of by the soul of Chivalry, should at last be accused of stealing onions! Enough! enough! I turned over, put my pipe away, and went fast to sleep; for I was callous to fleas now; they might bite me by millions; rats and mice might gnaw at my vitals, but I was totally resigned to all earthly afflictions that could be piled upon me; and the consequence was, I slept soundly till morning.[10]

Browne also followed a tried and true method of enlivening travel books by developing the characters in his narrative. Thus, George W. Curtis enlivened *The Howadji in Syria* by pretending to fall in love with a young Armenian girl while crossing the Sinai desert; he never got a chance before her party took its separate way to do more than smile at her. John Lloyd Stephens in his *Travels in Egypt, Arabia Petraea, and the Holy Land* took much pleasure in poking fun at his dragoman, Paul, who carried his Christianity so far as to wash the feet of pilgrims during Holy Week. John William DeForest in his *Oriental Acquaintance* delineated a crochety Yorkshireman in his party whose individualistic views on Palestine enlivened the narrative. And Mark Twain, in due time, caricatured his traveling companions, particularly such figures as "The Poet Lariat" and "The Oracle" in *The Innocents Abroad*.

Rather oddly, Ross Browne does little to individualize his two companions in *Yusef*; perhaps he felt reticent about building them into characters or perhaps they did not offer many peculiarities to work on. In one passage, he does expatiate a bit on their personal traits. The three were suffering terribly from the fleas as they tried to sleep in the hut of a Christian Arab in Djenin.

In the middle of the night, after tossing, rolling, and groaning, without even so much as a wink of sleep—for the fleas actually covered me as a live coating of black mail—I started up and looked around in search of sympathy. The tall Southerner was sitting up on the mud floor, his hair disheveled, his eyes wild and haggard, and his face dreadfully scarred and emaciated; he was in the act of aiming a blow, with an empty bottle, at the head of some hungry animal that had been trying to eat him. The English Captain, jolly as ever, was scratching himself with one hand, while with the other he held a pipe, which he smoked with great calmness and good-humor.

"Hallo!" said I, "what's the matter, Captain?"

"The fleas," said the Captain; "they're quite stunning, I assure you. Never saw so many in all my life."

"Why don't you catch 'em?"

"Too strong for me; can't hold 'em. 'Pon my honor, they won't let me sleep a wink. Awfully ferocious animals; stunning, quite stunning, I assure you. Sir, I don't think anything short of hot brandy-punch will cure them." [11]

Appropriately the three sufferers woke the tough-skinned Yusef, who heated them water so that they could spend the rest of the night drinking punch.

Browne devoted sections of *Yusef* to describing travelers he met; among them were Bimby, a dilettante American, and Bromley, a self-collected Englishman. Browne considered both of these characters to be types rather than individuals. The American is the wealthy expatriate who has more money than he knows what to do with and is ridden by his "wants." He cannot get the pants he likes in Paris, but must journey to Milan for them; he goes to Leipzig for his boots and to Smyrna for his tobacco, which he has always found inferior elsewhere. When Browne saw him in Smyrna, Bimby "was in the most exquisite distress in regard to the texture of a fez he was examining." He would never go back to America, he averred, for what would a man of taste do there? No pictures, no ruins, no society, no opera, etc. Browne concluded what he needed most was a job requiring him to work hard.

Bromley, the Englishman, is portrayed as calm even during the levanter which nearly swamped the boat headed for Palestine. He is reserved, serious, dogmatical, and English. He is a perfect gentleman, following all the rules and borrowing his taste from the guide book. A casually entered conversation with Browne leads to an animated contrast of English and American customs and attitudes— the tithe system in Ireland is weighed against the excesses of slavery in the Southern states, the "I guess" of American parlance is set against the "Now, I say" of the British, and so on, until the disputants get down to contrasting tobacco-chewing and wine-bibbing. Finally, both Englishman and American agree that their differences are only superficial and settle down to be friendly.

More specific and detailed are the characters of Dr. Mendoza and his wife, Portuguese travelers whom Browne met on the voyage from Naples to Palermo and kept in touch with all through his travels in the Levant. In a letter to Lucy from Constantinople Browne indicated that these were genuine acquaintances and that they were in fact Brazilians. He was both pleased and amused with the doctor, but he confided that he found Mendoza's wife "the crossest, and most childish and most unpleasant woman I ever was in company with." [12] She may have improved with acquaintance, for she is merely silly as portrayed in *Yusef*.

The portly and affable Dr. Mendoza was a man of the world, wealthy enough to travel "chiefly to kill time and hunt up the best hotels." He was always talking about the fine hotels he had visited, particularly those in St. Petersburg. His chatter specialized in the qualities of coffee and wine. His English was very imperfect and was larded with expressions in French and Italian; he was always finding things "poss" or "imposs," he frequently lamented that madame was "indispose," and he invariably confused the genders of his English pronouns. He was at his most affable when staying at the Orient in Athens and at the Misseri in Constantinople, for both hotels provided cuisines to suit his taste. In Beirut he hired the famous dragoman Emanual Bathos, who provided him with the most elaborate equipment imaginable. Browne frequently ran into the doctor and his madame as they wandered about Palestine. At the Dead Sea they appeared accompanied by the Roman Catholic Bishop of Jerusalem and a dozen priests, and Browne was sure that the Latin Convent in Jerusalem, which had been sheltering them assiduously, would benefit handsomely from their bounty.

At Tantura, where he was dislodged from the cupboard reserved for onions, Browne discovered in the morning that the Mendozas had been suffering in a private home next door. When Browne found them sitting upon a pile of baggage, groaning in a most disconsolate manner, he was greeted as a long lost friend.

We were always strictly Parisian in our politeness—no matter under what circumstances we met—especially the Madam, who had been educated in the true French school. It would have done any man of feeling good to see her when she rose from the baggage and returned my salutation; it was the most striking exhibition of politeness under difficulties that I ever beheld. Her skin was perfectly green, spotted over with red bites; her nose swollen to an unusual size by repeated attacks made by noxious reptiles; her hair disheveled and uncombed, and her dress and general exterior, covered with dirty straw and mud. Yet she bowed as gracefully and smiled as pleasantly, as ever bowed and smiled a lady in the dress circles of a Parisian Opera-house. It was really charming to behold such unruffled politeness.

"Oh, Monsieur Général! Monsieur Général!" was all she could say—"Quel jolie ville, Tantura! Quel hôtel Parisien! Oh, Mon Dieu!" and throwing up her hands, she sank down again upon the baggage in the most graceful manner. I verily believe if it were the fate of the Madam to be seized by a Royal Bengal tiger she would melt him by her politeness, or die gracefully in his teeth.

Her husband, however, was in no mood for politeness.

"Good morning, Doctor," said I; "how did you pass the night?"
"No pass de night!" replied the Doctor gloomily. " 'tis imposs to sleep. Very bad place dis. Hotel are not good in Tantura. . . . De Madam is indispose. He shall have pleasure to arrive at Beirut. Very good hotel in Beirut. I no like dis country. Tis interess for the ruin, but I no like the ruin for sleep in, cos 'tis imposs to sleep. Very much pulce for bite. No get much to eat here; no much flesh on the Arab for manger. 'Tis necess for eat de traveler. I shall be tres contents to leave Tantura—'Tis imposs to remain here." [13]

Yusef is sprinkled with short vignettes of native characters, usually accompanied by an amusing pencil sketch. Such is the portrait of the Greek patriarch being carried backwards in a basket by an Arab crossing a swollen stream and the amusing portrait of Old Ibrahim, the Jewish guide in Damascus, who was so wrapped in a brown study that one mistook him for a celebrated Rabbi; as a guide he was useless, as he refused to comment on St. Paul's adventures, the appearance of Damascene women, or anything else, for that matter. One pencil sketch, that of the Arab storyteller in Beirut, was signed in Arabic by the subject of the sketch who had been regaling his listeners with his oft-told story of the White Princess and the Grand Vizier while Browne took his likeness, to the joy of the onlookers. The sketch introduces a short discussion of the importance of the traditional storyteller in Arab culture; "he is a walking newspaper, a living history, a breathing essay, a personified book of travels, which evolves its stores of knowledge on self-acting principles." [14]

But of course the most fully developed native character in the book is the one for whom the book is named, the dragoman Yusef, Simon Badra, in this case a real person with his genuine name. Like other characters in *Yusef* he was introduced with a pencil sketch, which was accompanied with a lively description: "Face open and intelligent, eyes round and full of fire, temperament nervous-san-

A Gentleman of Elegant Leisure

guine, age twenty-eight, costume rich, careless, and dashing; figure well-knit and of medium height; manner frank, self-relying, and chivalrous; whole tone of character imposing, captivating, and Oriental." [15] From the time he was hired to take care of the party in Beirut to the last page of the book, where he was left lingering behind prison bars, he played a leading role both through his behavior and his remarks. A relative of both Miles Gloriosus and Sancho Panza, he soon wins his way with the reader.

As for Browne, he admitted that Yusef had about him a mesmeric quality: "He could have taken us to the public bazaars and sold us without the least opposition on our part, at almost any sacrifice, such was the power of his nature." His greatest boast was of bravery. He assured the Frangi that he was known throughout Syria as Badra the Destroyer of Robbers and that the last time he was out with a party he had killed six Bedouins single-handedly. Also he was resourceful, being not only a good cook but also a most accomplished rationalizer, ready after a soggy night to praise the rain because it cleared the air and always quick to invent a name or explanation when he was short on verified information. He could be enthusiastic about almost anything and yet when others were annoyed at bad luck he could outdo them all in blasphemy.

Yusef Dancing the Raas

He admitted to only one fault—a hatred of women—yet he was constantly on a lecherous lookout for one or another of his pretty "nieces" who lived in almost every village they visited and were invariably tied to jealous husbands. His schemes to outwit the husbands created situations which abounded in night maneuvers, creaking doors, and eventual frustration, after which Yusef would go out and beat one of the muleteers. Such a denouement culminated the night at Baalbek which had started so cheerfully with Browne on center stage entrancing the Arabs with his playing of the flute and singing of "Old Zip Coon." Most of the young women in the charmed circle had slipped their veils aside and were clearly entranced with the visiting stranger. But Yusef, in the burning enthusiasm of the occasion, grasped a sword and threw himself with unbounded zeal into dancing the raas. Frantically yet skillfully he whirled the sword around his head and whistled it within inches of the closest spectators; with the greatest agility he moved every part of his body in most complicated maneuvers as Browne's accompaniment on the flute became more and more agitated and as he tried to keep up with the rhythmic clapping; finally Yusef, having successfully passed through the fighting and dancing phases of the raas, reached the ultimate crescendo when he tried to rescue the daughter of the Grand Sultan and, mortally wounded, died slowly with his head in his lady-love's lap. He chose of course his host's pretty wife; Yusef was at the height of his powers. Still the husband eventually outwitted him with stealth, a bolted door, and a final recourse to staying up all night to argue with his wife and thus keep the intruder away.

This spirited episode, like the later episode of the fight of the muleteers, was followed by a calming dialogue between Badra, the Destroyer of Robbers, and Browne, the principal representative in those parts of the "City of Magnificent Distances," as Yusef habitually called Washington, D.C. These dialogues were clearly meant to echo the rich discourses which took place between Don Quixote and Sancho Panza after such moving incidents as the attack on the windmills; Browne and Yusef dealt with universal problems and searching truths such as the proper treatment of women, the nature of progress, and the secret of happiness. Sometimes the emphasis was placed on Yusef's Arab views, sometimes on Browne's versions of American society, usually described with a satirical turn. Thus Browne explained why Americans gave their women great freedom, while Arabs kept their consorts veiled and guarded.

General.—". . . Though they are free as air, many of them consider that they are barbarously limited in power, even now. It is nothing uncommon for them to hold conventions, for the purpose of denouncing the male sex, and asserting their right to seats in our National Legislature. Some of them even aspire to the Presidency. For all I know, there may be a female candidate nominated for that high office at this very moment."

YUSEF.—"Don't you whip 'em, sir? Don't you lock 'em up, and give 'em the bastinado?"

GENERAL (indignantly).—"The bastinado, forsooth! I'd like to see such a thing as that tried in our country. Why, we have ladies who would cowhide a man if they knew he entertained such a thought; and we have newspaper editors who compliment ladies for distinguishing themselves in that way. No, Yusef; we never use the bastinado. On the contrary, there are persons of the male sex, or who assume to be of that sex, ever ready to join these spunky ladies in their conventions, and act entirely under their dictation. That such men will eventually aspire to petticoats is not at all improbable."

YUSEF (highly excited).—"I'd shoot 'em; by Allah, sir, I'd gut 'em! Miserable dogs! . . ." [16]

This attack led into a discussion of the veiling of women in Muslim lands, a practice which Yusef stoutly supported on the grounds that it curbs women's instinctive vanity which, if unchecked, might do great damage. "Have you no customs in your country, sir, equally strange and incomprehensible at first sight?"

GENERAL.—"No, Yusef; thank heaven, we are clear of all such absurdities as this. Our most fashionable ladies not only keep their faces uncovered in public, but frequently appear in ball-rooms and opera-houses, with scarcely more than a piece of gauze above the waist."

YUSEF.—"And don't they feel ashamed at all?"

GENERAL.—"By no means. Those who desire to be distinguished in the world of fashion, never feel ashamed of anything that is fashionable." [17]

In the dialogue on the "Grand Secret of Human Happiness," which started with Browne's objections to the laziness of an Arab who spent most of the day smoking a narghile and most of the night sleeping, there developed a contrast between Yusef's concept of happiness—being content with as little as possible—and Browne's support of industry and progress, a creed which Browne admitted made him uneasy. After a diversion on the similarity between Yusef's beatings of the muleteer and the flogging of seamen on American ships, it proceeded to such a clear declaration of the virtues of industry that Yusef fell back on his enthusiasm for diversity: "That's the beauty of it—the very principle of existence! A Turk takes his ease in smoke; a Frenchman in dancing; a German in beer, talk, and pipes; an Englishman in beef-steak; an American—pardon me, O General, I mean no disrespect in referring to your own words—an American in being uneasy. When he is uneasy he is easy, and when he is easy he is uneasy." [18] After this sage remark, Yusef pointed out the famous Mill of Malaha looming up on the horizon, just as Don Quixote's squire had glimpsed the inn where Maritornes lived, after a similar discussion. And the events which took place that night were not unlike the violent activities in Cervantes' famous attic.

It was Browne's pleasure to build up Yusef by an ironical technique and then disgrace him in the end. Premonitions of his fate came when, before an illustrious audience containing several pretty and admiring women, he had abandoned himself to equestrian tricks, twirling brilliantly the very *djeered* above his head with which he had in Beirut belabored Browne's ugly, broken-backed, one-eyed, lame, and spavined Arabian steed, Saladin, shouting "Badra, Badra" and whirling past as he clung to his mount by mane and tail in his mad gallop. But on this occasion Yusef attempted the trick of dropping the *djeered* to the ground in order to retrieve it at a fast canter, only to find himself hanging like a cat by its tail unable to get back into his saddle. The ultimate humiliation was to have the muleteer, Mustapha, rescue him.

Yusef's braggadocio was much in evidence during the trip to Jerusalem. Such a remark as the following was not uncommon when he grew excited: "I could devour the seven-headed Dragon, and wallow in the blood of Rabadab, the four-handed Giant!" Sometimes it was hard to figure out whether he would rather gut his muleteers or slaughter Bedouins by the score. But under pressure, alas, his behavior did not live up to his boasting. In the rocky country above the Sea of Galilee he had been much perturbed at some ominous figures behind a rock but was much relieved to find them a quartet of old women and boys. At Sebastia it was clear that he was disturbed by the threatening Samaritans who surrounded the party while they were eating. In fact, Yusef turned pale and quickly led his party out of there towards Nablus, explaining as he fled that he had feared he would lose his temper, kill some of the Samaritans, and suffer punishment from the Turkish authorities when he reached Jerusalem.

Mustapha, the Arab Muleteer

At Jericho, when the party learned that the Bedouins had raided the area just a few nights earlier, Yusef was ordered to lie across the door of the hut to protect his pilgrims with his arsenal. In the dead of night there was much snoring, crawling about in the dark, and eventually a scramble, when a supposed Bedouin was caught by the throat only to turn out in the flare of a match to be Yusef. He was as full of explanations as Falstaff, laying most of his trouble to a fearsome nightmare he had suffered.

As the party returned up the coast from Jaffa to Beirut, Yusef showed signs of disintegration; he not only found more than the usual number of pretty nieces along the way, but he more and more frequently allowed them to fill him with the potent arrack. He explained to Browne that it hurt his conscience a great deal that he had killed no Bedouins during the trip; when Browne threatened to put him in a book and tell all the world about him, Yusef determined to destroy at least one badman. Fortified with arrack, he started to attack a camel driver in a defile approaching Tyre, but he changed his mind and shook hands instead. On the last day of the journey, however, again filled with arrack he went ahead of the party and, not far short of Beirut, beat up a withered little Turk, pretending he was a giant Bedouin.

The next morning in Beirut Yusef appeared in all his glory.

It was not until after breakfast the next morning, that we had the pleasure of seeing Yusef. He was standing out in the front yard, dressed in the most gorgeous of Oriental costumes. His turban was of the richest texture and most flashing colors; his vest actually glittered with gilded embroidery and silver buttons; his sash was of flaming vermilion; his sword and atagar of Damascus, dazzled the eye as they swung by his side in the morning sun-beams; his legs were swathed in crimson velvet; and his feet seemed to spurn the earth in the glory of yellow embroidered slippers, the richest productions of Aleppo. I declare, without exaggeration, when I saw him thus encircled by an admiring crowd, rolling out torrents of rich Arabic, as he gracefully waved his hands in the air, showing with what ease he had encountered the Bedouins from Damascus to the Dead Sea, I thought he was the most grateful, warlike, and distinguished looking man the world had ever produced. When I approached and said: "Good-morning, Yusef; how do you do?" it was really flattering to my feelings, the mingled dignity and deference with which he bowed to me, and the Oriental richness of the figures of speech which he made use of in returning the compliments of the morning.[19]

Yusef's glory was not to last long, however. The little Turk had gone to the authorities to obtain justice and the soldiers in Beirut soon had Yusef Badra, the Destroyer of Robbers, lodged in the local jail. It was here that Browne found him just before his steamer sailed for Alexandria. The fallen Yusef, with great tears running down his face, greeted him and some interested spectators from behind the bars. " 'My niece did it, gentlemen; she made me drunk. All my misfortunes have come from devils in the form of angels. Take warning, O Howadji, and never put faith in woman!' " [20]

The End of Yusef

Though the book *Yusef* brought its author some small fame and continued to appear in reprints until the turn of the century, it failed to turn the trick so that Browne the author could win out over Browne the government clerk. In the first flush of enthusiasm over its reception, Browne talked confidently of living off his royalties, which by that time were augmented by travel articles in *Harpers Magazine*, which published his account of his visit to Crusoe's Island during the very months that *Yusef* appeared. There was one other string to his bow if he couldn't make a living from his writing—that was the possibility of an appointment to a consular or ministerial position, something he had been hoping for for a long time. In those days, government patronage, particularly in the consular service, was the standard way of subsidizing authors, comparable to appointments to chairs in creative writing in colleges or Guggenheim fellowships today. Just after he came home from the Levant, Browne had some hopes of receiving an appointment to China but it failed to materialize; when a minor post in the Orient turned up a few years later he turned it down. But finally in 1868 he was appointed by President Johnson as United States Minister to China, to succeed the ebullient Anson Burlingame. He remained in Peking only a year, when he was recalled by President Grant after spending several cold months trying to carry out a policy set up by Burlingame which he felt was quite unrealistic.

Almost immediately after *Yusef* appeared, Browne, discouraged at the prospect of living on royalties or getting a diplomatic post, took a position with the Treasury Department as a confidential agent whose duty was to inspect custom houses along the borders of Western America. He was also ordered to inspect Indian agencies. For six years he was almost constantly traveling and sending in the detailed, honest, plain-spoken reports on custom officials and Indian agents which earned him a reputation as a government reformer. Because Browne's work, particularly as it turned to Indian affairs, concentrated on the Far West, he moved his family to Oakland, California. A visit which Bayard Taylor made to him there in 1859 may have encouraged him to try once more to support himself as a travel writer, for in that year he sent his wife and six children and two Indian servants to Washington, where he hoped to join them soon and take them to Germany. He felt he could live abroad more cheaply than in California, give the children a good education, and write travel letters about points in Europe which could be reached easily from Frankfort. Before he joined his family in the East, he went up to the newly discovered mines on the Comstock Lode in Nevada and obtained material for his lively illustrated "Peep at Washoe" which, together with his "Washoe Revisited," written four years later, anticipated Mark Twain's *Roughing It* (1872). He also anticipated to some degree the latter's *Tramp Abroad* (1880) in his *American Family in Germany* (1866) which with *The Land of Thor* (1867) told of his experiences during the three years he spent in Europe, with Frankfort as his base.

His personal contacts with Mark Twain are of some interest. He did not meet him in Virginia City, as he visited Washoe two years before Clemens arrived. However, we know that the two writers had met each other by the time Mark Twain returned from the Sandwich Islands to San Francisco and started on his very successful lecturing career, for Browne entertained him in Oakland soon after his first lecture. It has been said that Mark Twain went to Browne for advice about lecturing techniques but this seems unlikely. Browne also started lecturing about this time and was modestly successful; apparently he never drew upon the Holy Land for his material but concentrated on Iceland and Poland. Just before Browne was appointed minister to China, Mark Twain confided to his friend Mrs. Fairbanks that Browne was planning to get him a sinecure and take him to China with him.[21] The plan, which was probably concocted in Washington, D.C. while Mark Twain was working for Senator Stewart of Nevada and Browne was reporting to the Treasury Department, fell through somewhere along the line. Finally, in 1872 Browne wrote Lucy from London that he had run into "dry, quaint old Twain" in the English metropolis, where he was being feted for his successes with *The Innocents Abroad* and *Roughing It*.[22]

There is no indication that Browne ever met Herman Melville, although they both earned their daily bread in custom house work, one in the East, the other in the West. As time went on, Browne became involved in mining and real estate ventures—he became an expert on western mining, partly because of his skill in sketching mining properties—and he built a fantastic home called Pagoda Hill in an Oakland suburb where he planned to house all of his ramifying family. He died suddenly at fifty-four in 1875, presumably from an attack of appendicitis, and was buried in Oakland's Mountain View Cemetery as a revered California pioneer and humorist.

FIVE

Herman Melville

O F THE three travelers who are being considered in this study, Herman Melville had the most socially distinguished background. His father, who, when Herman was born, was a successful importer with home and offices in New York City, came from a prominent Revolutionary War family descended from Scots covenanters, some of whom belonged to the peerage in Scotland. Herman's mother was one of the Gansevoorts, a prominent Dutch family whose best-known member was Herman's grandfather, General Peter Gansevoort, celebrated as a hero in the Revolutionary War. As a boy Herman Melville had known the amenities of the child of well-to-do and socially prominent parents; not only was his father an experienced traveler who spoke French like a native but he was in a position to provide his children with a governess and to send Herman, when he was old enough, to an excellent private school. Up until the time Herman was eleven, the Melville family life offered the best of advantages to a growing genius. If we are to accept Newton Arvin's interpretation of Melville's heritage, we can even assume that his personality was well-balanced by the mixture of Melville and Gansevoort; from his father he inherited the "restless, excitable, mercurial, and experimental" part of his nature, and from his mother bodily vigor, reserve of stamina, "and even stolidity." Though he was not the "bright boy" of the family—that role was reserved for his older brother, Gansevoort—he was a boy of promise.

The almost idyllic home situation came to an abrupt end when Herman's father, through an unwise investment, lost his fortune and was forced into bankruptcy. The times were hard and the wretched merchant's health was failing; he moved his family to Albany, attempted without success to get back on his feet financially, collapsed, and died after two weeks of delirium in the dark days of January 1832, leaving his family in straightened circumstances and his son Herman the difficult task of facing the problems of "a decayed patrician." All during Herman's teens the fortune of the family fluctuated, with brother Gansevoort for awhile succeeding in business, only to go bankrupt in the end. Apparently Herman received a fairly good education, attending two Albany academies and eventually earning a certificate of proficiency in surveying and engineering from the Lansingburgh Academy, located in a little town a few miles up the Hudson from Albany to which Maria Melville, now almost fully dependent on the bounty of her relatives, moved her brood in hopes of finding simpler living than Albany could afford. Perhaps it was being forced by circumstances to teach a country school near Pittsfield, with all of the humiliations of boarding around and beating knowledge into the children, that caused Herman at the age of twenty to ship as cabin boy on a passenger vessel sailing for Europe. Back home, none the richer in money but much matured physically and emotionally, he tried again for a short time to put up with teaching, then, with the finality of a boy leaving home for good, boarded the *Acushnet* for his four years of wandering on the Pacific. When he returned home he wrote *Typee*, which appeared in 1846 and brought him an immediate public. One decade and eight books later, including *Moby-Dick*, he found that he was losing his reading audience, which cared far less for his domestic novel *Pierre* than it had for his tales dealing with the South Seas and whaling. By now he was married, had children to support, and realized that he could probably no longer make a living from his writing.

There is little question that his visit to Europe and the Near East in 1857 was in part an attempt to reclaim his health and spirits after working too intensely to survive in the writing game. For some time Melville had been suffering from rheumatism and sciatica, as well as some difficulties with his eyes, and no doubt the concern that he was written out gave the impression to his family that he was seriously disturbed—at least, very hard to live with. Such is the impression conveyed by a family letter written by Judge Lemuel Shaw, Melville's father-in-law, in which he revealed that his offer to finance a trip abroad for Herman through advancing some $1500 on is daughter's inheritance was prompted as much by concern over Elizabeth's comfort as Herman's welfare.

I suppose you have been informed by some of the family, how very ill, Herman has been. It is manifest to me from Elizabeth's letters, that she has felt great anxiety about him. When he is deeply engaged in one of his literary works, he confines him [self] to hard study many hours of the day, with little or no exercise, & this specially in winter for a great many days together. He thus probably overworks himself & brings on severe nervous affections. He has been advised strongly to break off this labor for some time, & take a voyage or a journey, & endeavour to recruit. No definite plan is arranged, but I think it may result, in this that in the autumn he will go away for four or five months, Elizabeth will come here with her younger children, Mrs. Griggs & Augusta will each take one of the boys, their house in Pittsfield will be shut up. I think he needs such a change & that it would be highly beneficial to him & probably restore him.[1]

The plan was a good one and was already bearing fruit when Melville, after closing down his western Massachusetts farmhouse for the winter and sending his wife and four children to their in-laws, reached New York where he visited his old friend Evert Duyckinck on the eve of sailing for Liverpool on 11 October 1856. Duyckinck found his friend revived in spirits.

Herman Melville passed the evening with me—fresh from his mountain charged to the muzzle with his sailor metaphysics and jargon of things unknowable. But a good stirring evening—plowing deep and bringing to the surface some rich fruits of thought and experience—Melville instanced old Burton as atheistical—in the exquisite irony of his passages on some sacred matters; cited a good story from the Decameron the *Enchantment* of the husband in the tree; a story from Judge Edmonds of a prayer meeting of female convicts at Sing Sing which the Judge was invited to witness and agreed to, provided he was introduced where he could not be seen. It was an orgy of indecency and blasphemy.[2]

During his short stay in New York, Melville also picked up his passport, filling out a description of himself—5′ 8¾″ high, blue eyes, dark brown hair, fair complexion, and a "round" chin[3] (which was effectually covered up by a handsome beard). Naturally he was not in the prime physical condition that he had been in during his whaling days, but his eagerness during his trip to take long walks and to climb any tower or eminence he came upon for a look around demonstrates that he had not been ruined by a sedentary life. Usually grave and reserved, he took to companionship with real warmth and thoroughly enjoyed a good laugh with such as Evert Duyckinck.

The grave side of Melville was most apparent during the short time he spent with Nathaniel Hawthorne, who was now serving as American Consul in Liverpool. This was doubtless partly because Melville reacted to a reserve—a holding back—in Hawthorne which he apparently had not been able to break down even during the close days in Pittsfield when this writer, the most stimulating literary companion Melville was to know, helped him so much in stirring the ferment that created *Moby-Dick*. It was undoubtedly partly because Hawthorne liked to talk of those deep things "of Providence and futurity, and of everything that lies beyond human ken" with which Melville was concerned. Hawthorne, who himself could hardly set a good example in firmness of religious convictions, noted in his journal after the visit that Melville would never rest "until he gets hold of a definite belief." Thus it is probably in terms of a denial of an afterlife that Hawthorne interpreted Melville's statement that he had "pretty much made up his mind to be annihilated." [4] However, knowing that Melville abandoned prose fiction after *The Confidence Man*, which he had brought with him in manuscript hoping to find an English publisher, critics have tended to interpret the much-quoted phrase to mean that Melville felt that he had pretty well made up his mind to being annihilated as a writer. This was far from the case, as the journal which he kept during his trip indicates.

This journal, which is our only on-the-spot record of Melville's Mediterranean trip, is the sort of account kept by a writer who intends to draw on it later for literary work. Kept fairly diligently in three notebooks, it usually included day-by-day items of observation or sentences of reflection on these observations; sometimes, however, when the excitement of sightseeing cut down on time for making journal entries, Melville resorted to lengthy summaries of his impressions written when he had time to catch his breath. Such was the case with his stimulating visit to Cairo and the Pyramids, written up in considerable detail with much comment as he awaited the steamer at Alexandria which would take him to Palestine. Such also was his method during most of his Holy Land visit, with only a few dated entries (many dated incorrectly) followed by a meaty account of his visit worked out while he rested for several days at Jaffa awaiting a change of weather which would make it possible for a ship to put in to that poorly sheltered port and take him on to Beirut.

The actual use of his travel journal, or his changing plans for its use, are not easily ascertainable at this date, particularly because many additional remarks have been added in the margin and many underlinings and directional marks superimposed in pen and pencil as Melville worked over the material during the twenty years that elapsed between his return home and the completion of his Holy Land poem, *Clarel*. Unlike Browne and Mark Twain, he was not preparing newsletters for a home public—he had made no such arrangement with a newspaper or magazine and it is doubtful that he would have found such an arrangement satisfactory. Later he was asked to contribute to the new *Atlantic Monthly* and agreed to do so, but never got around to it—he may have planned to use some of his diary material for this. In some entries he indicated that he might even use the material for a continuation of the enigmatic *Confidence Man*, which had ended with the teasing sentence: "Something further may follow of this Masquerade." It is certain that he used the diary to prepare two lectures entitled "Statuary in Rome" and "Travelling: Its Pleasures, Pains, and Profits" which he delivered during the three years he tried to support himself as a lecturer after returning home. At the end of his journal he wrote the cryptic words: "Frescoes for Travel by Three Brothers, Poet, Painter, and Scholar," which may suggest that he planned a travel book or may, more probably, be a step towards the development of *Clarel* which was to owe much of its appeal to the presentation of a number of contrasting points of view on the Holy Land. We do not know when he added the postscript, however.

The rather belabored points made above show that Melville kept his journal with the perceptivity and imagination that were the earmarks of a creative writer who ordinarily drew on his personal experiences for his writing. It is from this diary, then, that we will try to build up a picture of his reactions to the Levant, a part of the world he had long wanted to visit. In fact, during an earlier voyage across the Atlantic in 1849, he and a cousin of Bayard Taylor whom he had met on shipboard had cooked up a scheme to go to the Levant by a rather unusual route. Melville noted in his journal, "This afternoon Dr. Taylor & I sketched a plan for going down the Danube from Vienna to Constantinople; thence to Athens on the steamer; to Beyrouth & Jerusalem—Alexandria & the Pyramids . . . I am full (just now) of this glorious *Eastern* jaunt. Think of it! Jerusalem and the Pyramids—Constantinople, the Aegean, and old Athens!" [5] The plan may not have been too feasible with the hostile Ottoman Empire astride his path; however during this same trip he met in London Alexander William Kinglake, the author of the tremendously popular *Eōthen*, who had ridden by horseback to Constantinople through Hungary, Serbia, and Thrace more than a decade earlier. But the scheme fell through and Melville returned to America, still eager to visit the Near East. It was appropriate that Melville would long to visit the Holy Land; after all the Melville family motto was the Crusaders' cry "DENIQUE CŒLUM—Heaven at Last!" [6]

Though they were miles apart in temperament and ability, Melville and Browne shared a few important traits that made them both good travelers. Perhaps the most obvious of these was an ability to travel light. Browne had his knapsack and Melville his carpetbag, sometimes finding even this light load more than he liked to carry. Seven years earlier when he was making a short trip on the continent he had left his bag in Brussels and had carried "nothing" with him for four days in the Rhine country. When, during the week he spent in Liverpool on the present trip, Hawthorne invited him down to his home in Southport for a couple of days, Melville had taken only a nightshirt and toothbrush, much to his friend's surprise (and slight apprehension). But Hawthorne remembered that Melville had boasted of living for months in the South Seas with a red shirt and pair of duck trousers as his only possessions. Hawthorne could appreciate this point of view, although as American consul he could certainly not imitate it. Mrs. Hawthorne confided to a friend that she was afraid she would never get her husband on to the continent "because the thought of transporting a trunk or bundle deprives him of hope & peace and nearly of life." Thus it was that the favor which Hawthorne did for Melville which was even more helpful than listening to his doubts and fears, endorsing his passport for Constantinople, Egypt, etc., and even finalizing the contract with Longmans in London to publish *The Confidence Man*, was agreeing to keep Melville's trunk while he made his journey to the East. Commenting on Melville's departure with only his carpetbag, Hawthorne confided to his diary: "This is the next best thing to going naked; and as he wears his beard and moustache, and so needs no dressing case— nothing but a tooth-brush—I do not know a more independent personage." [7]

Not so independent as to be a loner, however, Melville, like Browne, was a gregarious soul, and though there is no doubt that he was ill and depressed during at least the early part of his Mediterranean trip, he was no Timon nor by nature a misanthrope. He struck up acquaintances easily on ship or land, enjoying convivial company and particularly taking to people who would discuss metaphysics with him or talk about "fixed fate, free will, and foreknowledge absolute." He almost invariably became acquainted with the captains of the ships on which he rode. He had convivial habits, illustrating one generalization he was to make in his lecture on "Travelling": the successful traveler, he maintained, must be "gifted with geniality and imagination, for if without these last he may as well stay home." He enjoyed wines and smoked cigars and pipes, though he does not seem to have taken up the long-stemmed chibouk as enthusiastically as Browne did. Neither man seems to have enjoyed the bubble pipe or narghile.

Melville was also willing, if necessary, to put up with cheap accommodations, the modest hotel or second class passage on the steamer. However, though he was not interested in traveling just to savor good hotels, as Dr. Mendoza preferred to do in *Yusef,* he made a point of occasionally trying a celebrated restaurant or staying at a famous hostelry like Shepheard's in Cairo. Though there is little evidence in his journal to support the idea he was a gourmet, or loved body comfort, he at least never spoke with contempt of epicurean delights as did Browne. Though he liked a daily bath— preferably in the morning—his behavior merited Hawthorne's observation that he was "a little heterodox in the manner of clean linen." While traveling on the Atlantic and Mediterranean by steamer, he had no opportunity to display his sailor experience and enthusiasm for exercise by scampering up the rigging as he had done when he crossed to England on a sailing packet in 1849; moreover, seven years of writing accompanied by sciatica and rheumatism had left him stocky rather than sturdy at thirty-seven; but it would be a mistake to take him too seriously in his remark to Hawthorne that he had lost his love of adventure. His walks, his frequent climbs, and his attempts to penetrate the labyrinths of a rabbit-warren like Constantinople all contradict his statement. Finally, he possessed the most valuable asset of a good traveler; he was observant and constantly subject to sense impressions. Though his granddaughter insisted his ear was so defective that he never became a good linguist, his journal bears witness to the effectiveness of his nose in detecting the trials and delights of the Near East.

Like Browne, he was subject to spurts of enthusiasm followed frequently by lonesomeness or depression; however, he was much more often down than up, slept poorly, sometimes tossing for several nights in a row, suffered nightmares, and at times almost lost the use of his eyes. There is little sign on this trip that he was homesick, as he had been on his earlier trip to London, which he had cut short in order to go home to his family. It was Browne, however, who better illustrated Melville's comment in "The Paradise of Bachelors": "Bachelors alone can travel freely, and without any twinges of their consciences touching desertion of the fireside."

As a lover of art, Melville was very different from Browne, who showed little genuine appreciation of painting or sculpture, or Mark Twain, who seemed proud of his philistine dislikes. Melville spent much time, particularly during the Italian visit which came at the end of his trip to the Near East, enjoying paintings and statues—his first and favorite lecture was to be on "The Statuary of Rome." He also esteemed the past as much as he distrusted the present, and history was constantly his study. Finally, quite unlike Browne or Mark Twain, he saw things with the eye of a poet and described what he saw with the method of one who thought in images and symbols. Thus, after making the most pedestrian of entries in his journal during the six days which the *Egyptian* took to sail from Liverpool to the Mediterranean, he spoke in his true voice when he wrote of the sunset view of Gibraltar: "Insular Rock. Sunset. Rock strongly lit, all the rest in shade. England throwing the rest of the world in shade."

It took more than a month (from 25 November to 28 December) for Melville to reach Alexandria, on the threshold of the Holy Land. After passing Gibraltar, the *Egyptian* took him leisurely eastward, stopping for a few hours at Malta, three days at the island of Syros, the principal Greek port in the heart of the Cyclades (which Melville like Browne was to visit three times during his trip), a similar leisurely stop at Salonica, a week at Constantinople, where Melville left his ship and stayed ashore in the Hotel du Globe in Pera, on to Smyrna in another coastal steamer, back to Syros for a few hours, and then on to Alexandria. This was a welcome month of relaxation. From the moment he entered the Mediterranean, Melville's spirits rose; with the exception of one squall he saw balmy sunshine for the entire period—"such weather as we might have in Paradise." It was like getting back to the South Seas, though the islands were brown instead of green. He was, like most travelers, surprised and disappointed at the barrenness of the fabled isles of the Aegean, but the local inhabitants delighted him, supplying the color he loved. He was fortunate in visiting the area when native costumes were still a matter of daily life rather than a display for tourists; from the moment he set foot on Greek soil at Syros he felt he was viewing an opera, with the characters welcoming him onstage. Aboard ship, the Turks, who preferred deck passage to cabin privacy and set up tents for their harems, constantly fascinated him; he particularly enjoyed "two 'beys effendi' in long furred robes of yellow, looking like Tom cats." Melville, what with the warm weather and renewed spirits, may have felt a bit like "a Tom cat" himself; he admitted to becoming entranced with the harem women, although he gained only fleeting glimpses of their flashing eyes and "fine busts." Though he was disappointed at seeing only old women in Salonica, he apparently had much better success in Constantinople where he noted among "Street sights": "The beauty of the human countenance. Among the women, ugly faces are rare.—Singular these races so exceed ours in this respect."

At Salonica, where he had a fine view of the snow-covered Mount Olympus, he had been amused when the English resident remarked casually that he had just spent a day's shooting in the Vale of Tempe ("Ye Gods! whortleberrying on Olympus, etc.") but at Smyrna he was disappointed in not being able to see slaves auctioned off in the Bazaar. Still, he saw plenty of camels in both places to furnish local color. Constantinople did not fail him. His seven days in that fabled city started appropriately when at dawn he saw from the ship the fog lifting coyly from the minarets and domes. ("Constantinople, like her Sultanas, was thus seen veiled in her 'ashmack.' ") The week ended with a glorious view of Scutari on the Asian shore glowing like a sapphire in the sunset. In between, he did all the usual things ashore—visited the famous mosques including Santa Sophia (where he was annoyed with a rascally priest who tried to sell him chunks of the fallen mosaics), wandered through the bazaars (where he thought he was being followed by a thug), rode around the Stamboul walls, penetrated as far as he could into the Seraglio, watched the flow of many races on the Galata pontoon bridge across the Golden Horn, rode over to Scutari lying in a caïque ("a boat bed"), and took a steamer trip up the Bosphorus to catch a glimpse of the Black Sea. The twisting Bosphorus reminded him of Lake George—he was as prone to be reminded of that lovely New York lake wherever he traveled as Mark Twain was of Lake Tahoe.

Of course, he "got up aloft" when he could. He went up into the gallery in Santa Sophia, clambered up the Genoese tower in Galata, and, best of all, mounted the Beyazit tower near the Blue Mosque in Stamboul ("My God, what a view!" he noted in his journal). His other specialty was visiting cemeteries—they always fascinated him although they sometimes depressed him. At Salonica he had seen his first Muslim tombs with their turbaned headstones. In Constantinople he discovered that a cemetery near his hotel also served as the garbage dump. Perhaps this was the very graveyard where the pariah dogs had so fascinated Browne when he was in Constantinople. Among the "forrests of cemeteries" Melville happened on one in Pera where signs of human tragedy moved him deeply. ". . . saw a woman over a new grave—no grass on it yet. Such abandonment of misery! Called to the dead, put her head down as close to it as possible; as if calling down a hatchway or cellar; besought—'Why dont you speak to me? My God!—It is I! Ah,—speak—but one word!' All deaf.—So much for consolation.—This woman and her cries haunt me horribly.—"

It was on the last day of the year that Melville discovered the Holy Land while climbing the Great Pyramid of Cheops. This was, he noted emphatically, a day he would never forget. He had enjoyed the dash from Cairo along the Nile on one of the scampering donkeys, had barely hesitated at Isle Roda, in the midst of the ford, where tradition had it that Moses was found in the bulrushes, and had started up the side of the Great Pyramid—"precipice on precipice,

cliff on cliff"—with an urgency that seemed automatic and irresistible. Later he noted in his diary: "In heyday holyday spirits arrived at
the eternal sorrow of the pyramids." He was sure that only the
phlegmatic take their time with such a climb, and he hurried, even
though a pain in his chest prompted him to rest at least once and the
wily guide offered to divert him part way up by leading him into a
sidehole which felt like a tunnel under the sea. Undaunted by a
feeling of awe and terror, he pressed on to the very top, where at first
he felt secure but then was quickly gripped by a nervousness, a final
giddiness and terror. It seemed to him that both immensity and age
were embodied in the monument. What sort of people could have
built it and why? Was it but one of a line of pyramids erected as a
bulwark against the desert, which pressed in relentlessly, creating a
border between brown waste and green verdure that was plainer
"than that between good an evil." The Pyramid was "vast, undefiled,
incomprehensible, and awful." No moss grew upon its stones and it
cast no shadow for most of the day. "I shudder at the idea of ancient
Egyptians. It was in these pyramids that was conceived the idea of
Jehovah. Terrible mixture of the cunning and awful. Moses learned
in all the lore of the Egyptians. The idea of Jehovah born here." The
Great Pyramid did not affect him as would have a comprehensible
work of Nature or of Man. Its creator was

that supernatural creature, the priest. They must needs have been terrible
inventors, those Egyptian wise men. And one seems to see that as out of the
crude forms of the natural earth they could evoke by art the transcendant
[novelty] of the pyramid so out of the rude elements of the insignificant
thoughts that are in all men, they could by an analogous art rear the
transcendant conception of a God. But for no holy purpose was the pyramid
founded.

For Melville, the secrets of the origins of the Jewish and Christian
religions lay buried in the Great Pyramid.

The notes which Melville made during his few days in Egypt are
full of images with symbolic flavor. One that persisted involved the
"contiguity of desert & verdure, splendor and squalor." But his only
comment on the Sphinx, which was to so fascinate Mark Twain, was:

"Back to desert & face to verdure. Solid rock." The splendor and squalor theme was also illustrated in Cairo by sights of handsome as well as ruined mosques and palaces, dim peeps at courts and walls in shadow, ghostly haunted houses, wretched beggars. The teeming life in street and square suggested to the recent author of *The Confidence Man* "one booth and Bartholemew Fair—a grand masquerade of humanity." The antiquity of Egypt was dramatized by the heavy coats of dust on many buildings, making Cairo minarets ashy in color, unlike the gleaming marble of Constantinople. The sense of the picturesque was strong—as Melville walked in the big square where Shepheard's Hotel stood he saw the crescent and star gradually appear in the evening sky. The next morning the early sun glimpsed through the foliage brought a balmy, dewy morning— "Paridise melted & poured into the air. Soft intoxication; no wonder these people never drink wine." He even playfully apostrophized the little donkeys, best fellows in the world. "As for his bray, that is the original Egyptian," he chuckled.

Melville celebrated New Year's day by riding the train back to Alexandria. He hated to leave Cairo but he rushed back expecting to find the steamer ready to sail for Jaffa, only to curse his fate while he waited until the fourth before it finally departed. All Alexandria had to offer were some second-rate catacombs, Pompey's Pillar, which he twice reported in his journal as looking like a huge stick of candy after being sucked, and an uncomfortably bright Mediterranean Sea. He feared for his eyes under the "scortching" sun of Egypt; in Cairo he had seen more blind men than he had ever seen before— "Too much light & no defence against it." The flies on the blindmen's eyes at noon reminded him that nature feeds on man. Now, as he waited for the steamer to sail he kept busy by writing in his diary and reading a book on Palestine. He was eager to catch his first glimpse of the Palestine coast, though he had been warned by his reading that it would be marked by rocks and sand and have a barren and dreary look. Doubtless he would continue feeling about that coast as he had felt about the Greek islands. Compared with those in the South Seas, they had lost their virginity, they "look worn, and are meagre, like life after enthusiasm is gone. The aspect of all of them is sterile & dry."

At last, after two days of steaming along the coast in the sun, he saw the breakers off Jaffa before sighting the little town. The swells were rolling and he landed not without danger, though he scorned the attempts of the Arab boatmen to "play upon my supposed fears." After all, he was an experienced sailor, about to set foot on holy soil in one of the oldest cities of the world. Even the date seemed propitious; it was the Epiphany.

He did not waste any time getting acquainted with Jaffa, however. Eager to be off to Jerusalem, he hired a Jewish dragoman and set out with excitement over the Plain of Sharon with the mountains of Ephraim beckoning him on. Darkness caught him at Ramla, where he put up at a so-called hotel and soon learned to agree wholeheartedly with his dragoman: " 'Dese Arab no know how to keep hotel.' " After attempting to eat a dinner of cold meat served on broken crockery attended by a host of mosquitoes and flies, he tried to get some sleep but failed. At two o'clock in the morning he and his guide were in their saddles and riding the pilgrim route once more. Darkness succeeded moonlight; a dawn of pale olive appeared, whereupon they breakfasted in a cave. More hours of "withered & desert country" followed by a "hot and wearisome ride over the arid hills" brought him at last to Jerusalem. Whether the first glimpse of the holy city on the hills quickened his heartbeat, we do not know, for he made no comment in his journal of that famous first view which brought tears to so many eyes. Rather, he indicates that by two o'clock that afternoon he was sheltered from the sun in the Mediterranean Hotel, which stood beside the Pool of Hezekiah, promising more mosquitoes but no Bathsheba, and run by a German named Hauser who had been converted to Judaism. Some three hundred yards away was the site where reverent pilgrims believed that Jesus was crucified and buried and rose from the dead.

In fact, Melville could see the battered dome of the Church of the Holy Sepulchre by stepping on a platform outside his chamber window. However, his afternoon excursion did not take him in the

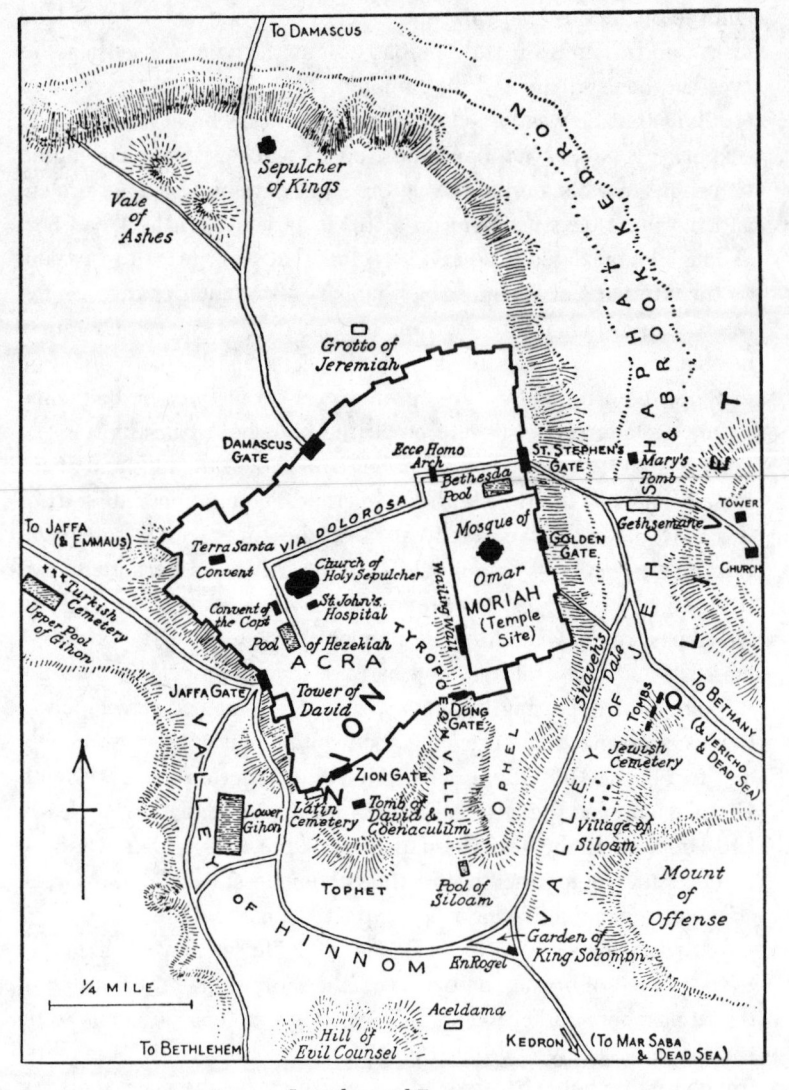

Jerusalem and Environs

direction of the church but, rather, beyond the city walls for a glimpse of the city and surrounding country from the elevated land to the north. Unfortunately he had to cut this venture short as his eyes had been so affected by the long morning's ride in the glare of arid hills that he was forced to take refuge in his hotel room.

It may possibly have been the trouble with his eyes that caused him to neglect his journal during the eight days he was in Jerusalem and the three days he spent on a trip to Jericho and the Dead Sea. (Though he misdated his diary, it is clear that he rode into Jerusalem on the afternoon of Wednesday, 7 January 1857, and departed on the return trip to Jaffa on the morning of Sunday, 18 January.) Or it may be that he was so busy obtaining impressions that he had no energy to write them up at the time, preferring to wait until he had some leisure at Jaffa or Beirut and could see his whole Palestine visit in perspective. He merely notes that he roamed over the hills and about the city, part of the time with his Jewish dragoman, possibly part of the time alone, and certainly part of the time with a congenial Bostonian, Frederick Cunningham, who arrived in Jerusalem two days after Melville. "A very prepossessing young man," Cunningham was thirty, seven years Melville's junior, a graduate of Harvard, was married, had four children, and had not long before taken over the shipping and importing business which his father had developed in the Mediterranean. He proved a good companion in this presumably first trip to the Holy Land; when Melville left Jerusalem it was with Cunningham and the latter's Druse dragoman, Abdallah, who clearly had supplanted the Jew. Perhaps that is the reason that when he reached Ramla for the second time, Melville stayed in the Greek convent rather than trying to put up with a native hotel.

Between these two visits to Ramla, Melville set himself diligently to the pursuit of his stated objective, "the saturation of my mind with the atmosphere of Jerusalem." To accomplish this, he spent some time almost every day in the Church of the Holy Sepulchre, frequently "hanging" from a little gallery inside the entrance from which he could see the Turkish policemen, stationed there to prevent members of Christian sects from warring with each other, sitting cross-legged on their divan, smoking leisurely and watching the pilgrims contemptuously. He could also see the stone where Christ's body was anointed, a spot which inevitably received the first attentions of the pilgrims. To Melville it looked, with its streaks of moldy red, like a butcher's slab. From his vantage point he could even see the pilgrims climb to the gallery of the "reputed Calvary" where, "by the smoky light of [an] old pawnbroker's lamp of dirty gold," they would be shown the hole in which the cross was fixed and gaze in awe through a grating (that looked to Melville like the opening to a coal-cellar) at the awesome crack in the rock created by the earthquake which accompanied Christ's crucifixion.

Nearby in the rotunda was the Holy Sepulchre itself, housed within a small structure that suggested "a church in a church." Because of the many lamps within, entering it from the dusky church seemed like entering a stuffy lighted lantern. "Wedged & half-dazzled, you stare for a moment on the ineloquence of the bedizened slab, and glad to come out, wipe your brow glad to escape as from the heat & jam of a show-box. All is glitter & nothing is gold. A sickening cheat." The chapels of the many sects in the main part of the church reminded Melville of the traders' booths in the New York stock exchange; the crypt where St. Helena was supposed to have found the true cross reminded him of a wine cellar. He felt that the whole church smelled like a deadhouse and that the pilgrims were either ghouls or cynics.

As he retreated from the gloomy interior, eager to get some fresh air, he returned through the entrance with a grate in the door like that of a jail. Out in the entrance court, the shabby carved façade looked "like so much spoiled pastry at which the mice have been at work" and the high and venerable tower beside the entrance reminded him of an ancient pine, "barked at bottom & all decay at top." This sty of a courtyard was filled with pertinacious hawkers of trinkets, while outside the gate, along the wall of the church which formed the upper part of the Via Dolorosa, human excrement (which he wryly hoped was exclusively Turkish) stank in piles in every nook and crevice. And to think that this was the main wall "of the fabric containing the tomb of one of the persons of the Godhead"!

About the rest of Jerusalem, Melville's journal says little. The crooked, narrow Via Dolorosa seemed deserted except for an occasional woman panting under a heavy burden or a man with a melancholy face. When his guide pointed out the stations of the cross, he was amused at the lack of reverence: "Yonder is the arch where Christ was shown to the people, & just by that open window is sold the best coffee in Jerusalem." He was pleased to discover that someone had built a little bachelor's abode atop the Ecco Homo Arch. Of course, he could not obtain entrance to Mt. Moriah so saw nothing of the Dome of the Rock and he does not mention visiting the Jewish Wailing Wall. Like Browne, however, he noted the wretched condition of the lepers near the Zion Gate, with their houses facing the city wall and their "park" a dungheap.

Clearly Melville did not like Jerusalem; he insisted that it inevitably drove any romantic illusions from his mind. The color of the whole city was grey and "looks at you like a cold grey eye in a cold grey man." The streets constantly smelled of burning rubbish— even the so-called Pool of Bethesda was an odorous, sooty place, full of debris. He was oppressed by "the insalubriousness of so small a city pent in by lofty walls obstructing ventilation, postponing the morning & hasting the unwholesome twilight." Being a man who tolerated discomfort only if he had to, he made a daily practice of rising with the sun and walking outside the walls and in the countryside in search of fresh air. He was surprised at the number of the city's inhabitants who did likewise.

Nevertheless, though he obtained better air outside the walls, his impressions remained almost uniformly gloomy. He does not even mention the Garden of Gethsamene, which many modern visitors have found a pleasant oasis among the many ugly churches; he merely remarks that olive trees resemble apples in being twisted but are still haunted and melancholy. He took some pleasure in the fancy of Christ coming to judge the dead from the beautiful Golden Gate, set and sealed cleanly above the Valley of Jehoshaphat. After visiting Mt. Zion he jotted down nothing about David's tomb or the room of the Last Supper. Rather, at sunrise, standing on Mt. Zion, he was fascinated by the red light on Aceldama, the field of blood where Judas killed himself, noting it was "confessing its inexpiable guilt by deeper dyes."

As he wandered around morning after morning, slipping down into the two valleys which embraced Jerusalem and joined together to the south forming the wadi through which the Kedron occasionally ran, the very names of Jehoshaphat and Hinnom—where Gihon or Gehanna lay—seemed ghostly and disturbing. Their symbol and principal feature was the grave—thousands of them in all directions. He found that the vale of Hinnom was filled with gravestones of infinite variety; he discovered that farther down the valley, in the wretched settlement of Siloam (Siloah), just above the Pool of Siloam, living persons dwelt in tombs in the hillside. And the gravestones which lay helter skelter in the Valley of Jehoshaphat, between Jerusalem and the Mount of Olives, frequently projected out from the hillsides "as if already in act of resurection." For this was the spot where tradition said that Muslims, Jews, and even Christians would rise on the Day of Judgment and be sent to eternal punishment or reward. Melville wandered among the tombs until he felt himself "one possessed with devils"; he stood outside St. Stephen's gate and watched the shadows enter tomb after tomb as night crawled up the slope of Mt. Olivet.

The ever-present stones, like the graves of Palestine, fascinated Melville. St. Stephen's Gate, named after the first Christian martyr, reminded him of the horrors of being stoned to death; the sight of piles of stones within and without the stately tomb of Absalom, stones thrown there over the centuries by passing Jews to express their hatred of the son who had betrayed King David, were visible signs of a melancholy amusement. The hillside view of Mt. Zion was one of "loose stones and gravel as if shot down by carts;" in another spot, the old-looking rocks reminded him of bones of mastodons. "Judea is one accumulation of stones—Stony mountains & stony plains; stony torrents & stony roads; stony walls & stony fields, stony houses & stony tombs; stony eyes & stony hearts." The more stones you removed the more stones you discovered. "It is like mending an old barn; the more you uncover, the more it grows." Melville grew facetious about the origin of all these stones: "*My* theory is that long ago, some whimsical King of the country took it into his head to pave all Judea, and entered into contracts to that effect; but the contractor becoming bankrupt mid-way in his business, the stones were only dumped on the ground, & there they lie to this day."

The mixture of peoples, particularly of Arabs, Jews, and Christians, in the Jerusalem area prompted Melville frequently to point out the irony of assuming one religion could outweigh another. Both Jew and Arab awaited judgment "in another faith than that of Him who ascended from the nigh Olivet." On the Via Dolorosa one heard the muezzin call to noontime prayers; the wall of Omar's Mosque rose from the foundations of Solomon's temple; the several tracks in the way from Jaffa to Jerusalem suggested the divergent faiths of the land. Over all was the indifference of nature; weeds grew on the side of Mt. Zion and the sun which rose over the Chapel of the Ascension on Mt. Olivet cast shadows impartially from church and mosque. Most ironic of all was the sight of a Muslim praying in the field below Bethlehem where the shepherds had heard the angels; naturally he had his back toward Jerusalem and was facing Mecca.

His visit to Bethlehem did not occur until the last day of the three-day excursion to Jericho and the Dead Sea which he undertook with Cunningham and possibly a fairly large party, with tents, equipment and escort. His notes on this venture principally stress the aridity of the Judean wilderness. The journey past Bethany (a "wretched Arab village") down the steep wadi which led to Jericho (which he mistakenly thought was the watercourse of the River Kedron) took him through black and funereal hillsides until it debouched on the plain of Jericho (more than a thousand feet below sea level) through what looked to Melville like the Gate of Hell. He admitted that there was some greenness around Jericho, but Quarantania, the Mountain of Temptation, due west of it, seemed to

Melville to be a strange place for the Devil to take Jesus to tempt him with the view.

In the evening when the glare had gone, after a good dinner and a "jolly time," Melville thoroughly enjoyed looking out from the tent door east toward the Moab Mountains. He felt that the tent was a "charmed circle, keeping off the curse" of the awful country. Though it rained during the night, not even thunder and lightning in the mountains could quite cancel out the effects of the cries of jackals and wolves. The next morning the party hastened on to the Jordan, the armed escort showing some fear of the Bedouins who had crossed from the opposite bank but proved to be merely looking for tobacco. Of the Jordan itself, Melville commented only that after the rain it was a turbid and yellow stream, with foliage on its banks but dry hills beyond. After a few hours of riding "on the mouldy plain" the party reached the Dead Sea, which looked like Lake George without verdure and was lined with foam which resembled the slaver of mad dogs. Melville apparently made no attempt to swim in the brackish water but he did take a gulp of it, discovering that the smarting bitter taste stayed with him the rest of the day; it inevitably caused him to speculate on the bitterness of life. These thoughts led to the searching for images to represent the barrenness of Judea—whitish mildew—leprosy—old cheese—rocks like bones—lime kilns—rubbish. He underlined the sentence, "*No moss as in other ruins—no grace of decay—no ivy—the unleavened nakedness of desolation.*" He was sure that such a landscape would have a dire effect on its inhabitants: "As the sight of haunted Haddon Hall suggested to Mrs Radcliffe her curdling romances, so I have little doubt, the diabolical landscapes [of a] great part of Judea must have suggested to the Jewish prophets, their ghastly theology."

Much of the afternoon was taken up in climbing steeply through this wilderness to the spot where the convent called Mar Saba hung on the side of its deep ravine. Melville recorded the many slimy trails of snails he passed on the way, the occasional wretched sheep or black goats he saw, the encampment of Bedouins whose tents looked to him like two rows of hearses. Finally the party reached the gate at the top of the monastery, went through the rigmarole of having their letter from the patriarch of Jerusalem raised in a basket, and were admitted. After they were taken to the room set aside for pilgrims, Melville relaxed. "Divans—St. Saba wine—*racka* [arrack]—comfortable . . . ," he noted. It was indeed a far cry from the shores of the Dead Sea where there was "nought to eat but bitumen & ashes with desert of Sodom apples washed down with water of Dead Sea." After dinner, Melville climbed down by ladders from level to level of the monastery until he was near the bottom of the ravine. As the light died out of the sky he visited the chapel, he saw the blackbirds fed, he discovered the one palm tree, half way down, which St. Saba was supposed to have planted with his own hands. Afterwards he enjoyed, for once, a "good bed & night's rest."

After a three-hour ride the following morning, the party reached Bethlehem, a town which apparently did not stir Melville to enthusiasm, though it failed to rouse him to ire as it had done Browne. He spent only a short time being shown through the Church of the Nativity, where lamps that burned with olive oil lit up the supposed spot where Christ was born and the manger in which he lay. He poked into the saints' cells without comment and took a look at the view from the top of the monastery.

The party was in a hurry to get on to Jerusalem because it was about to rain. With little thought of the boy David or of the maiden Ruth or even of the beloved wife Rachel, whose tomb stood by the wayside, they hurried on to Jerusalem, which, when viewed from a couple of miles away looked exactly like a mass of arid rocks. At the end of his journal Melville repeated this comment on the appearance of Jerusalem, savoring both the "arid" and the "rocks" as symbols of the Sacred City. It was not long before he was on his way home.

Although Melville spent a sleepless night in the Greek convent at Ramla on the return journey to the sea, he was in fine spirits the next day, enjoying the thrill of danger when news of an Arab raid forced his party, now defended by thirty armed guards, to detour by way of Lydda. There was much horseplay with cavorting and shooting at random (for no one seemed to take the threat of danger seriously), and it was invigorating to reach the green Plain of Sharon with its red poppies blooming profusely. Jaffa, itself, however, proved to be quite a trial. Cunningham and other friends Melville had met left on the steamer for Alexandria the next morning and Melville was stuck with five long days of lonesomeness in Jaffa while he waited for the weather to calm down so that the coastal steamer for Beirut could put into port. Call it Jaffa or its older name Joppa, as Melville was fond of doing, there was little to do in the antediluvian port except try to keep patient through "stern self-control and grim defiance." Though he was sure the walled town had existed before the flood, he could find no antiquities—Phoenician, Philistine, Jewish, or whatnot —worth visiting. Not even the house of Simon the Tanner stirred his blood! And of course there were no signs of Andromeda or Perseus or even of Jonah.

On the evening of his arrival he had plunged in for a swim in the Mediterranean but later the weather was too rough for any repetition of the experience. Though he was staying in the best hotel in town, the English Hotel on the highest spot in the city, and had a room at the very top of the hotel which had six windows and felt like a lighthouse, he soon became tired of the magnificent view and found himself inspecting the beams overhead to see whether they had once been part of a ship, gazing at the curious vial in the lintel over his door in which the German Jew who ran the hotel had inserted a page of Jewish scripture, and cutting tobacco in the middle of the night when the fleas would not let him sleep. In fact, he had done little sleeping since he left Jerusalem and, after four nights of insomnia, was definitely nursing a "genuine Jonah feeling." To occupy his mind, he started reading a Dumas novel which he found lying around the hotel; examined all the remarks in the visitors' book, musing that something comical could be made of them; and wrote extensively in his journal about Jerusalem and Judea. For company he turned to local missionaries, curious about their personalities and fortunes.

In both Smyrna and Jerusalem Melville had been easily persuaded of the ineffectiveness of the missionaries in the Levant; "might as well convert bricks into bride-cake as the Orientals into Christians. It is against the will of God that the East should be Christianized," he confided to his journal. Though the English Episcopal Church of Christ had spent seventy-five thousand dollars for a church on Mt. Zion, he concluded that the mission was palpably a failure, and the Protestant School offered nothing of interest to him except its graveyard. Melville was attracted, however, to odd characters representing smaller sects whom he saw or heard about in Palestine. He was fascinated with a curious old Connecticut man who was tottering about the streets of Jerusalem distributing tracts and Bibles without knowing a word of a native tongue. He found him more understandable than an American of good Quaker family who had turned Jew, divorced his American wife, married a Jewess, and settled down in Palestine—"Sad."

Now, as he waited for his ship, Melville was particularly struck with the efforts of a group of Seventh Day Baptists to make farmers and Christians out of Jews in the Jaffa area. Several years before his visit, a Mrs. C. S. Minor and some followers had come from Philadelphia with the belief that the scriptural prophecies concerning the return of the Jews to Palestine were about to be borne out; her purpose had been, as Melville put it, to help the Jews by "setting them right in their faith and their farming—in other words, preparing the soil literally & figuratively." Though Mrs. Minor had died the year before of cancer, Melville met a number of her followers, including a Rhode Island couple—Charles Saunders ("feeble by Nature & feebler by sickness") and Martha Saunders ("not without beauty, and of the heroine stamp, or desires to be"). Though both were diligently learning Arabic and Mrs. Saunders had "turned doctress to the poor" they had not succeeded in making farmers out of the few Jews at their disposal. Also in the group were an elderly English woman named Miss Williams, who was trying to help out by teaching, and the egregious Deacon Dickson and his family from Groton, Massachusetts. The Deacon, who was old and crotchety, still had hopes for the experiment, though his wife seemed resigned to failure. Their two daughters had married German members of the religious community and were apparently, as

Melville put it, "fated to beget a progeny of hybrid vagabonds." One of the sons-in-law was killed by the Arabs a year after Melville's visit, an event which possibly suggested one of the principal episodes in *Clarel*.

Melville found the whole experiment ridiculous: "The whole thing is half melancholy, half farcical—like the rest of the world." The idea of making farmers of the Jews was vain, he concluded ironically. Judea was a poor place in which to farm and Jews hated farming, he reasoned; moreover they were few in number and tended to cluster in towns and villages because of the animosity of the Arabs. "And how are the hosts of them scattered in other lands to be brought here? Only by a miracle." Thus, Melville, like many another, proved a poor prophet.

On Sunday, 25 January 1857 Melville at last got away from Jaffa by boarding the Austrian streamer *Acquila Imperiale* at one o'clock in the afternoon, although it did not sail until nearly midnight. The next afternoon he debarked at Beirut, where he spent a week at the hotel run by Nichola Bassoul, who was famous for having been Eliot Warburton's dragoman. At Beirut Melville seemed to be content to stroll along the beach asking "What is this fuss about?" Nothing in his diary indicates that he visited the Cedars of Lebanon or Baalbek; he may have gone up the coast a few miles to see the mouth of the muddy stream called the Adonis, but he surely saw nothing of the beautiful young man, beloved by Aphrodite, who was said to have been killed by a boar up on the side of the mountain from which the river flowed.

The steamer *Smyrne* which Melville boarded at Beirut was remembered by him for its ungracious captain, drunken engineer, and the host of fleas and bedbugs which kept him awake for the four nights he was aboard. But after stops at Cyprus, Smyrna, and the inescapable Syros he found himself at last in Piraeus, free of the captain and the bugs and eager to enjoy the Parthenon by moonlight. Athens provided no disappointment after Palestine and he thoroughly enjoyed his three days there. Then he left the Eastern Mediterranean, sailing first to Messina and Naples, then spending two months among the rich art treasures of Rome and northern Italy, after which he passed a couple of weeks going through Switzerland and the Rhine country to the Netherlands, and ten days in England, principally in London and Oxford. He sailed from Liverpool and arrived back in New York on 19 May, considerably revived in health and spirits and with three notebooks full of jottings for future use.

In the Near East particularly he had had trouble reconciling illusion and reality. No matter how hard he pressed his imagination into aiding him, he saw sterile ground rather than holy ground, dull fact rather than myth. When his ship put into Cyprus he wrote: "From these waters rose Venus from the foam. Found it as hard to realize such a thing as to realize on Mt. Olivet that from there Christ rose." When he sailed by the coast of Patmos where St. John wrote *Revelations*, he noted "Patmos is pretty high, & peculiarly barren looking. No inhabitants.—Was here again afflicted with the great curse of modern travel—skepticism. Could no more realize that St. John had ever had revelations here, than when off Juan Fernandez, could believe in Robinson Crusoe according to De Foe. When my eye rested on arid height, spirit partook of the barrenness." He was inclined to blame the leaders of the Higher Criticism, Niebuhr and Strauss, for his lack of vision, but he admitted that the presence on deck of a contemporary holy man who was all that was shabby more immediately undercut his faith. "Trying to be serious about St. John when from where I stood [the] figure of Santon a Arab holy man came between me & the island—almost naked—ludicrous chased away gravity—solemn idiocy—lunatic—opium eater—dreamer—yet treated with profoundest respect & reverence. . . . Wretched imbecile! base and beggarly Santon, miserable stumbling-block in way of the prophecies."

Perhaps he best expressed his difficulty in finding spiritual elevation in the Holy Land by commenting, "One finds that, after all, the most noted localities are made up of common elements of air, earth, & water."

SIX

"Clarel"

IT was not until the passing of nineteen years from the time he landed in Jaffa that Melville finally capitalized upon his Holy Land experiences by publishing *Clarel*. When he returned from Palestine he was thirty-seven; when *Clarel* appeared he was nearly fifty-seven. During those two decades he had done little writing, except for *Clarel* and a number of short poems. Of these he had published only *Battle-Pieces* (1866)—vivid vignettes showing some of his reactions to the Civil War. Supporting a wife and four children had occupied much of his energy and time. After returning from Europe in the year of the Panic of '57 he had turned somewhat in desperation to lecturing, grossing only $1237.50 in three years on the lyceum circuit; in these lectures he drew on his South Sea experiences and his observations of statuary in Rome but failed to use any of his Holy Land material. The acute financial pressure was somewhat relieved when his father-in-law died in 1861. Though he lost one of his most sympathetic and understanding friends, he gained financially because his wife inherited some of Justice Shaw's estate in Boston. Eventually, after nearly ten years of attempts to get some sort of government appointment, at home or abroad, Melville finally obtained a rather dull routine job in the New York Customs Service as an Inspector. This position, which he held for most of the rest of his life, gave him enough financial security so that he could work during his evenings and weekends on *Clarel*, a labor of love which he later was to describe as "a metrical affair, a pilgrimage or what not, of several thousand lines, eminently adapted for unpopularity." [1]

That he was able to produce *Clarel* even with some assurance of financial security was the striking result of his passion for writing. He not only had, like Thomas Hardy, changed his medium from prose to poetry, but he had persisted in completing his massive project with little hope that it would be received as a success. His family had not been very enthusiastic about his continuing to write. When he was still in Europe, his sister Augusta had written to his uncle Peter Gansevoort:

We all feel that it is of the utmost importance that something should be done to prevent the necessity of Herman's writing as he has been obliged to for several years past. Were he to return to the sedentary life which that of an author writing for his support necessitates, he would risk the loss of all the benefit to his health which he has gained by this tour, & possibly become a confirmed invalid. Of this his physicians have warned him . . . .[2]

Eighteen years later, as *Clarel* neared completion, his wife confided to her stepmother, "Herman is pretty well and very busy—pray do not mention it to *any one* that he is writing poetry—you know how such things spread. . . ." [3] Shortly before the long narrative poem was published, she stated to her cousin the fears she had long entertained; she had worried that "this dreadful *incubus* of a *book*" might unhinge him completely. In 1875 Peter Gansevoort, impressed by his nephew's pertinacity and perhaps fearful of his health, had given twelve hundred dollars to have the work published, and on 3 June of the following year, it appeared as a miracle in two volumes. In spite of nervous tension, bad eyes, and sciatica, working most of the time without any expectation that the work would be published, Herman Melville had completed eighteen thousand lines of poetry, producing a work the length of which exceeded in number of verses any epic written by Homer or Vergil or Milton. By the date of its appearance, Peter Gansevoort was dead; he was never to read the dedication to him, to exult that the work had at last been completed, or to read the reviews which, with one exception, consigned it to the waste heap as a failure.

Clarel may be looked upon as a tale of the spiritual struggle and unhappy love affair of a young student in search of a faith, or as a sort of *Moby-Dick* in verse in which many of the mysteries of the universe are probed, or as a modern Canterbury pilgrimage made by victims of a faithless age, or as an expanded travel document in which a rare imagination has transferred a factual journal into a vivid experience. Howard C. Horsford, in his introduction to his edition of Melville's Levant diary, remarks: "*Clarel*, so far as the narrative goes, is virtually an elaborated recapitulation of the Palestinian section of the journal." [4] This is true if one adds that a rather unlikely plot has been superimposed upon that basically uneventful journey. The title character, Clarel, is a young American who has given up his divinity training and has gone to the Holy Land in hopes of finding answers to some of the questions that plague him. In Jerusalem he meets several characters of various nationalities, creeds, and doubts, most of whom stimulate his imagination but answer none of his questions. He falls in love with Ruth, the daughter of an immigrant couple from America—a homesick Jewish woman named Agar and her husband Nathan, a Puritan zealot turned Jew who is devoting himself to farming a plot in sterile Palestine. When Nathan is killed by marauding Arabs, Clarel is denied access to the household during the period of mourning because of an ancient Jewish rule. This gives him a chance to make a pilgrimage to the Jordan, the Dead Sea, the convent of Mar Saba, and Bethlehem in the company of acquaintances he has made in Jerusalem and others who drop in during the journey. Much is made of their varying backgrounds and points-of-view; the party is a sort of traveling symposium as its members walk and ride on their way, view the holy places, and rest for the nine nights they are out. When they get back to Jerusalem, Clarel finds that both Agar and Ruth have died during his absence; he has returned at night only to run into the very process of their secret internment in the Valley of Jehoshaphat. Their deaths have not been wholly unanticipated, for two of the most prominent pilgrims have died with as little physical cause during the journey. Clarel remains in Jerusalem, still without a faith and with little hope of arriving at one.

Though the heroine Ruth and her family remain shadowy personalities during the few scenes in which they appear, this cannot be said of most of the remaining cast of thirty characters, individuals whom Clarel meets in Jerusalem or on the pilgrimage through the Judean wilderness. Their physical appearances as well as their dress and manners are usually described vividly, thus keeping them from being merely agents for expressing differing points of view. Their presence in the poem indicates that Melville had not abandoned his idea of turning his Palestine notes into "Frescoes of Travel by Three Brothers," originally thought of as a poet, a painter, and a scholar. They bear names almost as unusual as the ones invented by Melville for his allegorical *Mardi*—names like Abdon, Agath, Belex, Glaucon, Margoth, and Mortmain. Though differentiated in background, appearance, and personal tastes, five of the characters—Clarel, the student; Celio, a hunchback Roman who has come to doubt his Catholicism; Rolfe, a wanderer from the South Seas; Mortmain, a Swede who has found no happiness in revolutions; and Ungar, an ex-officer of the Southern Confederacy who has fled his country after defeat—are all Ishmaels who resemble to some degree Melville himself. Several of the characters, like Vine, who reflects Melville's concept of Hawthorne, and Nehemiah, an aged American millenni-alist, who was suggested by Warder Cresson whom Melville saw wandering around Jerusalem passing out tracts while he waited for the impending second coming, are based upon people Melville knew in America or met on his trip to the Levant.

Much of the appeal of the 150 canto poem lies in the many discussions into which the pilgrims fall, although, as Lewis Mumford has pointed out, a pilgrimage of "the harassed, the faithless, the doubting, the exiled" [5] lends a sobriety to the narrative and not even the presence of a genial Anglican clergyman named Derwent or an old salt named Agath, who has suffered many disasters but still loves life, lightens the tale. In spirit it is no Canterbury pilgrimage, though

Melville deliberately suggests the comparison in the departure from Jerusalem of his pilgrims at the beginning of Part II. The philosophical discussions are a poor substitute for "The Knight's Tale" and "The Miller's Tale"; however, as one critic has pointed out, they do treat the problems of a modern culture not based on religion, and the resultant spiritual and psychological turmoil of the members of that culture. They also allow Melville to present his own particularly personal world in iambic tetrameter lines and an occasional lyric studded with unusual metaphors, thus sometimes giving him a voice more effective than provided by the prose of *Moby-Dick.* In tune, this voice is almost always a discordant one, much more appealing to the modern ear than to mid-Victorian America.

Even while developing the structure of *Clarel* Melville effectively drew on his own experiences, organizing his poem around the holy days in the Christian calendar one of which had punctuated his own visit nineteen years before *Clarel* appeared. Thus, Clarel arrives in Jerusalem on the day of the Epiphany (6 January, in 1857, the date Melville had landed in Jaffa), leaves for the Jordan four weeks and one day later on Candlemas (2 February), returns from his tour during the early morning of Ash Wednesday (11 February), and remains in Jerusalem through Palm Sunday, Easter, and the seven weeks until Whitsuntide (17 May, in 1857). In spite of the timeliness of Clarel's experiences, he finds he must bear his cross alone (the cross symbolizing pain, not hope), having failed to have a vision of a resurrected Christ.

An extensive study of the prosody, structure, and thought of *Clarel* is not germane to this study, however, which concerns itself primarily with the manner in which Melville used his impressions of Palestine to build his poem. His portrayal of the Judea of 1857, particularly in its physical features, constitutes perhaps the most important aspect of his unusual narrative. In this portrayal he included more than he jotted down in his journal. Yet, though he "got up" his subject in his habitual manner, reading most of the important books about the area which were in print when he visited Palestine, like Stanley's *Sinai and Palestine* and Bartlett's *Walks*

About the City and Environs of Jerusalem as well as some others which had appeared after that visit, particularly Murray's *A Handbook of Travellers in Syria and Palestine*, he clearly depended to a very large degree on his own journal and his memories.[6] In the process, what otherwise might have glowed dully became incandescent in his verse.

Part I, the first of four sections into which *Clarel* is divided, concerns itself with Jerusalem. The poem opens with Clarel in his hotel room which is "much like a tomb new cut in stone." It is the Mediterranean Hotel where Melville had stayed, but it is run by a black Jew from Cochin (presumably a member of one of the ten lost tribes) who, like the hotelkeeper at Jaffa had inserted a vial holding quotations from the Torah into the lintel of the door and who had as his most valued possession a gravestone to cover his cadaver when he should at last achieve his ambition of being buried in the Valley of Jehoshaphat. As he tries in vain to pray, Clarel thinks of the disappointing ride up from Jaffa. Landing amid the "shouts and spray" from "the clear blue sea" he had hastened through the scarlet poppies on the Plain of Sharon toward the purple mountains of Ephraim which seemed all enchantment. However, an arduous ride at night across the rugged hills earned only a bleak view in a chilly dawn; disappointed, he struggled onward until, almost overcome by the scorch of noon "like hot desert sands thrown in the face of Louis, the crusade king," he reached the stony streets of El Khuds. Old Salem is not Samarcand, he realizes; "Like ice bastions around the Pole/Thy blank, blank towers, Jerusalem!"

At sunset Clarel climbs to his hotel roof for a view of "the tower which rides like an elephant," the Holy City. Around him circle the hills and toward the East rises Olivet, the mountain of hope. The city at his feet is another thing.

> Overlooked, the houses sloped from him—
> Terraced or dome, unchimnied, gray,
> All stone—a moor of roofs. No play
> Of life; no smoke went up, no sound
> Except low hum, and that half drowned.   (I, i, 141)

The fetid pool of Hezekiah lies glimmering below the dull walls of the Copt convent. No tarn among the Kaatskills looked as lonesome as "this dead pool."

Some weeks later he stood in the midst of night on the terrace outside his window and heard a cry of anguish break the silence—a cry of a Syrian woman who was caring for Celio, the renegade Catholic with the locks of Absalom and the hump of Aesop, at the time of his wretched death. And it was on the wall of his room that Clarel discovered the graffiti left by a lonesome Englishman, "B.L.:Oxford:St. Mary's Hall," apparently a radical who had become disillusioned with social revolution and the Higher Criticism and had found comfort from "the low lamps flickering in Syria's Tomb" in the Church of the Holy Sepulchre.

Clarel was to find no such comfort, although his reactions to the Church which housed so many holy scenes was more kindly than that of Melville as reflected in his diary. As was to be expected, Clarel hurried to the Church so near at hand on the first morning after his arrival in Jerusalem. His first reactions, as with most Protestants, was puzzlement over finding so many famous shrines under one roof; spots once separate were now close together, "now enroofed the whole coheres."

> What altars old in cluster rare
> And grotto-shrines engird the Tomb:
> Caves and a crag; and more is there;
> And halls monastic join their gloom.
> To sum in comprehensive bounds
> The Passion's drama with its grounds,
> Immense the temple winds and strays
> Finding each storied precinct out—
> Absorbs the sights all roundabout—
> Omniverous, and a world of maze.   (I, iii, 17)

Clarel's impressions consisted of rustlings, shadowy spaces, deep vistas, glowworm lights; of hermits in dim caves who came out at midnight unshod, with tapers lit, to anoint each holy place with fragrant oils; of friars who made a home here and truly believed that all was tradition and not fraud which motivated them. He found that

the sense of the past made up in a way for the incongruities of the
present; his mind dwelt with the kneeling crusaders and puzzled
over the phenomenon of pilgrimage adopted by countless creeds.

He was pleased that the dome was open above the Holy Sepulchre
(for when Melville was there it had not yet been repaired after the
disastrous earthquake which had nearly destroyed the church)—

> No blurring pane but open sky:
> In there day peeps, there stars go by,
> And, in still hours which these illume,
> Heaven's dews drop tears upon the Tomb.   (I, iii, 171)

But not even that gap in the roof made the confined quarters of the
Tomb acceptable to him.

> But he, the student, under dome
> Pauses: he stands before the Tomb.
> Through open door he sees the wicks
> Alight within, where six and six
> For Christ's apostles, night and day,
> Lamps, olden lamps do burn. In smoke
> Befogged they shed no vivid ray,
> But heat the cell and seem to choke.   (I, v, 25)

As Clarel wandered about the huge church he felt less and less
comfortable about being there. It was not only that he was weighed
down by the many ceremonies, or that he was disturbed by the signs
of clash among the sects; he simply realized that he could not believe
in a true fashion and did not belong there. Eventually, he "went
forth like a thing expelled."

Among traditional sights within the walls of Jerusalem, Melville
used the Via Dolorosa, leading up from St. Stephens Gate to the
Church of the Holy Sepulchre, not only for the scene of Clarel's last
appearance among the throng of pilgrims from many lands mingled
with "sour camels humped by heaven and man," but also as the
suffering path of the hunchback Celio, who just before his death
found that his passing under the Ecce Homo Arch and beside the
spot where the Wandering Jew had reputedly spurned Christ had
merely increased his burning doubts. Clarel lamented that on the

south side of the Via Dolorosa, Mt. Moriah, with its beautiful Dome
of the Rock, its El Aqsa Mosque, and its extensive gardens, was
denied to both Christian and Jew and could be glimpsed only from
nearby rooftops and from the slopes of the Mount of Olives.
Solomon's temple was long since gone and his gardens were now but
a cauliflower patch; the cry to prayer of the muezzin reminded
Clarel that "now the Crescent rides the Cross."

Melville was little concerned with Muslim characters in his poem,
however; the emphasis is rather on Christian visitors and Jewish
immigrants. The latter, though actually few in number in 1857,
played prominent parts in the poem; they were in Palestine either to
experiment with agriculture or to await their deaths. Like Thackeray
a decade earlier, Melville was struck with the uprooted plight of the
Hebrew in a land which had once been his. The Wailing Wall, part
of the foundations of the ancient temple, and now part of the
retaining wall of Mt. Moriah, was introduced into *Clarel* partly to
emphasize the concept of layers of antiquity piled one on another,
"wreck on wreck," and partly to give Clarel an opportunity to see
Ruth and her parents as they approach the wall on a Friday
afternoon, when Jews traditionally gathered to weep at the base of
their former temple.

The place of the lepers, inside the Zion Gate, was an appropriate
scene in the poem. The huts of the lepers facing the wall, surrounded
by filth and slime, were hardly less fearful than the disfigured lepers
themselves who begged within and without the gate which led to
David's tomb. Their "homes" prompted the lines on "Huts" which
vividly portray Melville's distress:

> The stone huts face the stony wall
> Inside—the city's towering screen—
> Leaving a reptile lane between;
> And streetward not a window small,
> Cranny nor loophole least is seen:
> Through excess of biting sympathies
> So hateful to the people's eyes
> Those lepers and their evil nook,
> No outlook from it will they brook:
> None enter: condolence is none.   (I, xxv, 1)

In addition to these traditional sites, Melville introduced glimpses into the byways of Jerusalem to bring Clarel to the abodes of the millennialist Nehemiah and of Ruth and her mother nearby. Nehemiah, who walked "like a somnambulist abroad" and was considered by the Arabs to be a Santon, had found a small room in a part of the city where the walls were crumbling, the houses "like plundered tombs" were inhabited by goats and goatherds, and dry feeble grasses sprouted in the crevices. It was a locale which suggested the spots where lizards survived in dry wells or stowaways hid down near the keelson. It could be approached only by foot; here were "no camels, which elsewhere in the Town,/Stalk through the street and brush the gown." Even the sparrows, whose twittering and chirping had seemed to Thackeray to be the most cheerful sound in Jerusalem, only reminded Clarel that they were commonly snared by the natives and sold two for a farthing for food in this wasteland. The house where Nehemiah dwelt was entered appropriately through "an arch, with keystone slipped half down/Like a dropped jaw."

The angelic Ruth dwelt in a more pleasant spot, a close where a creeper on the wall and flower pots on the window sill made for a small Eden, soon to be denied to Clarel. It was the only spot in the city that he looked on with favor.

As Walter E. Bezanson has pointed out in his excellent edition of *Clarel*, the image most prevalent in referring to Jerusalem is the labyrinth. The "feel" of the city is one of dryness, the air is stifling. Blank walls, high windows that cannot be peered into, doors like Bastille gates, heat and oppressive silence all encouraged one to escape outside of the city walls, and Clarel like Melville passed through the gates (open only in the daytime) as often as he could.

The wall which surrounds Jerusalem and the gates which pierce it at several places play a not inconsiderable part in the poem. Clarel had entered the city by the Jaffa Gate on the west and it was from this main portal that he started on the road to Emmaus where he first met Nehemiah and it is from the wall above this gate that he saw a brightly-arrayed Arab on a beautiful horse lit by the evening sun, as well as a mixed group of pilgrims and travelers entering on another evening. He says little of the Damascus Gate toward the north, although Clarel probably used it to reach the Vale of Ashes and the Sepulchre of Kings, but St. Stephens Gate on the east, which opened dramatically on the valley of the Kedron, played a prominent part. Processions were always moving in and out of this gate and it was the spot where Celio left the city with a group of Franciscans accompanying the sick and crippled to Lazarus' tomb in nearby Bethany. Also in the eastern wall was the Golden Gate, long sealed up by the Muslims, as it led directly into Mt. Moriah. There Nehemiah assured Clarel that Christ would soon come again, and enter the city, as he had entered on Palm Sunday.

Toward the south was Zion Gate, which one passed through to visit Mt. Zion and where the lepers begged beside the way; below it in the hollow between Mt. Moriah and Mt. Zion was the Dung Gate, a small door which was kept closed except when drought brought the water-donkeys in from Rogel. Tradition had it that this was the gate by which Jesus was slipped in quietly from Gethsemane to be taken to Pontius Pilate; fact had it that it was long used for dumping ordure from the city. It was here that Clarel and Nehemiah from a position of vantage on the flank of Mt. Zion peered down, like Dante and Vergil stooping to see spiteful sinners in the Inferno, and saw the taunting Margoth, a Jewish geologist who symbolized scientific materialism, poking around in the trash and muck. They climbed on without answering the taunts, thus completing one of the several imitations of Dante in *Clarel*.

So much for Jerusalem within the walls. Several cantos of Part I of *Clarel* are given over to describing a walk which Clarel and Nehemiah make down the valley of the Kedron to the pool of Siloam, and then back up the valley through the Garden of Gethsemane to the top of the Mount of Olives. At Siloam, beside the fountain with its miraculous properties to flow and ebb, they discovered a stranger "as quiet as in sleep" and, after Nehemiah washed his eyes in the pool which had once healed blind men, a kinship of understanding was quickly established between the stranger (the Hawthorne-like Vine) and Clarel. The three walk together to the Garden of Gethsemane:

> The student and companions win
> The wicket—pause and enter in.
> By roots strapped down in fold on fold—
> Gnarled into wens and knobs and knees—
> In olives, monumental trees,
> The Pang's survivors they behold.
> A wizened blue fruit drops from them,
> Nipped harvest of Jerusalem.   (I, xxx, 20)

Here, while Clarel thought of Christ's night-suffering and Vine stood aside, Nehemiah went to sleep, like James and Peter, and might have stayed asleep had not a tourist, a Paul Pry, rudely forced himself upon the trio.

They fled up the side of Olivet (the Mount of Olives), where for the first time they met Rolfe, South Seas mariner, with "a genial heart and a brain austere," who was to play a leading role in the poem as Melville's counterpart. Conversation and admiration of the view went hand-in-hand as the quartet reach the top of the hill with its familiar outlook over Jerusalem. As they commented on the juxtaposition of minaret, crusader tower, and the church which covered the holy shrines, Rolfe contrasted the graciousness of Caliph Omar, who refused to desecrate a Christian church, with the barbarity of the Crusaders, who waded in blood up to their ankles after they slaughtered the inhabitants of Jerusalem. Clarel went on to try to explain the psychology of St. Helena in her successful search for holy places while Rolfe shot holes in his theories and Vine remained quietly smiling. A little later, as they talked about the Holy City as seen from the spot where Jesus, according to tradition, wept over Jerusalem and its doom, Rolfe brought things down to date by commenting on the plight of its current inhabitants:

> "The very natives of the town
> Methinks would turn from it and flee
> But for that curse which is its crown—
> That curse which clogs so, poverty."   (I, xxxiii, 80)

In thoughtful, then skeptical mood they viewed Christ's footprint in the stone in the Chapel of the Ascension at the top of the Mount of Olives; from this height they also caught their first glimpse of the Judean Wilderness and the Dead Sea, where they were soon to travel.

> Far peep they gain
> Of waters which in caldron brood,
> Sunk mid the mounts of leaden bane:
> The Sodom Wave, or Putrid Sea,
> Or Sea of Salt, or Cities Five,
> Or Lot's, or Death's, Asphaltite,
> Of Asafœtida; all these
> Being names indeed with which they gyve
> That site of foul iniquities
> Abhored.   (I, xxxvi, 38)

Still in skeptical mood, they noted the paradox: "Hope's hill descries the pit Despair."

If one were to accept Melville's view, however, one did not need to go to the Dead Sea to find destruction; as he had pointed out in his journal and now expanded in *Clarel*, this destruction lay close at hand in the many graves and tombs with which the environs of Jerusalem abound. The "City of Dis" (Rolfe's term for Jerusalem) thus rises in the midst of a charnel house. Melville's images range from abandoned tomb to modern grave, from pre-Christian sepulchres to shallow ditches used surreptitiously by the Jews in defiance of Turkish edict.

Perhaps the least depressing of the burial areas described in *Clarel* were the Valley of Ashes on the Damascus road where strangely colored heaps of debris supported a local legend that the ash heaps were the remains of the animal sacrifices conducted in the early temples (Murray suggested they were detritus from a soapworks) and, also in the north, the imposing Sepulchre of Kings, "a grot now doubly dead," which had long ago been rifled of its contents. There Clarel found a touch of beauty in the frieze above the portico where chiseled grapes and vine-leaves suggested the poetry of Theocritus.

Melville also associated some of the many empty tombs of the

area, frequently carved out from the walls of the Valley of the
Kedron, with the last hours of the hunchback Celio. Thus Clarel
glimpsed him crying out in despair among "the silent cells/Cut in the
rock, void citadels/Of Death" near the pool of Lower Gihon and
melodramatically associated the unhappy Catholic renegade with
crazy men who hover near the pool like the mad Gadarenes. At
another point in the poem, Celio, after fleeing out St. Stephens Gate,
took refuge in the tomb attributed to St. James, one of three carved
from the rock, like Petra temples, and from there Celio saw a night
procession of monks from the Terra Santa monastery on their way
with the halt and blind to seek miraculous cures at Lazarus' tomb in
Bethany, just over the shoulder of Olivet. Celio joined them only to
find the "void cave named for Lazarus" repellent, revealing nothing
of raiser or raised, both being gone. Most fearful of all of these empty
tombs recalling the past is the hillside spot called Aceldama, or the
field of blood (purchased by Judas with his thirty pieces of silver) at
the foot of which for centuries the bodies of homeless strangers have
been interred: "A rotting charnel-house forlorn/Midway unearthed,
caved in and torn."

Melville's emphasis on tombs and graves in *Clarel* not only reflects
his reactions when he had visited Jerusalém but leads purposely to
the secret burial of Ruth and her mother which takes place after
Clarel returns from his pilgrimage into the Judean wilderness.

Part II of *Clarel*, titled "The Wilderness" opens with a reference
to Chaucer's *Canterbury Tales*, a reference which warns that this
nineteenth century pilgrimage started from the Mediterranean Hotel
rather than the Tabard Inn and proceeded down the Via Dolorosa
past Gethsemane and on—"down going, down, to Jericho"—rather
than through the pleasant spring fields to Becket's shrine; it was of
"another Age, and other men, and life an unfulfilled romance." The
journey, which was to take ten days to cover the circuit Melville
visited in three, was made by nine travelers to which a tenth, the
Jewish geologist Margoth, was added not far from Jericho. Clarel,
Vine, Rolfe, and the feeble Nehemiah, whose way Clarel was paying

so that he could see the Jordan River, constituted the nucleus of the party; to them were added the urbane, friendly Anglican priest named Derwent (who suffered from being the only meleorist in the many arguments which ensued) and the monomaniacal Swedish idealist-turned-misanthrope, Mortmain, who had been disappointed not only by the failure of the revolutionary movements of 1848 but had come to sense the evil which pervades God's universe as keenly and bitterly as had Captain Ahab. He wore a black skullcap, used a name which implied self-destruction, and was looked upon as mad by Derwent, the Episcopal optimist. There were also a prosperous Greek merchant from Salonika, his prospective son-in-law from Smyrna, and a narrow-minded protestant Elder from Scotland who was satirized for his dogmatic views about mystic events and holy places. His equipment for coping with the Holy Land consisted of ferule, pruning-knife, measuring tape, field-glasses, and horse pistols. The Salonika merchant and his youthful companion who, though full of bawdy songs, had never heard of Homer, furnished a Chaucerian touch of lightness to the early hours of the ride but, like the Scot presbyter (also a good subject for light satire), they left the party and returned to Jerusalem before the group reached Jericho. It was not long before both the action and conversation became more and more grim, although there was a light moment when Nehemiah tried to feed a tract to a camel.

The party was under the care of a dragoman named Djalea, a wise and sober Druze (probably suggested by Cunningham's dragoman who had guided Melville around Jerusalem), who displayed none of the humor and boastfulness of Browne's Yusef. Distinguished by his white turban and white sash, he carried chibouk, gun, yataghan, and pistols as his equipment. As was customary on trips to the Jordan area, the party was guarded by six Arabs equipped with pikes and rusty muskets; however, their leader had in addition to the customary arsenal a new revolver with which he was able to overawe a group of Bedouins who swam their horses across the Jordan to challenge Clarel's party. All of the travelers were adequately mounted; both the Druze guide and the Arab leader of the guard had handsome Arabian mounts, and three "sumpter mules" carried the camping equipment, including tents which were used only once during the pilgrimage. Finally, Nehemiah rode an ass which was perhaps as spirited as Browne's Tokina; he provided comic relief by braying most mockingly when the geologist Margoth, "a poor Simon Magus run to seed," became particularly blatant in his unimaginative materialism. Though he hailed from Germany, the geologist was a worthy precursor of Sinclair Lewis' Babbitt with his ideas of bringing Palestine up to date:

> Then mentions Salem: "Stale is she!
> Lay flat the walls, let in the air,
> That folks no more may sicken there!
> Wake up the dead; and let there be
> Rails, wires, from Olivet to the sea,
> With station in Gethsemane."   (II, xx, 91)

The pilgrims' route took them during the first day past the miserable huts which constituted Bethany, after which they descended for miles down a parched ravine—"Acheron run dry"— until they found themselves more than a thousand feet below sea level at Jericho. There at their back the ugly mountain called Quarantania—after the forty days Christ spent there in the desert being tempted by the devil—rose like a slagheap pocked with caves, many of which had been used as anchorite cells. It seemed most fearsome in its bleak loneliness.

> It shows from skirt of that wild path
> Bare as an iceberg seamed by rain
> Toppling in wash in foggy main
> Of Labrador.   (II, xiv, 100)

More pleasant were "Elisha's Spring" at its base and the oasis of Jericho itself. Unlike Melville, who had camped out at Jericho, Clarel's party chose to lodge in the largest Arab building in town, variously referred to as a crusader tower and an ugly refuge that resembled a burnt pine tree with a crow on top. Using fear of Bedouin marauders as an excuse for not venturing on immediately to the Jordan, the party spent two nights in this unsavory spot,

indulging themselves with discourse, speculating on which one of the
small protuberances on the Moab mountains opposite them was the
Pisgah from which Moses had viewed the Promised Land, and
growing lyrical over the "moonlit land of fear," soon swallowed up
by a wall of ugly fog. In fact, resting for two nights provided a
pleasant contrast to the hot ride from Jerusalem, which had
prompted speculation on dryness, stones (Nehemiah had tried to
clear some from the trail but found only more beneath) and the
appropriateness of the use of stones to kill people in a desert country.
However, speculation on the desert and its resemblance to the sea
had given rise to one of the best cantos in *Clarel* ("Of Deserts")
which told how man frequently gained inspiration from barren
places.

> Waste places are where yet is given
> A charm, a beauty from the heaven
> Above them, and clear air divine—
> Translucent ether opaline:
> . . . .   (II, xi, 21)

> For Judah here—
> Let Erebus her rival own:
> 'Tis horror absolute—severe,
> Dead, livid, honeycombed, dumb, fell—
> A caked depopulated hell;
> Yet so created, judged by sense,
> And visaged in significance
> Of settled anger terrible.   (II, xi, 68)

> . . . .

> But to pure hearts it yields no fear;
> And John, he found wild honey here.   (II, xi, 95)

After three hours of riding over a "sunken slimy plain" covered
with patches of fog the pilgrims found themselves on the third
morning beside the famed Jordan River, "swift Jordan swelled by
Lebanon rain." They sang a hymn by the stream (the traditional *Ave
maris stella*), some drank from its waters, others cooled wine in it,
and still others filled bottles with holy water for friends at home.
Nobody hazarded a bath in the rushing river with its slippery,

willow-covered banks; they did, however, pluck willow boughs to carry as simulated palm branches (there were no palms present) and even wrapped one around the ass's bridle, much to its disgust. Here, stimulated by the visit of a Dominican monk, there was much discussion of Roman Catholicism, as there had been of the ascetic life when an anchorite spending forty days on Quarantania had met them at Elisha's Spring.

Clarel and his friends then turned south to the point at which the Jordan entered the Dead Sea, riding across the Plain of Siddim, which Melville termed "Pluto's Park":

> Beslimed as after baleful floods:
> A nitrous, filmed and pallid mud,
> With shrubs to match. Salt specks they mark
> Or mildewed stunted twigs unclean
> Brushed by the stirrup, Stygean green,
> With shrivelled nut or apple small.   (II, xxviii, 2)

The persistent fog seemed to choke them and the salty air made the willow boughs they were carrying mottled. When they reached the Dead Sea, which Melville treats as the major symbol in this part of the poem, they were discouraged and dismayed. Nehemiah was obviously very ill; the suicidal Mortmain, who had left them in Jericho, was not awaiting them "by the marge" as he had promised to do, and the obnoxious geologist Margoth, who had attached himself to the party, was wearing their patiences thin with his jibing remarks. Not even the appearance of a rainbow in the fog picked up their spirits, for, reflected in the waters of the Dead Sea, it suggested "the rose that upon the coffin lies!" Not long after seeing this portent the bedraggled party came upon a huge rock with a face dropping sheerly toward the lake; it loomed up in such a way that Rolfe was reminded of the bleak rock at the tip of Cape Horn, beaten by wintry waves and constantly hidden with flying scud. They soon discovered a slanted cross marked on its surface, made from starlike figures arranged like the Southern Cross awry. That it was the Swedish Mortmain's work was made clear by the depressing verses he had inscribed below it.

Not long after this, they stopped to camp for the night.

Southward they find a strip at need '
Between the mount and marge, and make,
In expectation of the Swede,
Encampment there, nor shun the Lake.
'Twas afternoon. With Arab zest
The Bethlehemites their spears present,
Whereon they lift and spread the tent
And care for all.   (II, xxxii, 1)

As the pilgrims faced the icy waters, the sun set behind them,
lighting up the mountains across the Dead Sea in such a way as to
remind them of Lot and his daughters and the funeral pyre of
Sodom. Then both lake and wall grew fossil-like; the light disappeared and a dark night succeeded in which only one tawny star was
visible, a star which Mortmain, who had at last rejoined the party,
called Wormwood, after the star in *Revelations*. It is characteristic
that Mortmain alone drank of the bitter seawater—"madly tried the
gall." As evening wore on, against a background of tawny star,
drifting scud, and "waters of the lake/Whose bubbling air-beads
mount and break/As charged with breath of things alive," Mortmain
sat down upon "a camel's skull, late dragged/From forth the wave,
the eye-pits slagged/With crusty salt," and delivered an impassioned
discourse on the omnipresence of evil in the universe. The text for his
diatribe had to do with the destruction of the five cities which had
anciently stood beside the lake; these included the infamous Sodom
and Gomorrah. Not carnal harlotry but crimes of the spirit common
to all men were responsible for their destruction—crimes which were
inherent in the way men were made.

During the night, Nehemiah, who had continued to grow more
and more feeble, had an apocalyptic vision, wandered into the water
of Lot's Sea in his sleep, and was found drowned beside the camel's
skull when "the slurred day doth wanly break." His companions
buried him with his Bible beside him in a shallow grave dug out of
the salty crust with some camel ribs. While Derwent read the
service, the pilgrims were startled by the roar of an avalanche in the
distance.

Flints, dust, and showers of splintered stone,
An avalanche of rock down tore,

In somerset from each rebound—
Thud upon thump—down, down and down—
And landed. Lull. Then shore to shore
Rolled the deep echo, fold on fold,
Which, so reverberated, bowled
And bowled far down the long El Ghor.   (II, xxxix, 141)

Another portent, barely glimpsed, was somewhat more enhearten-
ing. It was a fog-bow, "a thing of heaven, and yet how frail":

. . . segment of an oval
Set in a colorless removal
Against a vertical shaft, or slight
Slim pencil of an aqueous light.
Suspended there, the segment hung
Like to the May-wreath that is swung
Against the pole. It showed half spent—
Hovered and trembled, paled away, and—went.
                                        (II, xxxix, 155)

The climax and most important part of *Clarel* is to be found in Part
III set in the fifteen hundred year old Greek monastery called Mar
Saba. In this book, titled "Mar Saba," Melville used every detail in
his journal and possibly his memory to build an unforgettable picture
of the convent which clung to the side of a dry canyon in the midst of
the Judean wilderness on the route which led from the Dead Sea to
Bethlehem. In doing so he expanded his experiences of a night's stop
to three days of suspenseful drama. The long approach to Mar Saba
was made into a fit prologue to the events within the convent. The
negotiating of the steep and dangerous climb up from the Dead Sea,
the discovery of the skeletons of two humans who died in mortal
struggle, the sight of snail trails in this great barrenness—"with gluey
track and streaky trail/Of some small slug or torpid snail"—and the
passing beside black Bedouin tents which looked like hearses were
followed by a long rest at the edge of the plateau of the high desert.
Here, under the "clear vault of hollow heaven" the pilgrims sat and
talked of sin, suffering, and eternity while Vine built a cairn, and a
gay young Cypriote on his way down to the Jordan attempted to
enhearten them with his songs. The sound of the chimes of Mar Saba,
which reached them late in the day, were more reassuring.

From the moment of the approach to Mar Saba the reader becomes aware that the bizarre convent is to be the center of a drama. Melville accentuates the unusual setting of the monastery by describing first the rarely-used approach from the bottom of the ravine:

> Through scuttle small, that keepeth place
> In floor of cellars which impend—
> Cellars or cloisters—men ascend
> By ladders which the monks let down
> And quick withdraw; and thence yet on
> Higher and higher, flight by flight,
> They mount from Erebus to light,
> And oft look, world wide, much in tone
> Of Uriel, warder in the sun,
> Who serious views this earthly scene
> Since Satan passed his guard and entered in.   (III, x, 8)

This entrance was, of course, forbidden to visitors; Clarel and his friends were forced to make the steep climb to the top of the wadi, where a wall and twin towers guarded the convent which had been so often attacked by marauders during previous centuries.

> But not by Kedron these now come
> Who ride from Siddim; no, they roam
> The roof of mountains—win the tall
>   Towers of Saba, and huge wall
> Builded along the steep, and there
> A postern with a door, full spare
> Yet strong, a clamped and bucklered mass
> Bolted.   (III, x, 19)

To enter this door, which looked as grim to Clarel as the Traitor's Gate in the Tower of London, it was necessary to place the required letter signed by the Patriarch of Jerusalem in a basket or "wallet" which was lowered from a hooded window high in the wall. Duly authenticated, the travelers passed through the little door, taking with them their horses, who had to stoop to enter, and the ass who slipped in easily: "Behold how through the crucial pass/Slips unabased the humble ass." Soon Clarel, Derwent, Rolfe, Vine, and Mortmain found themselves in "the frater-hall, Cliff hung" where they were given a simple meal which included the famous St. Saba Arrack, and then were offered "cool mats of dye sedate" upon which to rest their weary bones.

However, sleep was not at hand, for two other visitors, a jovial Greek from Lesbos and his Albanian companion, the giant Arnaut, were all for staging a revel with the newcomers. As the night wore on, the bacchanalian songs grew louder, the Lesbian and Rolfe began dancing, and even Clarel was persuaded to join in the drinking. The misanthropic Mortmain, as might be expected, remained aloof. The revelers woke an old Greek seaman, Agath, who obliged by telling some seatales. Eventually Clarel found his way to a lattice window, where he could hang out and see the monastery ledges in the moonlight. He was, in fact, disturbed about taking part in such revelry so soon after Nehemiah's death beside the Dead Sea. As he gazed out and pondered, he heard the midnight chanting of the monks, who were about to celebrate St. Saba's Day.

Most of this day was spent by Clarel and his friends attending services in the chapel with its tawdry pictures and hangings, like a "tarnished casket old"; visiting the library with its precious ancient manuscripts; and listening to the monks, whom Rolfe characterized as "an orthodoxy petrified," as they chanted beside the holy fire in the chantry, rekindled each Greek Easter from the mysterious Easter Fire which had caused so many panics among the crowds at the Church of the Holy Sepulchre in Jerusalem. Late in the day they climbed down to the bottom of the wadi, where in the light of the flaming red torches, the monks performed a masque dealing with the Wandering Jew, the arch-symbol of the spiritual exile. Startled by an owl who burst upward disturbed by the clamor and unusual light, Clarel drew back along the ravine to a spot from which he could see Mortmain sleeping on a ledge above him, his dark skullcap faintly lit by the flickering torches.

There was not to be much sleep for the others even that second night, and dawn found Clarel and Derwent high above the monastery in the watchtower where they could see the gray Judean wilderness backed by the mountains beyond the Dead Sea burning in the rising sun. Most of this day was spent in sightseeing, each man going his own way and following his own interest. The Anglican Derwent explored "this monkish capital":

> Chapels and oratories all,
> And shrines in coves of gilded bloom;
> The kitchen, too, and pantler's room—
> Naught came amiss. (III, xxii, 8)

Derwent also visited the blind old Abbot in charge of the convent who showed him the treasures and relics, including "the honey-combed gray-greenish bone/Of storied saint," fondling them with the touch of a dowager caressing her family plate. In the meantime Clarel, after passing the calm Druze who appeared to smoke his chibouk steadily during the entire visit, came upon a cenobite "busy at scuttle-hole in floor/Of rock" through which a ray of the sun revealed a "dim conclave of the dead,/Encircled where the shadow rules,/By sloping theater of skulls." This was the hole in which lay the skeletons of many monks, said to have been martyred by the ravagers of the convent. Further wandering brought Clarel to the caves on the opposite side of the ravine, rude depressions which had been used by desert hermits before the main convent was built. Back on the terraces of the convent itself, Clarel met a mad monk named Cyril who, while gnawing his own hand raw, demanded the password, "Death," and farther along he met a blue-robed friar, serene of countenance, who was busily feeding the many birds who depended upon the convent for their sustenance. The friar, who observed the rule of silence as well as of celibacy, made Clarel think once more of Ruth and his destiny in Jerusalem.

The last evening of the sojourn developed into a tableau, with the palm tree midway down the terraces the focus of attention. This palm tree, reputed to have been planted by St. Saba himself in the Fifth Century, was the only tree in the convent and a source of much interest to pilgrims visiting Mar Saba. Melville used it much as he had used the doubloon nailed to the mast by Ahab in *Moby-Dick*. Thus it symbolized something different to each of the main

characters. It was an object of curiosity to Clarel, who, from where
he stood, could see his friends perched at different levels of the
convent and ravine. As the afternoon sun faded to be replaced by
moonlight, Clarel continued to look at his friends for many hours.

> Over the gulf he hung alone:
> Alone, but for the comment caught
> Or dreamed, in face seen far below
> Upturned toward the Palm in thought,
> Or else on him—he scarce might know.
> Fixed seemed it in assent indeed
> Which indexed all? It was the Swede.
> Over the Swede, upon the stair—
> Long Bethel-stair of ledges brown
> Sloping as from the heaven let down—
> Apart lay Vine; lowermost there,
> Rolfe he discerned; nor less the three,
> While of each other unaware,
> In one consent of frame might be.   (III, xxx, 128)

In this scene Melville reveals in detail the meaning of the palm to
each character. To Vine it is a witness of the fleeting nature of
beauty, to Rolfe a reminder of happiness on a South Sea island, and
to Mortmain an almost mystical symbol of the lily which had stood
beside the Virgin Mary at the time of the Annunciation.

As Clarel lay on his ledge throughout the night, Mortmain, the
Swede, was dying from causes not made clear. For some time his
spirit had faltered. During the afternoon before Clarel's long night
vigil, a huge bird, probably an Egyptian vulture, had swooped down
with a savage cry and snatched Mortmain's skull cap, dropping it
into the ravine. Paying no attention Mortmain had continued lying
quietly, perhaps looking at the palm. When the party assembled the
next morning to set off for Bethlehem, the Swede did not join them;
they soon found his body lying at the foot of the Bethel-stairs, "the
filmed orbs fixed upon the Tree"; there was not only nightdew on his
eyelids but an eagle feather lying motionless upon his lips.

The pilgrims almost seemed little disturbed by Mortmain's death;
at least they departed in some haste for Bethlehem after providing
for his burial.

. . .
> With monks which round them stood
> Concerned, not discomposed in mood,
> Interment they provided for—
> Heaved a last sigh, nor tarried 'more. (III, xxxii, 48)

Mortmain's fate was to be buried in unconsecrated ground, a reward
which would not have bothered Mortmain had he known it.

> Where vulture unto vulture calls,
> And only ill things find a friend;
> There let the beak and claw contend.
> Where the hyena's cub be fed . . . . (III, xxxii, 72)

As the travelers, little changed by their experiences, left Mar Saba
for the uplands of Bethlehem, their final glimpse of the convent
presented a picture truly reminiscent of the sinking of the *Pequod* in
Moby-Dick.

> As on they ride
> And o'er the ridge begin to go,
> A parting glance they turn; and lo!
> The convent's twin towers disappear—
> Engulfed like a brig's mast below
> Submerging waters. (IV, i, 130)

After the vivid drama of the Mar Saba section, the fourth part of
Clarel, "Bethlehem," comes as a distinct anticlimax. It deals
primarily with the pilgrims' activities during their three day stay in
the town of the Nativity and ends with a series of short final cantos
presenting the lugubrious finale in nearby Jerusalem. In writing this
book Melville drew but sparsely from his journals—not surprising as
he had spent only a few hours in Bethlehem before rushing on to
Jerusalem to avoid the rain. The poem thus has little graphic
effectiveness in dealing with the Bethlehem scene. At the beginning
of Part IV we are first reminded that the travelers riding the rough
terrain from Mar Saba to Bethlehem had no star to guide them—they
were approaching a famous shrine during a disillusioned period. The
most notable incident in the day's journey came when a rise was
surmounted which gave them a view of Jerusalem, some ten miles to

the north. It appeared like a "stony metropolis of stones," a sight which caused the old mariner in the party to cry out: " 'Wreck ho! the wreck—Jerusalem.' " The country around Bethlehem came as a welcome relief to the pilgrims, however, for it showed much green and still displayed something of the idyllic quality captured in the Book of Ruth.

During the time the travelers spent in Bethlehem, housed in the Franciscan Convent, they dutifully visited the Shepherds' Field, noting its Muslim fieldhands praying faced toward Mecca; also they stood skeptically in the crypt of the Church of the Nativity with its silver star marking the spot where Mary bore Jesus and also noted the place of the manger nearby. Both holy shrines were located conveniently in a cave below the church. Other activities included rambles underground to such spots as the cave of St. Jerome, a visit to the Milk Grotto outside the town, and a long sojourn on the convent roof in the cool evening. Added characters—among them a worthy Franciscan guide, a genial one-legged Mexican revolutionist named Hannibal, and a "prodigal" young Lyonese Jew who was so goodlooking that Clarel almost forgot Ruth—joined the circle and participated in the almost interminable discussion of religion, history, myth, and progress. All of this left Clarel more confused than ever and he was particularly disturbed by the conflict which built up between the Anglican Derwent and a half-Indian Ishmael who had fought for the Confederacy in the Civil War and is, presumably, Melville's principal spokesman for his disappointment in post-war America. This important character is named Ungar and, like the old sailor Agath, had joined the party at Mar Saba. During the latter part of *Clarel* the cast becomes crowded indeed.

Clarel and his companions lingered on in Bethlehem to see the evening ceremonies attending Shrove Tuesday and did not depart for Jerusalem until after midnight. Though they had been away for only ten days Clarel had gone through many emotions; now he was eager to take Ruth and her mother back to America where he hoped they might live a happy life. But as Clarel approached the walled hill town, a feeling of foreboding came over him:

> The valley slept—
> Obscure in monitory dream
> Oppressive, roofed with awful skies
> Whose stars like silver nail-heads gleam
> Which stud some lid over lifeless eyes.   (IV, xxix, 151)

Instead of approaching the locked city by the normal route up the Hinnom Valley and through the Jaffa Gate, the pilgrims turned aside into the Valley of the Kedron, planning to try to enter Jerusalem through St. Stephens Gate, where their Arab guide felt sure he could bribe the porter, an acquaintance, to let them in. This approach effectively placed the party in Jehoshaphat, that sacred "Dale of Doom" where orthodox Jews desired to be buried so that their bodies would be present for the opening of the tombs at the Last Judgment.

Suddenly in the pitch dark the travelers surprised a party of Jews who, because the Turks had forbade them access to the holy area, had come by stealth to bury two of their members. They had brought their spades and grave-slabs with them, for this was to be a coffinless burial. A lantern revealed the strange sight to the returning travelers:

> New dug, between these, they behold
> Two narrow pits; and (nor remote)
> Twin figures on the ground they note
> Folded in cloaks.   (IV, xxx, 62)

When Clarel recognized the figures as those of Ruth and her mother (both of whom had died of grief or fever, which, it was not clear), there followed a scene embarrassingly reminiscent of *Hamlet* in which Clarel leaped down from his horse, grasped his sweetheart's hand, and cried out against burial, racial customs, and cruel fate. But to no avail:

> They laid them in the under-glooms—
> Each pale one in her portioned place.
> The gravel, from the bank raked down,
> Dull sounded on those slabs of stone,
> Grave answering grave—dull and more dull
> Each mass growing more, till either pit was full.
>
> As up from Kedron dumb they drew,
> Then first the shivering Clarel knew

Night's damp. The Martyr's port is won—
Stephen's; harsh grates the bolt withdrawn;
And, over Olivet, comes on
Ash Wednesday in the gray of dawn.   (IV, xxx, 145)

Long after Clarel's friends had gone their separate ways, the lad stayed on in Jerusalem ("Why lingers he, the stricken one?"). He suffered through the tedious days of Lent, watched without hope outside the gates as the colorful Palm Sunday processional passed, and, before dawn on Easter Sunday saw the ghosts of the six characters who had died during the duration of the poem (Celio, Nehemiah, Mortmain, Nathan, Agar, and Ruth) file before him wreathed in languid vapors, "like thaw-fogs curled from dankish snow." The joyful hymns sung by the many pilgrims in the Church of the Holy Sepulchre touched him no more than the spring colors in the valleys and on the hills outside the city.

Whitsuntide brought him no consciousness of a risen Savior. Rather, it is pictured in terms of long-suffering man and beast moving up the Via Crucis (Via Dolorosa), individuals and animals with no more purpose in life than he has had himself.

'Tis Whitsun-tide. From paths without,
Through Stephen's gate—by many a vein
Convergent brought within this lane,
Ere sundown shut the loiterer out—
As twere a frieze, behold the train!
Bowed water-carriers; Jews with staves,
Infirm gray monks; over-loaded slaves;
Turk soldiers—young, with home-sick eyes;
A Bey, bereaved through luxuries;
Strangers and exiles; Moslem dames
Long veiled in monumental white,
Dumb from the mounds which memory claims;
A half-starved vagrant Edomite;
Sore-footed Arab girls, which toil
Depressed under heap of garden-spoil;
The patient ass with panniered urn;
Sour camels humped by heaven and man,
Whose languid necks through habit turn
For ease—for ease they hardly gain.
In varied forms of fate they wend—

Or man or animal, 'tis one:
Cross-bearers all, alike they tend
And follow, slowly follow on.

But, lagging after, who is he
Called early every hope to test,
And now, at close of rare quest,
Finds so much more the heavier tree?
From slopes whence even Echo's gone
Wending, he murmurs in low tone:
"They wire the world—far under sea
They talk; but never comes to me
A message from beneath the stone."

Dusked Olivet he leaves behind,
And, taking now a slender wynd,
Vanishes in the obscurer town.   (IV, xxxiv, 22)

Our last glimpse of Clarel finds him lost in the heart of a Holy
Land which Melville has pictured in biting, corrosive terms.

SEVEN

Mark Twain

A<small>T</small> midafternoon on Wednesday, 11 September 1867 Mark Twain and seven companions set out from Beirut on the overland route to Jerusalem by way of Damascus. As they traveled single-file on the climb over the Lebanese range, they made a formidable party, a caravan numbering not only the eight principals but fourteen serving men in addition to Abraham of Malta, the chief dragoman, and his assistant, Mohammed of Alexandria. The riders and their duffle required two dozen horses and mules to transport them; their camp equipment included three sleeping tents, one kitchen tent, and one tent for dining—all large, finely furnished, and handsome. Before the day was over Mark Twain realized that it had been unnecessary for him to bring the blanket and shawl to sleep in or the towel and cake of soap he had included "to inspire respect in the Arabs, who would take me for a king in disguise." However, he was still thankful for the other possessions he had brought along; among them were pipes and plenty of tobacco, two or three woolen shirts, a portfolio with materials to write his newspaper letters, a guidebook—presumably Murray's guide to Syria and Palestine, which had appeared since Browne and Melville had made their trips—and a Bible purchased in Constantinople.

The eight who set out to ride for more than three weeks through the Syrian desert under the blazing September sun in order to visit the major pilgrimage spots of the Holy Land were perhaps the hardiest of the passengers on the *Quaker City*. This hybrid paddle-wheel steamer and sailing ship had put out from New York some three months earlier on what had been widely advertised as a luxury cruise to Europe and the Holy Land and was in fact one of the first transatlantic cruises ever offered to the traveling public. Mark Twain had called it "a picnic on a gigantic scale" before boarding but was later to refer to it as "a funeral procession without a corpse." Possibly the only working member among the seventy-odd excursionists, he had been busy earning his way by writing travel letters for the leading San Francisco daily, the *Alta California*, together with a handful for the *New York Tribune*. By the time he reached Beirut he had spent a very vigorous time visiting Gibraltar, Tangier (where he had obtained his first exciting glimpse of Muslim culture), France (where he was one of the many thousands of Americans visiting the celebrated Paris Exposition), Italy (from the palaces of Genoa and the canals of Venice to the frescoed ruins of Pompeii), Greece (where he had defied quarantine to slip ashore and visit the Acropolis by moonlight), Turkey (where the filth of the streets was to him more memorable than the beauties of Santa Sophia), and Russia (where he had written the presentation speech to the Czar for the *Quaker City* passengers, who had been received by royalty at Yalta). Now at last, pretty well worn down by weeks of hurried traveling and countless hours of keeping a journal and writing his newspaper correspond-ence, Mark Twain was on the threshold of Palestine. This was the climax, the principal goal of an expedition which had originally been organized by members of Henry Ward Beecher's Plymouth Church so that they could accompany the latter on a visit to the Holy Land where he intended to obtain first-hand impressions for a life of Christ which he planned to write. Beecher had decided not to go shortly before the *Quaker City* had sailed, whereupon some forty-five of his followers changed their minds and stayed home too, but the visit to the Holy Land had remained the focal point for the remaining members of the cruise. Mark Twain, while in Constantinople, had even drawn up a petition requesting that the trip to the Russian

Black Sea ports be eliminated so that more time could be spent in the Bible countries. The petition was never presented to the captain, however, and the *Quaker City* not only steamed off to Sebastopol but wasted five irksome days in Constantinople replacing the supply of coal that had been depleted on the Black Sea run.

It may have been because of the delay at Constantinople that the overland party which Mark Twain had helped organize the day the ship reached Beirut felt pressed for time and accomplished the trip over the Lebanon and Anti-Lebanon ranges, together with the side excursion to Baalbek, in three days. Mark Twain later asserted they were hurried unreasonably by members of the party who objected to traveling on Sunday and mistreated their animals in order to reach their Damascus hotel before the Sabbath. Browne had taken a more leisurely pace, using eight days to get to Damascus, but he had gone north by way of the Cedars of Lebanon; on the other hand, many of the less adventurous of the *Quaker City* party made the trip from Beirut to Damascus in a day, for not long before their arrival a French company had completed a passable road over the mountains and a diligence service had been established. However, as it was impossible to go south from Damascus to Jerusalem without packing in by trail, Mark Twain and his friends were forced to take a slower pace.

The first night they were out, when they camped on the shoulder of the mountains with a fine view of the Mediterranean as it stretched from Tyre and Sidon north to Byblos and Tripoli, Mark Twain was overwhelmed with the efficiency of his Arab guides in setting up their elaborate tents for cooking and eating and serving a dinner with plates and knives and forks and linen napkins—a dinner which excelled the cuisine on the boat. After cigars and port, the party split up to spend the night in comfortable beds in the three sleeping tents. Twain was with his best friend on the cruise—the Dan Slote whom he had met in New York before he had sailed and had described ecstatically to his mother as "a splendid, immoral, tobacco-smoking, wine-drinking, godless room-mate." [1] A thirty-nine-year-old bachelor, eight years older than Clemens (who himself would not be married for another three years, although he had already seen the picture of his future bride in the cabin of her brother, young Charley Langdon, a *Quaker City* fellow passenger), Slote was a partner in a New York banking firm. He was always ready for an adventure, as he had demonstrated by helping to celebrate during a very wet dinner in Tangier and by enthusiastically joining the moonlight tramp to the Acropolis in Athens. He was also considerate enough to let Mark Twain write a long enthusiastic letter to the *Alta California* before going to sleep that first night on the slope of Mt. Lebanon.

The sleepers in the other two tents, which were presumably bigger for they accommodated three persons in each, were of different ages and temperaments than Dan Slote and Samuel Clemens. In one there were two young chaps, Julius Moulton or "Moult" from St. Louis, and Jack Van Nostrand, whom Mark Twain had early in the voyage found so very youthful, green, and bumptious that he had caricatured him as "The Interrogation Point" in his *Alta* letters. However, Jack had worn well with time and had become one of the favorites in the small group Mark Twain found most congenial. About the young men's tent companion, J. W. Davis, of Staten Island, little is known; he was probably a much older man than his companions. According to Dewey Ganzel, who has done some remarkable detective work in his detailed study of the cruise of the *Quaker City* in his *Mark Twain Abroad*, Davis was one of the sanctimonious members of the party whom Mark Twain built up as the "pilgrims" in contrast with the "sinners," notably Dan and himself and their two juvenile friends, Jack and Moult, in his newspaper correspondence.

There is evidence to indicate that "Deacon" William F. Church of Ohio, in the third tent, was to Mark Twain possibly the most obnoxious of the pious pilgrims and it might well have been he who insisted on driving his horse lame in hurrying to reach Damascus before the Sabbath. Clemens probably felt toward Church much as he did toward Stephen M. Griswold, another pious pilgrim who had joined the expedition in Naples; years later Mark Twain was to write below Griswold's picture, which formed the frontispiece of the latter's *Sixty Years with the Plymouth Church*: "The real old familiar Plymouth-Church complacency. . . . It is the way God looks when He has had a successful season." [2]

Church, like Ross Browne, played the flute, but there is no evidence that he entertained the Arabs with "Old Zip Coon"; perhaps his talents were displayed in the ship's amateur orchestra which Mark Twain described as "the flute, the asthmatic melodeon, and the consumptive clarinet." It crippled the "Star Spangled Banner" on the Fourth of July while the choir (probably aided by Clemens' sweet tenor voice) chased it to cover. In the same tent with Church was Dr. G. B. Birch of Hannibal, Missouri, one of the eight physicians aboard the *Quaker City*. Assumedly most of the time Birch stood well with Clemens, for he had had the spirit to defy quarantine and accompany Mark Twain on his hazardous night jaunt to the Acropolis, as did Colonel W. R. Denny, the tent companion of Church and Birch. Colonel Denny, one of several Civil War veterans on the cruise, was from Virginia and had fought for the Confederacy, yet was sufficiently congenial with the Northerners aboard the ship that the Czar remarked on his presence among the visitors, indicating that the wounds of the war were being healed only two years after its last gun was fired. The Czar might have added, had he been less discreet, that it was the financial boom following the war which had made it possible for Americans to come in throngs as European tourists.

The beginning of that same Civil War had put an end to Sam Clemens' career as a river pilot and had turned him to the Far West where, in Nevada, he had gained a reputation as a newspaper humorist under the nom-de-plume of Mark Twain. After a few years in Virginia City he had moved to a larger audience in San Francisco, then at its height as a literary frontier; there he added some narrative sketches to his repertoire of burlesques of customs and satirical attacks on local abuses and abusers, attacks which had earned him a reputation as something of a moralist; and it was from there, a year before the *Quaker City* trip, that he had sailed to the Sandwich Islands as a roving reporter. His letters to the *Sacramento Union* helped him develop his descriptive powers as well as his social criticism; after he returned he discovered, almost by accident, that he was also very gifted as a lecturer. Ever restless, eager for a wider audience, and determined to visit his family in St. Louis, now that the war was behind him (and them) he traveled to New York via Nicaragua, arriving in the midst of a cold January in 1867.

Mark Twain had come east with the intention of going far afield as a roving correspondent, possibly even circling the globe by way of China, a country which long had fascinated him but which was one of the few in the world he was never to visit. He had brought to New York many letters of introduction, including one to Henry Ward Beecher, and it may have been contact with Beecher, or at least with his church, that turned him toward the *Quaker City* cruise. He was delighted to learn that the *Alta California* was prepared to pay the $1250 for his passage as well as $20 for each of his letters written en route. Early in May his first book had appeared, *The Celebrated Jumping Frog of Calaveras County, and other Sketches*; not long after that event he had proved to himself that he could lecture to a New York audience as effectively as to a California one; and by the time he sailed for Europe he had already confided to a fellow humorist that he intended to make a book of his trip to Europe and the Holy Land. Restless, over-sensitive, and given to fits of depression (as well as quick rages followed by lingering remorse), uncertain as to how well an uneducated, profane, western newspaper man would be accepted by a cultured, and to a large extent, sanctimonious eastern crowd on a luxury tour, he set out to sail the Atlantic and the Mediterranean in search of name and fortune.

He was, in fact, surprised to find that he was one of the most celebrated passengers on the cruise. Though Henry Ward Beecher, General Sherman, and several other luminaries had been billed to sail on the *Quaker City*, they had changed their minds for one reason or another. Thus, a journalist with a growing reputation as a humorist with a book to his credit (even though it was a financial failure made up of republished sketches from San Francisco journals) had possibilities of favor and Mark Twain's personality and talent made up the rest. It is true that he did not at first make a good impression—he did not appear to be genteel. Even Mrs. Mary Fairbanks of Cleveland, who was to become a lifelong friend and mentor, had found him odd and slovenly and had been put off by his attenuated drawl and uncertain shuffle; she first noticed him when he was lolling about the ship, as one "committed to utter indolence." But with his ready wit and his grave manner, he soon won his way, so that the slight figure of middle height, with sloping shoulders and delicate hands, came to be recognized as an important person— unruly, carrot-colored hair, drooping mustache, blue eyes and shaggy eyebrows, hawk nose, sensitive mouth, and all.

Clemens woke early on the second day out from Beirut, sure that the fresh air breathed in camping out was responsible for his good spirits. With a fine appetite he tackled the hot mutton chops, fried chicken, omelette, fried potatoes, and coffee he and his companions were served for breakfast. By the time he reached his second cup of coffee he was startled to find that most of the tents and paraphernalia were packed and on their way. Shortly thereafter (he says by half-past six) the eight pilgrims and sinners were also on their way up the mountain, amazed at the considerable space their many animals took up on a road crowded with commerce moving in both directions. Though the new road to Damascus was lined on both sides with telegraph poles, it still served as a caravan route, with camels the chief beasts of burden. Mark Twain, who was still looking for the picturesque, even after being exposed to Tangier, Constantinople, and Beirut, found camels viewed close up less appealing than they had been from a distance. "This reminds me," he wrote to the *Alta California*,

that I have been trying for some time to think what a camel looks like, and now I have made it out. When he is down on all his knees, flat on his breast to receive his load, he looks like a goose swimming; and when he is upright he looks like a bob-tailed ostrich with fore-legs to it. Camels are not beautiful, and their long under lip gives them an exceedingly "gallus" expression. They have immense, flat, forked cushions of feet, that make a track in the dust like a pie with a slice cut out of it. They are not particular about their diet. They would eat a tomb-stone if they could bite it. A thistle grows about here which has needles on it that would pierce through leather, I think; if one touches you, you can find relief in nothing but profanity. The camels eat these. They show by their actions that they enjoy them. I expect it would be a real treat to a camel to have a keg of nails for dinner.[3]

Mark Twain had even less complimentary things to say about the Syrian horses, which, like Ross Browne, he found a sad contrast to the traditional concept of an Arab steed. When the travelers had been invited during their short stay in Beirut to pick out their mounts, they had found them a most nondescript lot of horseflesh. He described them vividly to his *Alta* readers:

One brute had an eye out; another had his tail sawed off close, like a jack-ass rabbit, and was proud of it; another had a bony ridge running from his neck to his tail, like one of those ruined aqueducts one sees about Rome, and then had a neck on him like a bowsprit; they all limped, and had sore backs, and likewise raw places and old scales scattered about their persons like brass nails in an old hair trunk; their gaits were marvellous to contemplate, and replete with variety—under way the procession looked like a fleet in a storm.[4]

Mark Twain picked out for himself a horse which he named Jericho; he wrote that he chose it because he found it had enough spirit to shy; he later discovered that it merely staggered. Jericho was a mare whose "tail had been chopped off and driven up" and who shied all over the road until she finally went lame going over the mountains, after which Mark Twain chose walking in preference to riding. She was abandoned at Damascus for another mount, which the humorist named Baalbek because it was such a magnificent ruin.

Of course the making fun of horses was common enough in the arsenal of a humorist writing in the tradition of the old Southwest, and Mark Twain was later to reach a high point in this genre with his description of his "Genuine Mexican Plug" in *Roughing It*, but that he really had trouble with his first mount in Syria is indicated by a nonhumorous comment in his journal; both he and Jack had to lead their horses for four hours at the end of a much too strenuous day when the party visited Baalbek and then traveled on toward Damascus until eleven at night. By this time, the journey which Clemens had entered into in fine spirits was rapidly becoming a nightmare. The last long day—a Saturday—during which the pilgrims pushed on relentlessly in order to reach Damascus before the gates closed at night was a torture of sore riding over rough country in "the hot oven of Syria," relieved for only a short time by a stop for lunch and swim in the ice-cold water of the celebrated Fountain of Figia. He was indeed happy to fall into a bed in the leading hotel of Damascus.

Street Cars of Damascus

The fact that Mark Twain woke at four o'clock the following morning sick with what he called "cholera morbus" suggests that he had not been fit to travel the previous day, that the plunge in the cold water of Figia, which he later insisted brought on his illness, was possibly done in hopes of calming his fever, and that the resentment he had developed at the rush to reach Damascus before Sunday was partly a reflection of his discomfort. As he lay in bed all that Sabbath day, with Dr. Birch doctoring him in a manner for which he was very grateful, he may indeed have felt that he had become a victim of the dread cholera, which had killed eight passengers during his sea voyage from Nicaragua to New York the previous winter; which had been epidemic in Italy, where more than once the *Quaker City* had had to avoid a port because of the quarantine restrictions; and which had been responsible for the ship being quarantined off Piraeus so that only by breaking the law could he reach Athens. But, as he was well enough on Monday not only to see the routine sights of Damascus in a whirlwind tour on donkey but to travel over a rough trail half the way to Baniyas, at the headwaters of the Jordan, one is persuaded that what Clemens was suffering from was not the deadly cholera but rather an attack of that disorder which is such an inevitable scourge of travelers, enteritis or "tourist tummy." Still, such a seizure under the circumstances was enough to account for a rapid shift in attitude toward both his companions and the country he was passing through.

It was the day following his seige in the sickbed in Damascus that Mark Twain seemed to be at his most miserable. As his party pushed steadily southward, he was sure that the September sun was the hottest ever—"the sun flowed down like the shafts of fire that stream out before a blow-pipe." His eyes were swimming from the glare and his rump was burning from riding on a ragged spoon of an Arabian saddle that constantly slipped on his mount's sore back. To add to his discomfort Mark Twain had scorned to carry the umbrella which guidebooks considered essential for tourists riding under the Syrian sun. It was packed up, far ahead with the tents. When he later wrote to his California readers of his distress, he had recovered enough to make fun of umbrellas (who ever saw an Arab carry one?), thus creating one of his liveliest portraits of himself and his companions.

No Arab wears a brim to his fez, or uses an umbrella, or anything to shade his eyes or his face, and he always looks comfortable and proper in the sun. But of all the ridiculous sights I ever have seen, our party of eight is the most so—they cut the most outlandish figure you can imagine. They travel single file; they all wear the endless white rag of Constantinople wrapped round and round their hats and dangling down their backs; they all wear thick green spectacles, with side-glasses to them; they all hold white umbrellas, lined with green, over their heads; without exception their stirrups are too short—they are the very worst gang of horsemen on earth; their animals to a horse trot fearfully hard—and lo! when these pilgrims get strung out one after the other; glaring straight ahead and breathless; bouncing high and out of turn, all along the line, and coming down one after the other like the stamps of a quartz mill; knees well up and stiff, elbows flapping like a rooster's that is going to crow, and the long file of umbrellas popping convulsively up and down—when one sees this outrageous picture exposed to the light of day, he is astounded that the gods don't get out their thunderbolts and just haze these pilgrims from Julesburg to Jericho! [5]

In his newspaper reports covering the week it took him to go from Beirut to Baniyas, where he first stepped on Palestinian soil, Mark Twain dutifully recorded the "sights" for which he, as a California correspondent reporting on the Old World, was responsible. These included principally the ruins of Baalbek and the city of Damascus. Although Baalbek impressed him with its antiquity and the mystery of its origin, much of his lengthy description was devoted to impressing his readers with the size of the great stones with which the temples had been built, and the puzzle as to how they were dragged from the quarry and raised into place. His account was full of homely comparisons; he wrote of columns of blocks as large as omnibuses, capitals as big as a cottage, tunnels large enough to admit a train of cars, horizontal blocks as huge as a street car or even the hull of a steamboat.

Ancient Damascus, beautiful from a distance, proved a wretched place on closer examination. True, it was a real oasis with plentiful water allowing many gardens to flourish, but all of these were located behind forbidding walls—only in the courtyard of his hotel did he get a glimpse of the local Arabs' adept way of mixing greenery and water which was to be echoed when the Moors built the Alhambra. The "oldest city in the world" proved to be "a very sink of pollution and uncomeliness"; it was filled with beggars, many of them loathsome lepers. Moreover, the inhabitants were notoriously hostile toward Christians—Twain knew it was only six years since they had massacred thousands in the crooked streets. Even the Street

Full-Dressed Tourist

called Straight was a disappointment; it was "straighter than a corkscrew but not as straight as a rainbow"; to call it straight was "a fine piece of irony—the only facetious remark in the Bible, I believe."

As a dutiful correspondent, he also recorded his visits to sites in Damascus associated with St. Paul. He even retold the story of the conversion of Saul—of his temporary blindness when he was hidden

in the house of Judas, of his recognition by Ananias, and of his escape
from that cruel city when he was lowered over the city wall in a
basket. This account he gave more or less in a straightforward
fashion, a method hardly his custom when dealing with Bible stories,
which he liked to dress up with a mixture of skepticism, travesty, and
piety—with the last usually losing out. For instance, near Baalbek he
had visited "Noah's tomb," only to puzzle on how it could be two
hundred and ten feet long and only four feet high; the once rich
country that lay between the two Lebanon ranges, where he had
thrilled at sleeping under the "dews of Hermon," reminded him of
the illustration he had seen in his family Bible of Joshua and his
companion carrying a burden of grapes so big that a single bunch
hung from the pole to the ground. He found no such grapes now nor
any signs of rich farmland. He had remained completely skeptical
when some of his pious companions had insisted that the Fountain of
Figia had been associated with Balaam's Ass. Having passed the
supposed burial place of Nimrod the Hunter, he paid tribute to
Nimrod's founding of Babylon but joshed about the confusion of
tongues which brought the erection of the Tower of Babel to a close:
"When things got so mixed that when a mason sung out for bricks
they brought him mortar, Nimrod saw the game was up."

As he traveled south plagued by fatigue, fever, and daily
discomfort, the dream of a picturesque land of Arabian Nights or
Biblical patriarch dissolved under the glaring Syrian sun into an
awareness of a people more miserable than any he had ever
seen—even than the Goshoot Indians of Nevada. This had not been
true at the beginning of the journey. He had declared Beirut a
beautiful city, and an afternoon spent roaming about its streets
persuaded him that the costumes were picturesque and fanciful,
though not as varied as those he had seen in Constantinople and
Smyrna. Still, there was one variation that interested him more than
a little; the veiled women elsewhere had occasionally shown an
ankle—here, though swathed about the head like mummies they
exposed their breasts to the public. He was not as ecstatic about this
practice as was Lamartine, but, as an outsider, Mark Twain had had

no opportunity of being introduced to a charming fifteen-year-old with firm, pert breasts, an incident which caused the great romantic to claim he had discovered another Haidee.[6] After two days on the trail, while passing through the valley of the Lebanon near Baalbek, Mark Twain was still disposed to blame the neglect of a once fertile area on the oppressive taxes and the mistreatment of the Lebanese by the Turks. "These people are naturally good-hearted and intelligent, and with education and liberty, would be a happy and contented race."

As he moved farther into Syria, however, his mood changed; embarrassed at having to eat his lunch surrounded by beggars at the Fountain of Figia, he confided his discomfort to his diary: "Wretched nest of human vermin about the fountain—rags, dirt, sunken cheeks, pallor of sickness, sores, projecting bones, dull, aching misery in their eyes and ravenous hunger speaking from every eloquent fibre and muscle from head to foot." [7] True, these were but the beggars, the castoffs, but after a sick day in Damascus he pronounced the inhabitants to be "the ugliest, wickedest looking villains I have ever seen," and he lumped all Turks and Arabs together as despicable. (During his visit to the Levant, Mark Twain made little attempt to distinguish among Arabs, Turks, and Jews, much less to recognize a Druze, a Maronite, or a Bedouin. As with most visitors new to the area, he had little chance or knowledge to make such distinctions.) And when he reached Kafr Hawar, on the east slope of Mt. Hermon about halfway between Damascus and Baniyas, he was ready to describe it as the "typical" village, just what one would expect in "the God-forsaken barrenness and desolation of Syria."

A Syrian village is a hive of huts one story high (six feet,) and as square as a dry goods box; it is mudplaster all over, flat roof and all, and generally white-washed after a fashion. The same roof often extends over half the town, covering many of the streets, which are generally about a yard wide. When you ride through one of these villages at noonday, you first meet a melancholy dog, that looks up at you and silently begs that you won't run over him, but he does not offer to get out of the way; next you meet a young boy without any clothes on, and he holds out his hand and says "Bucksheesh!" —he don't really expect a cent, but then he learned to say that before he learned to say mother, and now he cannot break himself of it; next you meet a woman with a black veil drawn closely over her face, and her bust exposed; finally, you come to several sore-eyed children and children in all stages of mutilation and decay; and sitting humbly in the dust, and all fringed with filthy rags, is a poor devil whose arms and legs are gnarled and twisted like grapevines. These are all the people you are likely to see. The balance of the population are asleep within doors, or abroad tending goats in the plains and on the hill sides. . . . A Syrian village is the sorriest sight in the world, and its surroundings are eminently in keeping with it.[8]

As he moved farther into Palestine, Mark Twain became more and more distressed over the conditions of the natives. Even in Baniyas, the site of ancient Caesarea Philippi where the headwaters of the Jordan River burst forth from a cliff once sacred to Pan, he was less impressed with the tradition that it was here that Jesus had spoken the famous words, "Thou art Peter, and upon this rock will I build my church," than he was with an incident which took place the morning after the party arrived at the spring which reminded him that Christ was a healer of the sick. When the usual motley collection of natives gathered around the visitors, Mark Twain noticed with horror that many of the children had diseased eyes. No longer was he in the mood which had prompted him to write:

Yesterday we met a woman riding on a little jackass, and she had a child in her arms; honestly, I thought the child had goggles on as we approached, and I wondered how its mother could afford so much style. But when we drew near, we saw the goggles were nothing but a camp-meeting of flies assembled around each of the child's eyes, and at the same time there was a detachment prospecting its nose.[9]

Now he was delighted to find that Dr. Birch—like Jesus—could do something to relieve the children's suffering. All morning the doctor treated the young ones as the mothers brought them in for help. "When each individual got his portion of medicine, his eyes were radiant with joy." Mark Twain's story for his *New York Tribune* readers of Dr. Birch's help for the sick children became a glowing tribute to Christ as a healer.[10] The incident at Baniyas was one of the few times that the American humorist felt the presence of Jesus as a real person in the Holy Land.

Once having entered Palestine Mark Twain and his companions seemed almost driven by devils to move rapidly on toward Jerusalem. A short visit to Dan, another "source" of the Jordan, followed by two days of reasonably lengthy rides over ground sometimes stony, sometimes swampy, with an overnight camp near the Mill of Malaha where Browne had spent such a miserable night, brought them to the Sea of Galilee, where the only settlement they passed before reaching Tiberias was the wretched village of Magdala, traditional birthplace of Mary Magdalene. Mark Twain, who had bathed in the cold waters of the Fountain of Figia—"it generally gives me the cholera to take a bath"—and the bubbling waters at Baniyas took three swims in the Sea of Galilee. These dips more than compensensated for the failure to take the long-anticipated boatride on the lake; this expedition, particularly desired by the "pilgrims," never was undertaken because they found the boatman's fee too high. After sleeping just inside the ruined walls of Tiberias, the party moved on, under special guard, toward Nazareth, enjoying good views from the hills above Tiberias and from the mound of Mt. Tabor, where they lunched. Their tents were in the process of being pitched by early afternoon in an olive grove not far from Mary's Well in Nazareth and they profited by the several remaining hours of sunlight to visit the holy shrines associated with Jesus' boyhood.

Early the next day both sinners and pilgrims were racing their horses across the Plain of Esdraelon, shooting off their sidearms to the alarm of both Christians and Arabs. Cooling off from their gallop they next came upon "a ruinous old buzzard roost on a hill" where, they were told, the notorious King Ahab had "lived in splendor with his awful heifer, Jezebel." Further rough going over stony hills brought them into Jenin, tired but pleased to meet some of their *Quaker City* companions, who had come up from Haifa on the shorter route to the Holy City. Very early the next morning, which was a Sunday, several of the party, including Mark Twain, decided to press on and try to get as close to Jerusalem as they could, even though they knew they would outstrip their tents. As they actually set out at one o'clock in the morning they were able to cover much of the remaining distance by nightfall, passing rapidly through Samaria

with its fertile valley at Nablus. Nineteen hours of travel found both
the horses and men terribly fatigued and still short of their goal; that
night was spent rolled up on the ground outside an Arab hut in the
village of Lubia, where according to his journal, Mark Twain's
companions included "lice, fleas, horses, jackasses, chickens, and,
worse than all, Arabs for company all night." They were on their way
again by two o'clock the next morning; cold and sleepy, they
stumbled on, while the path grew rockier and rockier as they
climbed toward the heights of Jerusalem. "All the way to Jerusalem,
rocks—rocks—rocks. Roads infernal. Thought we never *would* get
there." [11] Shortly after noon the exhausted travelers looked down
upon the object of their quest; though they could discern many of
the famous landmarks, they had no emotion left to exult or weep. As
Emily Severance, who was one of the *Quaker City* party who had
come up from Haifa to join them in their final spurt, put it: "All of us
were too tired to feel enthusiastic or the least bit solemn." [12] A
couple of hours later, Mark Twain and his companions were taking a
well-deserved rest in the Mediterranean Hotel.

It was to be hoped that Jerusalem would not prove as disappointing as had the Sea of Galilee and Nazareth. Mark Twain had found
that in September the hills which bordered the lake were dry and
desolate, bare of cultivated fields or natural verdure. The water was
not even notably blue, not blue, that is, in the sense that Lake Tahoe
was blue. There was not much to see on its shores. Capernaum had
proved to be an unexcavated ruin, Magdala a group of filthy hovels,
and Tiberias still a wreck from the earthquake that had struck it
twenty years earlier.

Twain had disliked Nazareth from the moment he saw it; the
inhabitants were dark and hostile; the much-vaunted women ugly;
the grottoes where he was assured the Annunciation took place and
Jesus spent his childhood—the "Virgin's kitchen" and "Joseph's
Workroom"—all were down in the crypts of Roman Catholic
Churches and were, in Mark Twain's mind, simply "swindles."
"Imagine Christ's thirty years of life in the slow village of Nazareth,"
he confided to his journal. He concluded that his reverence for holy
events did not stand up effectively in the glare of day or the darkness

of the cavern. Just as he had insisted that the view from Mt. Tabor became beautiful only when framed by an old window, so the Sea of Galilee was attractive only at night when the stars shown boldly in the sky. As for believing that the Angel of the Lord spoke to the Virgin Mary in the grotto in Nazareth, his imagination failed him. "I saw the little recess from which the angel stepped, but could not fill its void. The angels that I know are creatures of unstable fancy— they will not fit in niches of substantial stone. Imagination labors best in distant fields." [13]

Two of the things which had come to bother Mark Twain most about Palestine were its smallness and its barrenness. He swore it was no larger than a typical county in the United States—"a small strip of rocks and deserts and mountains." And was this the land of milk and honey? Occasionally he came upon a patch of arable land—at Dan, on the upper Jordan on the shores of Lake Huleh, in the Samaritan valley where Nablus lay, but even these areas were being cultivated but sparsely. Was this the Promised Land: "Palestine, where every hundred acres of arable land is protected by three mountains on each side and a desert at each end to keep it from bolting for want of company." He was convinced that the land had never bloomed like a rose, much less supported six million souls. He was convinced that it had always been a rocky desert inhabited, even in Biblical times, by people no different from the shiftless Arabs he met daily. He asserted dogmatically that the Holy Land had not changed since the times of Christ "in manners, customs, architecture, or people."

The contemporary manners were demonstrated in the constant demand for "bucksheesh," the occasional throwing of stones at him and his friends and their horses, and the architecture in the flat plastered Syrian box, frequently ornamented in a manner which Mark Twain obviously enjoyed reporting to his California public. This ornamentation consisted of camel dung frescoes. The sides of the houses were

daubed with a smooth white plaster, and tastefully frescoed aloft and alow with disks of camel-dung placed there to dry. This gives the edifice the romantic appearance of having been riddled with canon-balls, and imparts to it a very pleasing effect. When the artist has arranged his materials with an eye to just proportion—the small and the large flakes in alternate rows, and separated by carefully-considered intervals—I know of nothing more cheerful to look upon than a spirited Syrian fresco. . . . I have seen the *chef d'oeuvres* of Vernet, Tinteretto, Titian and a host of others whose fame is known in every land, but few of them ever affected me like the battle-pieces of these nameless sons of Art. Yet who speaks of them? No one. . . . Like the lost art of painting on glass, it will pass from the knowledge of men, and then, too late, the world will mourn.[14]

Syrian House

His descriptions of the natives remained either marked by invective or humorously pejorative. At least he was meeting with more variety as he worked his way south. At first, the tall, muscular, dark-skinned Bedouins with their picturesque black tents seemed to have a "kingly stateliness of being." However, by the time he had seen a number of them in action he was ready to call them "tatterdemalion vagrants"—they reminded him of Digger Indians as they cavorted around on "old crowbait horses, spearing imaginary enemies;. whooping, and fluttering their rags in the wind, and carrying on in every respect like a pack of hopeless lunatics." "To glance at the genuine son of the desert is to take the romance out of him forever." Mark Twain particularly enjoyed himself in making fun of the appearance and armament of the Arab guard whom the

party was forced to hire to protect them from these same ineffectual
Bedouins on the trip from Tiberias to Nazareth. This apparition, this
"infamous star-spangled scum of the desert," this "King Solomon, in
all his glory," was a ridiculous "chaos of paraphernalia" with his
"Arab gun of Saladin's time," his formidable battery of old brass-
mounted horse-pistols, his blood-thirsty knives, and his crooked,
silver-clad scimitar.[15] And this fantastic vagabond had been hired to
protect eight armed Christians (one of them from the Wild West).

He was constantly disappointed in another particular. He had
expected to find the sons of the desert mounted on beautiful Arabian
steeds but he saw only sorry-looking hacks who were "spined and
necked like the ichthyosaurus in the museum, and humped and
cornered like a dromedary!" He maintained he saw more Arabs on
pigmy donkeys than on spirited horses.

When I see these hooded, full-robed, bearded, swarthy Arabs riding on a
mighty-eared jackass the size of a young calf, and swinging their prodigious
feet contentedly to and fro within four inches of the ground, and pouring
forth that maddening caterwauling which they call music, my heart goes
back to the old days of the patriarchs and I behold the pride of Canaan and
the hope of the world—Israel the blest! [16]

And he insisted the paintings of the "Flight into Egypt" were
invariably in error, because certainly in Palestine Mary would have
been walking with the young Child in her arms while Joseph rode
stolidly on the donkey—"whoever heard of a Syrian walking while
his wife or his mother or his sister rode?"

The process of enlivening Biblical days by transporting the scenes
and characters he saw on his travels into the past (constantly
assuming that there had been little change in Palestine since
Abraham's day) resulted in Mark Twain retelling many Bible stories,
imparting to them a broad flavor of burlesque familiar enough to his
Alta readers. He had discovered that the Murray guide to Palestine
contained an index which conveniently listed Bible passages applying
to each of the spots he visited; with this aid, and with the Bible he
had purchased in Constantinople, he had no dearth of material for
filling out his letters. Thus, the short stop at Dan, which he renamed

Dutch Flat according to his practice of giving California names to Palestinian places (he felt that "From Dutch Flat to Beersheba" sounded better than "From Dan to Beersheba"), suggested the story of Jeroboam setting up a golden calf for the Israelites, for whom a golden calf was "pleasantly suggestive of free lunch." Learning that Lot had passed through Dan after Sodom was destroyed, Mark Twain chose the occasion to sympathize with Lot's wife, left behind looking "unpleasantly conspicuous." A few miles farther on, the thieving Bedouins reminded him that the captive Jews stole everything in sight before they "*vamoosed* the Egyptian ranch"; and the sight of the Waters of Merom recalled the fact that it was here that Joshua fell upon his enemies and "utterly destroyed them, root and branch," thus providing evidence for his theory that the ancient Hebrews were noted, not for cultural attainments, but for the savagery with which they massacred their enemies. This concept led naturally to reflections on the savage behavior of Jael when she drove a hideous ten-penny spike into Sisera's brain after offering the fleeing general a drink of water and inviting him to share her bed: "It was very funny." This vein of macabre humor, so typical of a frontier journalism which had produced an Ambrose Bierce, reached its nadir in Mark Twain's newspaper letters when he joked about the woman of Samaria protesting to the King that, after she had agreed with a neighbor mother that they should boil and eat their sons to relieve the famine, the neighbor had refused to boil hers after the complainer had carried out her end of the pact. "Maternal love . . . was proof against the claims of justice. This love rose up before the fond, sad mother, and she would not boil her son."

Although Mark Twain commented to his *Alta* readers, "I can't go on finding out things and telling them to your subscribers all night" he continued to locate subjects at every hand. He smacked his lips as he retold the "Shibboleth" story, got gruesome pleasure out of Jehu's method of disposing of Jezebel after Ahab's blood had been duly licked by the dogs, and made much of Jehu's behavior as the King of Judah in slaying practically every Samaritan in sight. At Jezreel's Fountain in Ain Jelud (renamed Jacksonville) he was reminded of

Gideon's clever stunt of managing to rout and destroy an entire army by blowing horns and exposing lamps which had been hidden in pots until the strategic moment. Told at great length were the stories of Joseph and of the Prodigal Son. The Joseph story provided an occasion for much throwing about of commodity market jargon in telling of Joseph's financial successes under Pharaoh and ended with the dramatic moment when Joseph recognized Benjamin, crying " 'Ha! the strawberry upon your left arm!—it is! it is my long-lost brothers!' (Slow music.)"

Mark Twain thought up his version of the story of the Prodigal Son as he pondered the children with sore eyes and the camel-dung frescoes in Deburich,. a little village at the foot of Mt. Tabor where the prodigal was supposed to have lived. Here even romantic moments had their earthy sides: "As in the days of old, the pensive youth, in curtailed shirt and naked shins, still breathes soft nothings in the ear of his adored, while she gathers her camel-dung and sorts it with a critical eye." After this introduction, Clemens built up the famous story of the wanderer's return home by emphasizing the threadbare quality of life as the humorist saw it in this small village, expounding on the scarcity of shoes and shirts and even the simplest of foods. He concluded:

When I was in Sunday School I always regarded that Prodigal Son as the stupidest youth that ever lived, to go away from his father's palace where he had a dozen courses for dinner, and wore handsome clothes, and had fast horses, and dogs, and plenty of money to spend, and could go to the circus whenever he wanted to (I had an idea that this was a peculiar privilege of rich men's sons all the world over), and travel off to some strange land and get swamped and have to feed hogs for a living. But I always rejoiced to think he went back home again, and I took pleasure in thinking he must have appreciated its riches and its luxury so unspeakably then. I could not understand the fatted calf, but I never allowed him to interfere materially with the unities of my romance. But my dream is over, now. It is just about an even matter between the Prodigal's two homes. If he had had a shirt and something to eat when he was feeding swine, the difference between that place and his old home would not have paid for the trouble of the journey back again—save that one was *home* and the other was not.[17]

Mark Twain spent a week in Jerusalem and its environs, arriving on Monday afternoon and departing for the coast about three o'clock in the afternoon the following Sunday. He apparently rested on what remained of his day of arrival, staying at the best hotel in town, and doubtless enjoying the change from camping. Tuesday was devoted to sightseeing, principally at the Church of the Holy Sepulchre, but early Wednesday morning, he joined the dragoman Abraham and some of the pilgrims from the *Quaker City* in a three day circuit to the Jordan River, the Dead Sea, and Bethlehem, arriving back in Jerusalem early on Friday afternoon and collapsing at his hotel: "I never have enjoyed rest as I have enjoyed it during the last few hours," [18] he noted. Probably it was the next day (Saturday) that he luxuriated in a breakfast at *noon* at the hotel. He was enjoying a well-deserved pause in sightseeing; he had been at it almost constantly throughout the summer. It is clear that most of the members of the *Quaker City* cruise were worn out even before they reached Jerusalem, especially the eight hardy souls who had come overland by the Damascus route. Mark Twain admitted there were only two of that group (and he did not include himself) who had had any eagerness for performing their stint as pilgrims by the time they arrived at the principal shrine in Christendom. Many of the main party were sick, according to Mrs. Severance; others did not even take the trouble to make the short jaunt to Bethlehem. It is not surprising, therefore, that Mark Twain's journal of this period is filled with terse comments and jottings, that he gave up trying to keep his newspaper letters current, and that, when he finally left Palestine, he recorded in his notes: "I have only one pleasant reminiscence of this Palestine excursion—time I had the cholera in Damascus." [19]

He conscientiously visited most of the traditional sites in Jerusalem, sometimes so hastily that he failed to appreciate truly beautiful spots, such as the Garden of Gethsemane (where his mood was so vile that he paid little attention to the "eight hoary live trees") and the lovely Dome of the Rock. Unlike Browne and Melville he had arrived late enough in history to gain access to the jealously guarded Mt. Moriah with its Muslim architectural treasures only to admit in his notebook that he did not have time to enjoy the experience.

Rather, he concentrated on the Church of the Holy Sepulchre, which he maintained he visited everyday he was in Jerusalem. Surprisingly, his attitude toward its many sacred sites was somewhat more tolerant than those of Browne and Melville. He wrote in his diary: "Oh for the ignorance & the confidingness of ignorance that could enable a man to kneel at the Sepulchre & look at the rift in the rock, & the socket of the cross & the tomb of Adam & feel & know & never question that they were genuine." [20] He had less tendency to be outraged by what Murray's guidebook titled "bare-faced impostures" than the majority of Protestant visitors of the period; perhaps this was because he acknowledged less religious belief to be violated than most. As Arthur L. Scott has pointed out in his study of Mark Twain's attitudes during foreign travel in *Mark Twain at Large*, even as early as *The Innocents Abroad* trip he was inclined to be more tolerant of practices which he thought were superstitious than were other more orthodox pilgrims.

It is not surprising, then, to find that even in his letters to the *Alta California*, which were considerably more outspoken than *The Innocents Abroad*, he soft-pedalled his customary humor when dealing with the Holy Sepulchre itself and the nearby chapel which housed the tip of Golgotha (or the Hill of Calvary), where three holes in the marble floor opened into the recesses where the three crosses stood; of the former he was respectful though he mentioned the "tawdry gee-gaws and tawdry ornamentation" which he found within the little edifice which had been erected over the rock shelf termed a sepulchre; actually he was moved emotionally by the sight of the place of crucifixion and suggested that one "fully believes that he is looking upon the very spot where the Savior gave up his life."

As for the rest of the offerings of the Church of the Holy Sepulchre, "with all its clap-trap, side-shows and unseemly hum-buggery of every kind," he was inclined to take things in his stride, noting that "everything was ingeniously massed together," including even the center of the earth, the spot from which the dirt was taken to make Adam, and the grave of the venerable Melchizedek. He thoroughly enjoyed joking about St. Helena's miraculous knack for discovering sacred sites and noteworthy relics, such as the three crosses, the crown of thorns, and even the copper plate with its initials I.N.R.I. He assured his readers that the pertinacious mother of Constantine went all over Palestine, prospecting with remarkable luck. "Whenever she found a thing mentioned in her Bible, Old or New, she would take her umbrella and start out after that thing and never, never stop until she found it. . . . She did best here on Calvary, no doubt. She had a claim here that she worked as long as she lived." Down in the cellar where she did much of her most important exploring, she was about to let up for awhile when a dream told her to continue for a day longer. "She put in one more blast and raised out the cross of the penitent thief." [21] Good work!

The site in the church containing the formidable sword with which the crusader Godfrey had sliced up Saracens not only threw Mark Twain into a fit of historical reverie but gave him added opportunity to deal in the macabre. "I can never forget old Godfrey's sword, now. I tried it on a Moslem, and clove him in twain like a doughnut. The spirit of its ancient owner was upon me, and if I had had a graveyard I would have destroyed all the infidels in Jerusalem. I never like to kill a man when I have no place to bury him." [22] The assurance that Adam's grave was actually to be found in a chapel which was side-by-side with Golgotha moved him to lengthy speculation on the experiences of his noted ancestor. Mostly this had to do with what Adam had missed by dying so early. Pretending to shed a tear over poor old Adam, the frontier humorist lamented: "He had not seen the telegraph, or the locomotive, or the steamboat; he did not even see the flood. He missed the Paris Exposition." He went on to exclaim that Adam, on the other hand, had escaped having his shirts ruined by the laundry and that he had never had the misfortune to swap his fig leaf for "a claw-hammered coat, white kids, and a moustache." [23] All these references to the magnificent aspects of progress that Adam missed were to be omitted in *The Innocents Abroad*, where they were replaced with Adam's misfortune at not having lived long enough to know Mark Twain.

His journal notes about the rest of Jerusalem and its surroundings are but desiccated jottings, without expansion, and his comments for his *Alta* readers stress his fatigue and ennui. He was surfeited with sights, packed close together in a Jerusalem which was so small one could walk around its walls in an hour. He considered Jerusalem one of the "knobbiest" cities in the world when viewed from the top of one of those walls, whose streets were invariably crooked, badly paved and so narrow that he more than once saw cats jump across a street from roof to roof. Like Browne and Melville, he was much disturbed at the "maimed, malformed, and diseased humanity" which swarmed the narrow passages and choked the gates. He tried to become interested in the most famous of Jerusalem's streets, the Via Dolorosa, but recorded only his cynical reaction on being told that a hole in one of the rock walls lining the street was made when Jesus fell with the cross. The house on the Via Dolorosa attributed to the Wandering Jew prompted him to expand on that unfortunate wanderer's attempts to meet death, on his gradually developed interest in executions and funerals, and on his visit to Jerusalem every fifty years to collect the rent.

He found that the Pool of Bethesda was a slimy cesspool and he called the Pool of Hezekiah, where Bathsheba was bathing when David caught sight of her, a "frog-pond." He regretted that David had been provided with a tomb, for he felt he had to visit it as a result, and he could not bring himself to forgive Judas for hanging himself on a hill outside the city instead of inside its walls, for it meant one more stiff climb for the visitors. He discussed with his readers his progress in "doing" Jerusalem:

We cast up the account. It footed up pretty fairly. There was nothing more in Jerusalem to be seen, except the houses of Dives and Lazarus of the parable, and "Moreover the dog;" the Tombs of the Kings; ditto of the Judges; the spot where they stoned one disciple to death, and beheaded another; the room and the table made celebrated by the Last Supper; the fig-tree that Jesus withered; a dozen of historical places about Gethsemane and the Mount of Olives, and fifteen or twenty others in different portions of the city itself. We began to see our way through. It was suggested that we might hire parties to visit these things for us and thus see them by proxy, but after some deliberation it was decided that such a course would be discreditable. Still, we had got altogether enough, for the present. There was open rebellion in the camp—undisguised mutiny. There was a strong disposition to lie around the hotel and smoke. A diversion must be tried, or demoralization would ensue.[24]

Charge on Bedouins

The diversion was the trip to Jericho, the Jordan, and the Dead Sea which has already been mentioned.

The diversion had with it a touch of excitement, for, during Mark Twain's visit the Bedouins had been carrying on raids in the Jordan Valley and two of the parties from the *Quaker City* had had some trouble while visiting the area. As was customary, a squad of guards was required to accompany the eight tourists and their dragoman; though Mark made much of the supposed pusillanimity of himself and his companions during the ride down to Jericho, he was in fact disappointed that they didn't see a single Bedouin en route. As for the Arab guards, the final indignity came when one of them even "wanted to smouch me." [25] Like most Palestine visitors from America he concluded that "the nuisance of an Arab guard is one which is created by the Sheiks and Bedouins together, for mutual profit it is said" and suggested that the two enemies frequently got together for lunch and divided the backsheesh.

Thus the hot ride through the Judean wilderness down, down to the Jordan Valley was accomplished without even a reference to the troubles of the man rescued by the Good Samaritan beside that dusty trail; the only stop en route was at the "miserable mud village of Bethany" where the party visited Lazarus' house and his tomb, Mark Twain exclaiming on the affluence of Lazarus and declaring that he'd rather live in his tomb than in any house in the ratty town. Down in the plain where ancient Jericho had stood, he was struck with the lack of cultivation in an area noted at one time as the most fertile spot in Palestine. Now, like most of the Holy Land, it was a terrible wilderness; here "the ravens could hardly have made their own living, let alone board Elijah" and even the lizards were emigrating. "No Second Advent—Christ been here once, will never come again," he noted in his diary. Later, in his *Alta* letters, he applied the judgment to all of Palestine.

The party camped none too comfortably in a fig orchard near the new Jericho, for their dragoman was having trouble with the local Arabs as to where he could pitch his tents, and at two o'clock the next morning they were dragged out of bed so that they would arrive at the Jordan early. They did so, so early that after arrival Mark Twain and Jack slipped away and slept under a bush for two hours, catching cold in the process. It was still dark when the members of the party removed most of their clothes and plunged into the icy water of the Jordan, low enough at this season so that they could wade across it without danger. As might be expected, its size disappointed Sam Clemens, the ex-Mississippi River pilot; "a good many streets in America are double as wide as the Jordan," he commented.

Not long after dawn the party set off for the Dead Sea, riding across "the scorching, arid repulsive solitude" where grew the

Sodom Apples (called Hell's Pippins by Melville), which didn't even have the traditional dust within them. When they reached the sea and everybody slipped into its slimy waters, Mark Twain found that none of the terrible things that were supposed to happen to him took place. According to his journal, he even took his horse in with him as an experiment and saw it upset by its buoyancy; he himself enjoyed the brackish bath enough to stay in for an hour, get sunburned, and emerge with enough salt crystals in his hair to suggest icicles. Then, presumably after having had some lunch, the party set off toward the steep trail to Mar Saba. He commented dryly that he had had no glimpse of Lot's wife, but that he rode off smelling badly.

The five-and-one-half-hour climb in the heat of late September to the wadi where the convent hung on the canyon wall was particularly hard on Mark Twain and his tired companions. However, he barely mentioned this grim ordeal and the night spent in the convent in his journal or in his *Alta* letters. Later in *The Innocents Abroad* he gave considerable emphasis to the hot ride:

I cannot describe the hideous afternoon's ride from the Dead Sea to Mars Saba [sic]. It oppresses me yet, to think of it. The sun so pelted us that the tears ran down our cheeks once or twice. The ghastly, treeless, grassless, breathless canons smothered us as if we had been in an oven. The sun had positive *weight* to it, I think. Not a man could sit erect under it. All drooped low in the saddles. . . . What a very heaven the massy towers and ramparts of vast Mars Saba looked to us when we caught the first glimpse of them! [26]

Yet the monastery in the wilderness made no such impression on him as it had on Melville. Most of the details he used in his description of it seem to come straight from the guidebook. It is probable that he arrived too tired for sightseeing and it is known that he left after a "good night's rest" at three o'clock the following morning (their dragoman apparently got them up two hours too early as usual). In his account of the visit, in *The Innocents Abroad*, Mark Twain expanded at length, however, on two subjects concerning the monks in the convent. He very much regretted that they chose to bar women from their lives ("They have banished the tender grace of life and left only the sapped and skinny mockery"); and he praised them for their hospitality.

Here, as elsewhere in Syria, he had noted the kindliness of cloistered monks to pilgrims, particularly the poor ones. He admitted that he had been "educated to enmity toward everything that is Catholic"; however, he felt moved to testify in favor of their hospitality. Of course, in Mar Saba he was dealing with the Greek Orthodox, not the Roman Catholics, whom he had so disliked in Italy, but he made little of the difference between the communicants of the two Faiths.

They knew we were foreigners and Protestants, and not likely to feel admiration or much friendliness toward them. But their large charity was above considering such things. They simply saw in us men who were hungry, and thirsty, and tired, and that was sufficient. They opened their doors and gave us welcome. They asked no questions, and they made no self-righteous display of their hospitality. They fished for no compliments. They moved quietly about, setting the table for us, making the beds, and bringing water to wash in, and paid no heed when we said it was wrong for them to do that when we had men whose business it was to perform such offices. We fared most comfortably, and sat late at dinner. We walked over the building with the hermits afterward, and then sat on the lofty battlements and smoked while we enjoyed the cool air, the wild scenery, and the sunset.[27]

The visit to Bethlehem came as an anticlimax. It was early morning when the party reached the Shepherd's Field, a spot which failed to impress Mark Twain, and much of the time before lunch was spent in the Church of the Nativity, the site of which was chosen by "the inveterate St. Helena." He was probably not surprised to find that both manger and birthplace were located in a single grotto in the crypt. "The grotto was tricked out in the usual tasteless style observable in all the holy places of Palestine," he noted. His visit to this holy spot, marred by the presence of "beggars, cripples, and greasy monks," was soon over; "I was glad to get out of there, and glad when we had trotted through the grottoes where Eusebius wrote, and Jerome fasted, and Joseph prepared for the flight into Egypt, and the dozen other distinguished grottoes, and knew we were done." [28] The party hastened back to Jerusalem, stopping during their two hour ride to take a look at Rachel's tomb, which Mark Twain noted in his diary as "authentic," thus implying doubt about everything else he had seen that day.

He spent two more days in Jerusalem, visiting a few of the spots he knew he would be expected to describe for his readers in California. Diversion, however, came in the form of a night on the town with the visiting officers from the gunboat *Swatara*, met first in Smyrna: "A rather high time . . . for such a slow old camp as the Holy City," he confided to his notebook. He also found time to visit an "infernal Turkish bath" which he pronounced to be much inferior to one he had patronized in Constantinople. At midafternoon on Sunday he set out from the Damascus gate for Jaffa where the *Quaker City* was riding at anchor, due to sail early Tuesday, 1 October. He broke the journey to the coast by spending Sunday night in the Latin convent in Ramla, where he appreciated the warm hospitality provided by the Roman Catholic monks. The next morning the travelers indulged in the customary practice of galloping their horses across the Plain of Sharon; by early afternoon, after the shortest of obligation visits to such sites in Jaffa as the house of Peter the Tanner, Mark Twain was back aboard the ship, eager to relax a moment before he began catching up on his newspaper correspondence.

Likewise aboard the *Quaker City* on their way to America were his relics and momentoes. After constantly accusing the pilgrims in his party of being confirmed vandals in his *Alta* letters, he was bringing back some snatchings of his own. These included a branch plucked from a Cedar of Lebanon planted just outside the Jerusalem walls "by Godfrey de Bouillon, first King of Jerusalem, about 1085 to 1099";[29] fragments of stone purportedly from Solomon's temple, which he had found lying about on holy Muslim soil near the Dome of the Rock; and bits of the wall of the Milk Grotto in Bethlehem, which were said to cure barrenness in women. "We took many specimens, to the end that we might confer happiness upon certain household we wot of." He had also obtained more legitimately a Bible bound in balsam and olive wood for his mother, olive beads for his sister, an olive wood cardcase, two or three paper knives purportedly made from wood from "Abraham's Oak," and bottles of water from the Pool of Bethesda, the Jordan River, and the Dead Sea.[30]

The *Quaker City* carried on its decks to Alexandria some forty members of an abortive American agricultural colony which had failed to establish itself outside Jaffa; Mark Twain used them as the subject of a newspaper letter to the *New York Tribune*, but his imagination failed to be stimulated by them as Melville's had been when he had visited similar American agriculturists outside Jaffa ten years before. Egypt, where Mark Twain had spent five days, proved a happy contrast to Palestine and brought from the western humorist almost nothing but praise. He had looked forward to visiting Egypt so much that he and Jack Van Nostrand debarked from the *Quaker City* at Alexandria fourteen hours early just to spend a night in the town. He enjoyed traveling on the railroad to Cairo—at last he was back among signs of progress, even in this country which had harbored one of the oldest civilizations in the world. He was pleased to see green fields and orchards again and he found the Nile a genuine river, unlike the Jordan. He clambered up the Great Pyramid with zest and was so moved by the Sphinx that when he wrote *The Innocents Abroad* he devoted to it one of his most celebrated purple passages. He even liked the looks of the inhabitants, or at least some of them, recording in his notes his delight at one unusual sight: "Naked girls in the streets—finely built." [31] Before sailing for New York, which he reached late in November after stops in Spain and Bermuda, he indulged in one more wisecrack at the expense of Judea in his notebook: "The idea of the Children of Israel leaving Egypt to hunt up a better thing in Palestine is rich!" [32]

EIGHT

"*The Innocents Abroad*"

THOUGH the *Quaker City* reached New York late in November 1867, *The Innocents Abroad* did not appear until July 1869. During the interim Mark Twain, as usual, was a very busy man. He worked for awhile in Washington, D.C. as the private secretary to Senator Stewart of Nevada and gained many of the impressions that he would use in his first novel, *The Gilded Age*. He made a trip West by way of the Isthmus to San Francisco where he arranged for the release of his *Alta California* letters, revised them and added enough comment to bring them to book length, and made a lecture tour of the California hinterland and Virginia City and the Nevada communities near it. His *Innocents Abroad* manuscript was ready for the American Publishing Company a year before book publication, and he busied himself with an eastern lecture tour, planned in part to advertise the book, and gave such moments as he could snatch from following an extensive itinerary to courting Olivia ("Livy") Langdon, the sister of one of his companions on the *Quaker City* and the daughter of a successful coal merchant who lived in Elmira, New York. Before the appearance of *The Innocents Abroad* and his marriage seven months later, he was still the restless western journalist, unsure of what his ultimate profession would be; as late as the summer of 1868 he was still thinking of San Francisco as his home. By the time the book came out he had definitely decided to live in the East and he had matured in his writing enough so that he felt that he could make a career of it. Earlier during this period he had considered taking a job as postmaster in San Francisco and also, during the first winter after the Holy Land excursion, he had been tempted by an offer to go to China as an assistant to Ross Browne, who was succeeding Mark Twain's friend, Anson Burlingame, as American Minister to China.

In spite of the several temptations to take nonwriting jobs, Mark Twain had concentrated on making the most of his experiences as a traveler to Europe and the Levant. His newspaper letters in the *Alta California* supplemented by the few he had written for the *New York Tribune*, had reached a good many readers and, with the *Jumping Frog* book, had given him something of a reputation as the coming American humorist. Though he undoubtedly had had the idea of a travel book in mind even before he sailed on the *Quaker City*, it appears that the first medium in which he attempted further to capitalize on his travels was the drama, always a tempting field because of the gambling possibility that it might pay well quickly. The fact that a fragment of the play is to be found in the notebook he kept on the trip suggests that he started it on the voyage home.[1]

In the incomplete *"Quaker City* Holy Land Excursion," made up of parts of two acts and a very short fragment dealing with a drunk, who was confused about the bells aboard ship and the use of the sails, Mark Twain emphasizes the contrast between the pious "pilgrims" who constitute most of the members of the party and the "sinners," who in the play are two newspaper men (one named Mark Twain) and their boon companion. This was a contrast he had made most evident in a letter written hostilely for the *New York Herald* the day he returned to New York in which he rather ungraciously made fun of the concept of the *Quaker City* voyage as a pleasure cruise, maintaining that most of the passengers were venerable fossils whose favorite pastimes were playing dominoes and attending daily prayer meetings. The focus of their voyage was the visit to Palestine: "The pleasure ship was a synagogue, and the pleasure trip was a funeral excursion without a corpse." "The pilgrimage part of the excursion was its pet feature," he averred. The day the *Herald* diatribe appeared, he wrote his last letter for the *Alta* in which he continued the theme, stressing once more the decrepitude and intolerance of the pilgrims and asserting that "there were not blackguards enough on board in proportion to the saints—there was not genuine piety enough to offset the hypocrisy." [2] After exploding in the public print, Mark Twain wrote to his good friend Mrs. Fairbanks that he had found only eight of his companions on the trip genuine friends and the rest were beyond the pale as far as he was concerned.

Though the causes of friction are evident enough when one considers Mark Twain's frontier background, his religious skepticism, and his preference for younger men (and women) as companions, and the testimony of other members of the expedition support Mark Twain's conclusion that Captain Duncan's administration of the excursion was seriously at fault, the emphasis in the crudely-developed play indicates that one of the real sources of trouble lay in the behavior of Mark Twain and his companions who gathered nightly in Cabin 10. Not only did they flaunt the rules of the ship by drinking and smoking, but, if the play is to be used as evidence, they kept the lights burning all night while they played seven-up in a profane fashion. The pilgrims, who appeared on deck in formations moving to and from prayer meetings, were led by an Elder Homily, whose first remark was: "How wonderful is prophecy." It reflected Mark Twain's annoyance with the pilgrim members of the overland party in Syria, who constantly found that everything, whether ruined or surviving, carried out the prophecies they found in their well-thumbed Bibles. Fortunately the play was never completed—its burlesque was too heavy-handed to make for good drama—and less than a week after landing, Mark Twain wrote to his friend Charles Henry Webb, who had published the *Jumping Frog* volume for him and was interested in the play, that he was much too busy with newspaper commitments to finish the drama.

It was almost inevitable that Mark Twain, like Herman Melville, would turn to lecturing as a medium for use of his travel experiences, particularly as, unlike Melville, he had already had some success in lecturing on his Sandwich Island trip and knew that he could both draw and hold an audience. Some six weeks after sailing into New York he delivered his first *Quaker City* lecture in Washington, D.C. under the title "The Frozen Truth." He had just returned from a visit to New York City where he had stayed with Dan Slote and thoroughly enjoyed a get-together at Dan's with Charley Langdon (Livy's young brother) and Jack Van Nostrand. They were all four "Quaker City night hawks" and had a lively talk over old times. "We went through the Holy Land together, & I just laughed till my sides ached, at some of our reminiscences. It was the unholiest gang that ever cavorted through Palestine, but those are the best boys in the world," [3] he wrote his family. About the same time as the Palestine get-together he had taken Livy to hear Charles Dickens speak. Dickens, making his second trip to America, was drawing huge crowds, some of whom would stand all night to get tickets. Mark Twain must have been tempted to try to follow in his footsteps.

"The Frozen Truth" was apparently almost an impromptu affair, as Mark Twain wrote his mother: "I hardly knew what I was going to talk about, but it went off in splendid style." [4] Apparently he followed his practice of speaking from notes and accordingly left no manuscript record of his remarks. However, Paul Fatout, in preparing his *Mark Twain on the Lecture Circuit*, was able to find newspaper reports that indicate he dealt with the type of material he had used in his *Alta* letters but had paid little attention to the visit to the Holy Land and localized his lectures principally by saying that the Turks probably had a government something like ours, "citing a Turkish office-holder who had built himself a palace after three years in office." Probably some of the material he used in this lecture was embodied in the one he was soon to give on numerous occasions in the Far West, which he was to reach in March. He did not try it again in the nation's capital, resorting rather to a return to his Sandwich Island lecture.

When Mark Twain arrived in San Francisco on 2 April 1868, his views on Palestine were already well-known to the Western public, for his travel letters had been appearing regularly and recently and the last of the series did not come out until three days after his arrival. Thus he got the full benefit of the criticism of his views, which was widespread but by no means unanimous. Newspaper files show that he, who had written that Christ would never come to Palestine a second time as he had been there once, was called by one minister "this son of the devil" and by another "this person, Mark Twain, who visits the Holy Land and ridicules sacred scenes and things." [5] When he opened his new lecture titled "Pilgrim Life" before an overflow audience in Platt's Hall in San Francisco, he said that he would not discuss the Holy Land because he "had already been scolded for remarks on that subject." He probably was no more concerned with the few attacks on his newspaper letters than he was with his sister Pamela's fears that he might be profane about holy things. (He had promised her "there would be no scoffing at sacred things in my book or lectures.") Instead of ridiculing the Holy Sites he concentrated on those "bald-headed, spectacled and sedate old pilgrims," spiced his talk with drollery about the Sultan's difficulties with eight hundred wives, and grew serious in commenting on the departed glories of such cities as Athens and Damascus. During his two weeks tour of the Mother Lode towns and the Virginia City area he probably did not repeat his take of sixteen hundred dollars in San Francisco for his opening lecture but he did well enough to encourage him to give one more lecture in that city on 2 July, after finishing his manuscript for *The Innocents Abroad.* This time he spoke on "Venice, Past and Present": reports of this lecture, which apparently was never repeated, indicate that, though concentrating on Venice, he roamed over many topics he had covered in his earlier talks.

Though no notes, with the exception of some fragmentary passages embodying a conclusion, remain from these lectures to make certain what he covered, it is probable that during his western tour he introduced the elaborate "Moses Who?" anecdote which was to be one of the high points of his "The American Vandal Abroad" talk with which he toured the East the following winter, and which he introduced as a digression in *Roughing It.* In the latter book the occasion for the story was a tribute to the skill of Ben Holliday in

getting stagecoaches across the country in record time; the butt of
the story was the goodnatured Jack Van Nostrand ("The Interrogation Point" or most innocent of the innocents) who had sat by a pool
in Palestine for hours waiting to hear the voice of the turtle in the
land. According to Mark Twain, the likable nineteen-year-old New
Yorker had done little Bible reading and "all Holy Land history was
fresh and new to him." He was thus an open target for one of the
older pilgrims in the party, "our encyclopedia," who "never passed a
celebrated locality, from Bashan to Bethlehem, without illuminating
it with an oration." Thus, when the group of eight were camped in
Jericho, with the mountains of Moab turning dark blue with the
dusk, the learned pilgrim had tried to impress the boy with the idea
that " 'our eyes may be resting at this very moment upon the spot
where lies the mysterious grave of Moses.' " " 'Moses who?' " asked
Jack. This inquiry of course brought a sermon on how wonderfully
Moses held the children of Israel together as they wandered in the
wilderness which lay between Egypt and the Jordan Valley, bringing
them through to this very spot in forty years. " *'Forty years? Only
three hundred miles?* Humph! Ben Holliday would have fetched
them through in thirty-six hours.' " [6] Thus Mark Twain amused his
Roughing It readers as he combined a dig at a loquacious pilgrim
with skepticism about the skills of Moses and admiration for modern
progress in transportation. After all, Ben Holliday had moved his
coaches successfully over country that was almost as rough as the
Sinai and Judean wildernesses, and the Palestinians (descendants of
Moses) after thousands of years did not yet have a road that would
accommodate a four wheel cart.

It was during the winter following his trip to the Far West that
Mark Twain embarked on his first professionally directed lecture
tour. Having delivered the bulky manuscript of *The Innocents
Abroad* to the American Publishing Company in Hartford, Connecticut, he turned most of his energies to lecturing not only to support
himself but also to advertise the book, which he hoped would appear
before spring was over. Working as one of the "second-class stars"
sent out by James Redpath in his newly-founded Boston Lyceum
Bureau, Mark Twain spent nearly four months in the dead of winter

hopping back and forth between the East and Middle West and appearing before both appreciative and critical audiences in cities as large as Cleveland and Pittsburgh and as small as Charlotte, Michigan, and Ottawa, Illinois. Not yet able to draw the numbers or command the pay of the big guns of the lyceum circuit, oldtimers like Henry Ward Beecher and the reformed drunkard, the gymnastic John B. Gough, he was more or less content to earn his one hundred dollars a night during some forty engagements involving seven thousand miles of train travel. As befitted a more earnest commitment than those which had produced "The Frozen Truth" in Washington and "Pilgrim Life" and "Venice" in San Francisco, he now wrote out his lecture and memorized it, learning shortly to make it sound spontaneous, partly by inserting new anecdotes and partly by playing on his audience in an impromptu fashion. A portion of the lecture, "The American Vandal Abroad" (titled for one audience "Brother Jonathan Abroad") remains in manuscript in the Mark Twain papers and was published in part in *Mark Twain's Speeches*.

The text of "The American Vandal Abroad" disproves the contention of one small-town critic that "there is nothing in his lectures, for he very properly sacrifices everything to make his audience roar, and they do," yet the testimony of another hearer that Mark Twain followed his semilyrical apostrophe to the Sphinx with the remark that the American Vandal stood unconcernedly picking his teeth in its shadow shows that he did frequently stretch for his laughs. The substance of the lecture, alternating between humor and set-pieces and including the tried and true pictures of gondola life in Venice, moonlight and adventure on the Acropolis, and international contact in the visit to Alexander II of Russia, contained little about the visit to the Holy Land but remains of interest because of Mark Twain's somewhat complicated concept of the American Vandal, who might be baiting guides or criticizing Old Masters or exploring a harem in Damascus.

The trait most clearly implied in the title was the proclivity of tourists to pick up momentoes legitimately and illegitimately as they traveled through foreign lands, and Mark Twain had consistently criticized the *Quaker City* travelers for this propensity. Even one of

The Relic Hunter

his best friends, Dan Slote, was twitted for buying a Muslim tombstone with his name carved on it in Constantinople; his cabinmate suspected that his next purchase would be a Circassian slave.[7] "Your genuine Vandal is an intolerable and incorrigible relic gatherer," he stated in his lecture; some time earlier he had entered in his notebook the comment: "God protect the relics of Jerusalem when our tribe gets there." Yet he himself was not without blame, for he well knew that he had brought home in his luggage the six-inch head of a female statue, possibly picked up the night he broke quarantine in Greece and visited the Acropolis by moonlight. The temptation to take home one of the many fragments which lay about near the Parthenon must have been irresistible. To his *Alta* readers he had marveled over the sculptured faces as they seemed to stare upward in the moonlight: "What a world of ruined sculpture was about us! Stood up in rows—stacked up in piles—scattered broadcast over the wide area—of the Acropolis—were hundreds of crippled statues of all sizes and most exquisite workmanship." [8] For years the charming head was used as a paperweight by members of Mark Twain's family; now it is one of the prize exhibits in the Mark Twain Papers at the University of California in Berkeley.

Only part of the time did the lecturer attack the American vandal. "I treat him gently and kindly," Mark Twain admitted. In much of the lecture he was delivering an apology for the untutored American traveler, a new type who doubtless belonged as much in Europe and the Holy Land as his countless precursors from many lands. The term "vandal," he asserted, "best describes the roving, independent, free-and-easy character of that class of traveling Americans who are *not* elaborately educated, cultivated, and refined, and gilded and filigreed with the ineffable graces of the first society." [9] And it was as a spokesman for this type of American, now going abroad in greater and greater numbers, that Mark Twain wrote *The Innocents Abroad*.

As we have seen, plans for *The Innocents Abroad* were developed almost as soon as Mark Twain returned from Europe. As a matter of fact the humorist received an offer from Elisha Bliss, the president of the American Publishing Company early in December 1867, a few days after his return from the Holy Land, and at once acknowledged that, though he had had other offers of interest, he was almost convinced that subscription publication was what he wanted. He knew that this method of selling books, through the high-pressure salesmanship of company peddlers throughout the country, and particularly in the rural areas, would probably make him the most money, a matter which held a degree of interest for him "almost beyond comprehension." In his reply to Bliss he outlined what he proposed to do to turn his newspaper correspondence into just such a book as Bliss wanted.

I wrote fifty-two letters for the San Francisco "Alta California" during the Quaker City excursion, about half of which number have been printed, thus far. The "Alta" has few exchanges in the east, and I suppose scarcely any of these letters have been copied on this side of the Rocky Mountains. I could weed them of their chief faults of construction and inelegancies of expression, and make a volume which would be more acceptable in many respects than any I could now write. When those letters were written my impressions were fresh, but now they have lost their freshness; they were warm then—they are cold, now. I could strike out certain letters, and write new ones to supply their places.[10]

It was not long before the terms were worked out; Mark Twain was to prepare a manuscript which would number about six hundred pages when printed (he estimated he had about half of that length available in his newspaper letters) and he was to have the manuscript in Hartford by the 1 August 1868. Bliss, in turn, would manufacture the book with adequate format and illustrations and see to it that it was widely subscribed to in advance. Mark Twain was to realize 5 percent of the subscription price. After some consideration of alternate titles, it was decided to call the volume *The Innocents Abroad, or The New Pilgrim's Progress*; as Mark Twain put it, this title "seems to be the neatest and easiest understood—by farmers and everybody—suppose we adopt it." [11]

Almost as soon as Mark Twain came to his agreement with Bliss, he set about revising his newspaper letters for the proposed book. Knowing that he would have to add new materials, he borrowed copies of the newspaper correspondence by several of his friends, most notably Mrs. Fairbanks and Mrs. Severance, in order to aid his memory; he does not seem to have used them materially in accomplishing his task, however. He soon found he was not getting much done in Washington, where he was still working as a correspondent for at least three newspapers, and, as we have seen, set out in mid-March 1868 for San Francisco primarily to settle a dispute over his right to use the *Alta* letters, which the San Francisco newspaper had copyrighted in their own name (having paid hand-somely for them) and proposed to publish as a book. Once on the scene, the controversy was soon settled amicably and Mark Twain set about using his short stay in the West to lecture and to prepare the manuscript of his travel book, due in Hartford at the end of July. In an early estimate he made to Mrs. Fairbanks he judged that his newspaper letters would provide him with less than half of his text, but the evidence presented by D. M. McKeithan in reprinting all of the *Alta, Tribune,* and *Herald* letters in *Travelling with the Innocents Abroad* indicates that Mark Twain had much underestimated the bulk of his printed letters. He used all but one of them in his book text, with extensive revisions; his principal additions were to supply approximately ten chapters dealing with France and Italy, which presumably took the place of letters that had been lost in transit from the *Quaker City* to San Francisco, and five chapters dealing with Egypt and the trip home. Both of these large sections may have been written on the voyage home, as, according to Dewey Ganzel, Mark Twain learned before leaving Alexandria that some of his letters had failed to reach the *Alta.* However, as none of this material appeared in newspaper form, it is quite possible that he did not write it until after he made a contract for his book. It is noteworthy that the chapters dealing with France and Italy were published in four articles which appeared in San Francisco in the first four issues of the *Overland Monthly,* starting on almost the day that Mark Twain completed his manuscript and left San Francisco for Hartford. This material, which had not appeared in print earlier, was all included verbatim in *The Innocents Abroad.*

Still, that six-hundred-page book took a good deal of effort. In his *Autobiography* Mark Twain spoke of the enthusiasm with which he worked during the two months he spent at the Lick House in San Francisco.

I was very young in those days, exceedingly young, marvelously young, younger than I am now [he was in his late sixties], younger than I shall ever be again, by hundreds of years. I worked every night from eleven or twelve until broad day in the morning, and as I did 200,000 words in the sixty days, the average was more than 3000 words a day—nothing for Sir Walter Scott, nothing for Louis Stevenson, nothing for plenty of other people, but quite handsome for me.[12]

Allowing for seven-day weeks, some rough figuring, and the assumption that revising sixty newspaper letters was as hard as writing a new text, this comes out about right.

As we have seen, much of the new material for the book consisted of introductory chapters taken in part from the letters he had written for the *Alta* before embarking, the completion of the sections on travel in France and Italy to replace letters which had gone astray, and the half-dozen chapters dealing with his experiences in Egypt and on the way home, the copy for which, as Mark Twain says, was brought home in his pocket. He also included, apparently at the publishers' request, the ill-spirited letter he had written for the *New York Herald* on the day of his arrival in which he had taken the management of the *Quaker City* to task and had ridiculed the pilgrims. Otherwise, preparing *The Innocents Abroad* consisted of carefully reworking the newspaper letters which he had written, mostly to the *Alta California*. Though he had assured Bliss that he "could strike out certain letters, and write new ones to supply their places" he found when he turned to the task, he preferred to use at least parts of all of the letters, making alterations in style, cutting occasionally, and adding detail, such as bizarre stories from an apocryphal New Testament he had found in a New York library and background material garnered from guidebooks such as Murray's. Much of his effort while writing nights in San Francisco was turned toward weeding his newspaper correspondence of their "inelegancies of expression" and turning them toward a national rather than a local audience. As this was his first developed book, it is of value to watch in some detail how Mark Twain made his revisions.[13]

The most mechanical and obvious changes made to suit the newspaper letters to a wider public were the alterations in geographical reference. Thus, San Francisco became "an American city of 150,000"; the *Alta* was changed to "American metropolitan newspapers"; and "self-reliant Californians" were generalized into "self-reliant Americans." At least twice Mark Twain saw fit to remove slurs on his old friends, the San Francisco police; in one case policemen in general rather than San Francisco police alone received gold watches; and in the other, a reference to an Arab market smelling "like a San Francisco police court" was altered to simply "like a police court."

A few references to the California and Nevada hinterlands were also changed or omitted. Deleted was a paragraph comparing the topography of Palestine and Washoe, as was also a comparison of the camels of Syria with the camels he had seen in Virginia City. In the letters, he assured his readers that the rivers of Syria did "not amount to quite as much as the Carson and the Humboldt," but he apparently felt that his larger audience would not recognize the validity of that comparison. In the book, he retained his name Jacksonville for Temmin-el Foka but gave up his substitution of Dutch Flat for Dan. He omitted his statement that two Syrian towns were as much alike as two Chinamen, perhaps on the assumption that Easterners knew no Chinamen.

Changes in diction aimed to rid his manuscript of localisms were fairly numerous. Thus, not only did he substitute whist for seven-up as an amusement for his passengers, but he also frequently altered metaphors based on gambling games familiar to all westerners. In one tale the exclamation "Let us ante up and pass the buck" became simply "Let us die!" He had said that the self-righteousness of the Pharisees was their "long suit," but he changed it to their "specialty." He cut out the exclamation "I pass!" following his description of the effects of leprosy, substituting for it the trite "Horrible!" In his colloquial account of the sulking of Ahab over his failure to obtain Naboth's vineyard, he not only deleted the statement that Ahab "pouted over it and would not take his regular squills," but also changed Jezebel's query on discovering her spouse in the dumps from "wherefore he had renegged" to "wherefore he sorrowed." (He apparently felt the whole story should be toned down, because he had already changed his description of Jezreel from the vivid "ruinous old buzzard roost on a hill" to the colorless "ruinous old town on a hill.") Finally, while describing the disillusionment awaiting the visitor to the Plain of Esdraelon he substituted the commonplace phrase "suffer sorrow and disappointment" for the more localized one "fare no better than he that betteth his substance on 'deuces and' when the thing the worldling calleth a flush is out against him."

There was a similar weeding out of mining terms. Thus the statement that Nimrod "preempted a claim" on the site of Babylon was altered to Nimrod "settled." Originally, the green-spectacled Yanks riding horseback through Syria were pictured as novices bouncing high "and coming down one after the other like the stamps of a quartz mill." He abandoned that technical phrase as well as his wish that he "had a magazine under those fellows, with 4 or 500 lbs. of powder in it." He also changed his account of St. Helena's search for the cross by discarding the word "prospecting" from "she was prospecting here in the 3rd Century," and in addition eliminated completely his picturesque account of her discovery of the second thief's cross: "She put in one more blast and raised it." He thought better of his explanation of the appeal of the Golden Calf to the Israelites: "It was pleasantly suggestive of a free lunch," substituting for it the cliché, "human nature has not changed much since then." He deleted his reference to Hero as "Leander's squaw," and he changed the "filibusters who captured Dan" to the "adventurers who captured Dan."

Such are some of the typical changes Mark Twain made in order to rid his manuscript of localisms. The general revision of the letters, however, is of greater importance in showing his concept of the difference in demand and taste between his local and national audiences. When he had first heard that the owners of the *Alta* were planning to publish his letters in book form without revision, he had lamented to Mrs. Fairbanks: "If the *Alta*'s book were to come out with those wretched, slangy letters unrevised, I should be utterly ruined." [14] And, as Justin Kaplan has pointed out, the "slang" Mrs. Fairbanks objected to in her pupil's writings embraced "indecorums, colloquialisms, indelicacies, and vulgarities of all sorts and degrees." [15] Thus, Mark Twain applied himself seriously to improving his style, toning down his prejudices, and reducing the number of his vulgarities. The first of these tasks called for countless alterations; as he had written the *Alta* letters at an estimated speed of fifteen hundred words each day, days which had been filled with travel and excitement, he had had no time to revise his manuscript before it appeared in the newspaper. Though he by no means removed all the errors, grammatical and otherwise, in this revision, he did correct many of the more flagrant ones. Of course, we have no way of knowing how many of these changes were made by professional proofreaders in Hartford. Thus, little weight can be accorded to the changing of "don't" to "does not" and "have got" to "have" in many passages, or of elementary corrections such as the shift of "that" to "who," "who" to "whom," "rung" to "rang," "lay" to "lie," "like" to "as if," and the impersonal "you" to "one."

More significant was his revision of diction, since he frequently changed colloquial and slang expression to formal usage, not always to the improvement of his style. Some changes, like the following, were probably for the better: "reckon" to "suppose," "we dusted" to "we travelled," "hanker for" to "long for," "bother" to "trouble," and "gang" to "mob." On the other hand, his respect for conventional usage impaired his effectiveness when "old fogy" became "old fossil," "fill you up to the chin" became "gorge," "scare up a bath" became "hunt up a bath," "Lord High Chancellors of the Busted Exchequer" became "Lord High Chancellors of the Exploded Exchequer," the "jolly old brick of a nobleman" became simply an "old nobleman," and Nimrod's grave was altered from "the place where he was planted" to "the place his ashes inhabit." And a distinct loss was the omission of a phrase likening the whirling of a dervish to "a granddaddy long-legs with one foot in a candle."

Mark Twain also toned down some of his exaggerations. Thus, "gallons" of coins became "quarts," and the ninth wonder of the world was returned to its natural place as the eighth wonder. Other typical changes were "exquisitely beautiful" to "very charming to the eye," "eternally polite" to "polite," and "superbly" to "finely." Typical of a general practice was his moderation of his skepticism about the fulfillment of Biblical prophecy by substituting such phrases as "trenches upon the absurd" for "is absurd," and the softening of his diatribe against modern Greeks by calling them "questionable characters," "confiscators," and "falsifiers," rather than "thieves," "thieves," and "liars."

Frequently he made his diction more specific or vivid, though improvement was doubtful in changing "a swindle" to "an imposture," the "squirt" of a jet of water to the "discharge" of same, and (in his description of a camel) "a bob-tailed ostrich with four legs to it" to "an ostrich with an extra pair of legs." Typical of many alterations for the better were the changes of "absurd" to "overdone," "affair" to "edifice," "got after them" to "reduce their numbers," "prance" to "swagger," "only too proud" to "glad."

In softening his attacks for a larger public, Mark Twain apparently felt that his philistinism would be less objectionable than his racial prejudices and his irreverence. He left most of his art criticism unaltered, though he omitted a few remarks such as, "We don't know any more about pictures than a kangaroo does about metaphysics," and references to the paintings of the Old Masters such as "ghastly old nightmares done in lampblack and lightning." He either eliminated or tempered allusions to the homeliness of French women, the character of the Turkish Sultan (whom he had said he itched to assassinate), and his condemnation of the Turks, Arabs, and particularly the Israelites. In his *Alta* letters he had frequently attacked the last: "How they ever came to be the chosen people of the Lord is a mystery which will stagger me from this day forth until I perish." The alteration of his wholehearted condemnation of the inhabitants of the biblical lands was in keeping with his desire to make his book less irreverent than his letters, and, as we shall see, he finally cut out an entire section.

Mark Twain's expurgation of assumed profanities in his text bears evidence of the social censorship he felt he faced. Though he did not remove all possible offenses, he made changes such as: "devil" to "vagrant," "dang bed-chambers" to "bed-chambers," "damn it" to "execrate it," "I thanked God" to "I thanked fortune," and "wild with religious ecstasy" to "light-hearted and happy." And he omitted a statement that he told a guide in Tangier "to go to the hottest place he could in the other world."

More interesting are the expurgations of vulgarity. Thus, he decided it was more refined to say "male Moor" than "he-Moor," to change "one might spit across the narrow canal" to "jump across" it, and to alter "kept our snouts buried in our handkerchiefs" to "kept our nostrils buried," etc. He cut out some of his similes about bad smells: "Turks smell like a slaughter house in summer" became "Turks smell like—like Turks," and a breath which was "like the sigh of a buzzard" was reduced to a simple bad breath. He apparently decided it was vulgar to say his horse's tail had been shortened by being "driven up" and so accused the animal of sitting on it. He deleted an allusion to scribbling names on toilet walls, and he reduced the number of his jokes about the camel-dung frescoes in Syria and his comparison of them to the works of the Old Masters. In his original version of the method adopted by Moroccan robbers in recovering coins swallowed by a courier, the marauders gave the courier a physic, and waited; in *The Innocents Abroad* they resorted, more politely, to an emetic.

The major expurgation in the book, however, comes with the exclusion of the fictitious Mr. Brown. Brown had been used in the Sandwich Island letters and in the New York correspondence as a figure who frequently expressed more vulgar sentiments than Mark Twain wished ascribed to himself.[16] He was also a good butt for jokes and somewhat of a clown, though he sometimes displayed the shrewdness of a Sancho Panza. A few of his experiences, as related in the *Alta*, are retained in *The Innocents* and assigned to an equally fictitious Blucher; such are his seasickness, his 21,000 rei dinner in Fayal, and his attempt to ride a donkey into a mosque. But most of Brown's experiences, like his person, were omitted from the book. In the letters, for instance, Brown attacked da Vinci's *Last Supper*, he called the Czar's attendants "roosters," and he thought a dragoman was an animal like a rhinoceros. His succinct report on Gibraltar read: "All nations of the earth are represented in its population and an English shilling buys four drinks." Confused by the French watercloset signs, he complained that nearly every railway station in France was called "Côte des Hommes." He aided Mark Twain in an experiment to see whether the fumes in the Grotto del Cane would kill a dog, as reputed; they found a dog, were just about to try the experiment, and "then—just then, after all my trouble and vexation, the dog went up and smelt Brown's breath and laid down and died."

And it was Brown who looked on cynically while Mark Twain watched the Russian women bathing at Odessa, an episode omitted from a book to be sold in the refined American East. Mark Twain noticed that the women wore only a single thin dress, which, as he says "would be a very good apology for a bathing dress, if it would only stay down. But it won't do it. It will float up around their necks in the most scandalous way, and the water is clear, and yet they don't seem to know enough to kick up the mud in the bottom. I was never so outraged in my life." Mark Twain says he stayed there for seven hours, feeling that he might be of help. One girl, the prettiest in the party, bathed in nothing but a shawl and particularly worried him; he was afraid she would tangle her feet in the fringe and drown. He even offered to hold the shawl. Finally he said to Brown: "It makes my heart bleed to look upon this unhallowed scene." "We better go then," Brown said, "If you stay here seven more hours you might bleed to death." Twain added: "So we went away. But it was marvelously cheerful bathing." [17] Mr. Brown's disappearance marked an important step in the conversion of Mark Twain to politeness.

No doubt part of the reason Mark Twain dropped Mr. Brown was that he was busy developing other characters, not only minor figures based on actual people particularly prominent in the cruise, like the Oracle, the Interrogation Point, and the Poet Lariat, but a bolder concept of himself as traveler and narrator. As Bret Harte put it in a discerning review of *The Innocents Abroad*, "the irascible pilgrim, 'Mark Twain,' is a very eccentric creation of Mr. Clemens'." [18] This character which Mark Twain imposed upon himself was not always consistent; sometimes he was a barbarian, scoffing at aspects of culture which he did not understand, particularly in the fields of art and religion; sometimes he was the naive boy, delighted with Europe and the Middle East—the seeing of things he had read about and dreamed about. This was the role he stressed when years later he wrote an introduction to the Tauchnitz edition of the book; but most often he was the skeptic, constantly amused and sometimes annoyed at the seriousness of the "pilgrims." These pilgrims moved into central roles as Mark Twain moved with his party of eight through the dry reaches of Syria. There seem to have been three of the party who provided contrasts to Mark Twain, with his objections to a fundamentalist interpretation of the Scriptures, his worship of science and progress, particularly in technology, and his enthusiasm for democracy, particularly as exemplified on the frontier. Thus, "Mark Twain" was sometimes deeply moved by relics of the past, at other times scornful of the absence of modern improvements such as good roads and railways. He also could be nearly as irreverent as he chose to be, even though Mrs. Fairbanks or his bride, Livy, might object; as he wrote to Bliss after publication of *The Innocents Abroad*: "The irreverence of the volume appears to be a tip-top good feature of it, diplomatically speaking." (He had first written "financially" but had crossed that word out; however, in another letter, this time to Gov. Frank Fuller, he admitted to being most concerned with the "bucksheesh" the book would elicit.) As an afterthought he noted to Bliss "though I wish with all my heart there wasn't an irreverent passage in it." [19]

The "pilgrim" who received the most excoriating attention in *The Innocents Abroad* was not one of the party, however, but a traveler who had visited Palestine a dozen years before Mark Twain's trip, William C. Prime, author of *Tent Life in the Holy Land* to which we have referred several times in the first chapter. Prime, member of a distinguished New York family which had produced more than one outstanding Presbyterian minister, had graduated from Princeton before setting out to explore the Levant with his wife and good friend Whitely. Full of energy—in time he was to be president of the Associated Press as well as one of the outstanding promotors of the Metropolitan Museum of Art and Professor of Art at Princeton—he had by the time he was thirty experienced the adventures in Egypt which he described in *Boat Life in Egypt and Nubia* and had gone on to visit the Holy Land, following much the same route as did Ross Browne and Mark Twain but reversing directions, going north from Jaffa to Beirut by way of Jerusalem and Damascus. Though he was in Palestine a few months before Melville made his visit, he saw it in quite a different way. Unlike Browne, he had enough money to be a real adventurer; he brought with him from Egypt a tent outfit that he had had made specially for the trip; he imported his own Egyptian dragoman who had been with him on the Nile; and he brought an American flag which, topped by an eagle, he flew defiantly from his wife Miriam's tent wherever the party camped in Syria. He was already a skilled collector of art objects, he could quote Latin and he spoke some Arabic, and he, like his fellow spirits Kinglake and Warburton, affected Arab dress. He prided himself on his eye for good horseflesh, on his riding ability, and on the keenness of his marksmanship with revolver and rifle. He also believed that the best way to keep Arabs in their places was to punish them severely if they misbehaved.

Prime wrote his *Tent Life in the Holy Land* with a great deal of enthusiasm and not a little humor. Though he found the natives of Palestine superstitious, dirty, and unprogressive, though he declared "the curse of God appears to rest on all the country, and the desolation of the land of Israel could scarcely be more total and complete," [20] he, unlike the majority of Protestant pilgrims, made much of the sacredness of holy places and thrilled to the stimuli of geography and history. He had no difficulty accepting the filthy sewers called streets in Jerusalem, and a typical day was almost uniformly described in lyrical terms. "To rise in the morning early, and go along the Way of Grief to the gate of St. Stephen, and out on the brow of Moriah, there to see the sun rise over Olivet; to go down and wash your eyes, heavy with sleep, in the soft waters of Siloam, that they might never ache again; to climb the sides of Mt. Zion, and come in by the Zion gate, and so up the streets of the city to the Holy Sepulchre; to visit Calvary and the Tomb; to press our knee on the cold rock where the first footsteps of the risen Saviour were pressed; and then, as the twilight came on, and the moonlight fell softly in the valley, to go down to Gethsemane and to pray! Think of days thus spent!" [21] He enjoyed his Palestine visit to the full, from distant Alexandria seeing a star fall over Jerusalem, from St. Stephen's Gate noting the halo over Mt. Olivet, and at Bethlehem hearing music in the sky. The water of the Dead Sea turned his eyes to "balls of

anguish" and made his nostrils "hot as the nostrils of Lucifer."
Walking in the evening he could relive within his imagination the
crucifixion and the raising of Lazarus. He also thrilled at riding his
horse around the walls of Jerusalem in twenty-eight minutes. And, as
a seasoned desert traveler, he could relax in strange places: "Our
long chibouks, with fresh sticks of lemon-tree, were fragrant with
Latakea, and our glasses filled with that delicious wine of Lebanon,
the memory whereof is aromatic." Also he hired a stonemason to cut
chunks from Jerusalem's Golden Gate so that he could take them
home to America.

While writing his *Alta* letters, Mark Twain mentioned William C.
Prime only once (although he twice spoke of carrying the latter's
book with him as a guide); the occasion was Clemens' first view of
Jerusalem at which time he perhaps felt somewhat at fault because
he could not weep. Prime had made quite a thing of it, as had many
other travelers; Prime had had trouble seeing the city through his
tears and, according to Mark Twain, all of his companions, including
two Muslim servants, a Latin monk, and a Jew, also broke out
weeping. Mark Twain added he was surprised that the camels and
asses did not weep too. To cap his amused description of "the water
company," he noted "Prime got such a start then that he never could
shut himself off; and he went through Palestine and irrigated it from
one end to the other." [22]

When he began revising his letters for *The Innocents Abroad*,
Mark Twain used Prime as a romantic whipping boy much as
Browne had used Lamartine. Thus, when Mark Twain first came in
contact with Bedouins he found them tame and had fun in taunting
Prime (who had become "Grimes" for book publication) for his
readiness to use an arsenal, made up of a Navy Colt, a "volcanic
repeater," and a bowie-knife to take pot shots at elusive Bedouins.
Later he took exception to Prime's description of the Sea of Galilee,
objecting particularly to his calling it deep blue and referring to the
distant Mt. Hermon towering over it in the north. "I do not object to
the witness dragging a mountain forty-five miles to help the scenery
under consideration, because it is entirely proper to do it, and,
besides, the picture needs it." He decided that Prime saw Palestine

through Presbyterian glasses; many years later he affirmed that his scapegoat took religion as "his daily tipple." [23] The humorist pretended to suspect that the "pilgrims" he was traveling with were taking their cues from Prime; he was sure of it when they reached Nazareth and, like the author of *Tent Life in the Holy Land*, declared a plain-looking Syrian woman they saw at Mary's Fountain to be Madonna-like in her beauty. "Commend me to Fenimore Cooper to find beauty in the Indians, and to Grimes to find it in the Arabs," [24] he announced, anticipating his famous essay on Cooper which he wrote years later.

'I Wept'

It was hard to say which annoyed him more, Prime's shooting or his weeping; he insisted "Grimes" went through Palestine "with one hand forever on his revolver, and the other on his pocket handkerchief." When Mark Twain gazed on Godfrey's crusader sword hanging in the Church of the Holy Sepulchre he said it was the spirit of "Grimes" that made him thirst to kill every Arab in sight with it. He found Prime's spirit less than admirable when the latter wrote that he sat by willingly while an Arab boy who had stolen some powder from him was treated to the bastinado by the Lebanese authorities. Here Mark Twain seemed really angry and contemptuous of his target; elsewhere he merely used him as a foil to contrast with his own views. The climax came when, knowing that Prime had written "I wept, when I saw Jerusalem, I wept when I lay in the starlight at Bethlehem, I wept on the blessed shores of Galilee," Mark Twain revised his famous passage on bursting into tears at the grave of his ancestor Adam and repeated the lines he had quoted from Prime shortly before: "Let him who would sneer at my emotion close this volume here, for he will find little to his taste in my journeyings through Holy Land." [25]

The idea of ridiculing Prime at length may have come from Bret Harte, who, according to a letter which Mark Twain wrote to Charles Henry Webb in 1870, gave him considerable help with the revision in San Francisco. "Harte read all the MS. of the 'Innocents' and told me what passages, paragraphs, and *chapters* to leave out—and I followed orders strictly. It was a kind thing for Harte to do, and I think I appreciated it." [26] Harte, who had worked with Mark Twain on the *Californian* was about to issue the new *Overland Monthly*, the first memorable issue of which appeared in July 1868—the month Mark Twain left for the East with his completed manuscript. In addition to including a chapter of *Innocents Abroad*, this issue carried a review by Harte of *Going to Jericho* by John Franklin Swift. Swift, like Mark Twain, was from Missouri and had come to California during the gold rush; ex-blacksmith and ex-mule-skinner he had established himself in law and had seen something of politics in San Francisco and Virginia City. In midcareer he had taken off time to travel in Europe and had made the trek from Jaffa to Damascus via Jerusalem in the spring of the year that Mark Twain covered the route in the opposite direction. Swift's travel letters had appeared in the *San Francisco Bulletin* and were now collected in book form, giving more attention to factual details than Mark Twain's letters in the *Alta* but sharing with Mark Twain's writing not only traits of frontier humor but the attitude, "Show me, I'm from Missouri." After stating that his lack of veneration was due "to an education that has been practical to the fullest extent of the American idea, and an education that demands proofs to sustain averments," he suggested that the guide at the house of Simon the Tanner in Jaffa was wearing a "cast-off dressing gown of the host who charitably entertained St. Peter," insisted that Jerusalem itself should have been filled with mastodons instead of camels, and described the canopy over the Holy Sepulchre as looking like "a fancy baker's Oven." [27]

In his review of the book, Bret Harte, who had been working with Mark Twain's manuscript, welcomed Swift into the company of "the exuberant image-breakers," anti-romantics who included Ross Browne, William Dean Howells, whose *Venetian Life* came out in 1866, and Mark Twain. "A race of good-humored, engaging iconoclasts seem to have precipitated themselves upon the old altars of mankind," he wrote; the days of sentimental journeying were over and Kinglake, Curtis, Prime, and Lamartine were out-of-date. He particularly singled out Prime among the outmoded pilgrims: "The spectacle of good Mr. Prime with a revolver in one hand and a Bible in the other is somewhat ludicrous." [28]

While helping Mark Twain with his revisions, Bret Harte seems to have concentrated on making cuts. Perhaps he was responsible for Mark Twain's modifying his accounts of camel-dung frescoes, or condensing the story of "The Fall and Rise of Joseph," or cutting out entirely his burlesques of the search of Naaman for a cure for leprosy and of the adventures of the Prodigal Son. Of more interest is the speculation on whether Harte, one-quarter Jew, was responsible for Mark Twain deleting a long passage attacking the ancient Israelites, a passage which did not appear in the *Alta* but which has survived in manuscript form in the Mark Twain Papers.[29] Curiously, in his newspaper letters he had paid little attention to the six thousand Jewish refugees in Jerusalem who were living in miserable ghettoes and who were being supported by friends in other countries. Rather, justifying his stand by vaguely citing Robinson and Thomson, he assumed that the contemporary Arab was the true descendant of the people of the Bible and had changed very little since the days of Abraham or the days of Jesus. In a statement in an *Alta* letter which he omitted from his book, Mark Twain had presented his thesis: "It is pretty safe, no doubt, to believe that from Abraham's time till now, Palestine has been peopled only with ignorant, degraded, lazy, unwashed loafers and savages. Arabs they were, they are, and always will be. . . . The difference between a prowling varlet of an Arab to-day and an Israelite of old amounts to nothing more, perhaps, than that you spell the nationality of the one with four letters and of the other with nine." [30]

In his discarded manuscript, Mark Twain omitted the "no doubts" and "perhapses" and went after the Israelites hammer and tongs, thus leading into an attack on the credibility of the Bible narrative. Part of his attack rested upon his dislike for the Arabs he had met in Palestine; the other part was based on his disapproval of the ethics of Old Testament leaders. For instance, he asked why we should revere the prophet Samuel when the latter demanded that Saul exterminate all unbelievers? It seemed to him that the cruel Israelites devoted themselves to genocide. Why revere Joseph who had proved to be a heartless financier in Egypt or Jacob who was perfidious in his relations with Laban and Esau? Why esteem a people who had left no signs of greatness behind them, such as roads and impressive buildings? "Seen afar off,—as far as from America to the Holy Land—the ancient children of Israel seem almost too lovely & too holy for this coarse earth; but seen face to face, in their legitimate descendants, with no hope of distance to soften their harsh features and no glamor of sabbath-school glory to beautify them, they are like any other savages. . . . Many of them [i.e. the patriarchs of old] were superior to the digger Indians of California, but not all of them could rank the Sioux of the Great Plains." Once again he asserted that one must keep away from the Great Plains and the Holy Land if he wanted to retain a romantic admiration for Indians and Israelites.

He went on to insist that he saw Jacob and Abraham in the Holy Land nearly every day:

"I have seen Jacob in Palestine, many a time. He is six feet high, & very lean; his beard is long & grizzled; he wears a soiled turban shaped like a vast swathed door-knob, on his head; a long, torn and shredded black-striped robe sweeps down from his shoulders; his face is as brown as an Indian's; his shins are bare; he wears a cut-away slipper which exposes the entire rear half of his unwashed foot; he rides an ass the size of a young calf; its monstrous ears reach up to the middle of his breast, & work contentedly, something in the manner of shears blades; the man punches the ass in the flank with his staff, he swings his slippered foot back and forth, comfortably, within a short ten inches of the ground, & keeping up a barbarous catarwauling, which stands for singing, he vibrates along much as a long-bodied man might who was running upon his knees." [31]

True to his promise, Mark Twain delivered the manuscript of *The Innocents Abroad* to Elisha Bliss in Hartford, Connecticut, in July 1868. It was another year, however, before the book appeared—a year during which Bliss won a set-to with some of the directors of the American Publishing Company who feared that the book was too irreverent for their clientele; a year during which Mark Twain lectured on the "American Vandal Abroad" while he fumed at delays in his book's publication; and, most important of all, a year during which he finally became engaged to Livy Langdon in spite of the doubts her parents felt about his life as a robust bachelor on the frontier. It was during the spring of 1869 that Livy helped her fiancé with the second proofs of the forthcoming book. Years later when dictating his autobiography Mark Twain started a legend about Livy's emasculating his writing with the following statement: "In the beginning of our engagement the proofs of my first book, *The Innocents Abroad*, began to arrive, and she read them with me. She also edited them. She was my faithful, judicious, and painstaking editor from that day forth until within three or four months of her death—a stretch of more than a third of a century." [32] Still later Albert Bigelow Paine, in his biography of Mark Twain, expanded the concept of Livy's influence on the book: "What he [Mark Twain] lacked in delicacy—and his lack was likely to be large enough in that direction—she detected, and together they pruned it away." [33] It is not likely, however, that many alterations or omissions resulted from Livy's advice, for the two were reading revised or page proofs in which alterations were expensive affairs. Moreover, a comparison of the four articles dealing with France and Italy that Mark Twain turned over to Harte to use in the *Overland Monthly* (July–November 1868) with the corresponding chapters in the book shows very slight alteration indeed, suggesting that Livy's delicacy had little influence on *The Innocents Abroad.* Also Mrs. Fairbanks, to whom Mark Twain read some of his newspaper letters on the *Quaker City,* is reputed to have advised him to abandon certain passages to the waves, but, again, the effect on the total book was probably slight.

As Mark Twain put it nearly twenty years later, he felt that his manuscript could well have stood cutting. "When the Lord finished the world, he pronounced it good. That is what I said about my first work too. But Time, I tell you, Time takes the confidence out of these incautious early opinions. It is more likely He thinks about the world, now, pretty much as I think about the 'Innocents Abroad.' The fact is, there is a trifle too much water in both." [34] He had worked so energetically expanding his newspaper letters that by late April, as the page proofs continued to come in, he even became panicky over the manuscript being *too* long. He wrote Bliss to cut if necessary: "Certainly—snatch out *Samson*—it isn't even necessary to mention him. Yes, snatch out the *Jaffa Colony,* too. Also, snatch out my *Temperance Society experience.*" [35] The book at last appeared three months later, 651 pages long (with its illustrations), sans Sampson and Temperance Society but including the chapter on the Jaffa Colony.

In one of his letters to Bliss, Mark Twain wrote that the theme of *The Innocents Abroad* was the contrast between what the travelers had *expected* to see and what they *did* see on their journey. Surely this remark applies most pointedly to the portion of the book dealing with the Holy Land. Reality had simply not lived up to anticipation. As he was to point out after being disappointed with the Taj Mahal in *Following the Equator*: "It is a mistake for a person with an unregulated imagination to go and look at an illustrious world's wonder. . . . I ought never to hunt up the reality, but stay miles away from it. . . ." [36] But even as he worked on the book, his "unregulated imagination" began to build a romantic mist about what he had seen a year before—this process was most evidently stimulated by his love for Livy. During the Christmas season he was so overjoyed that Livy had agreed to be his wife that he wrote to Mrs. Fairbanks:

About this time, (past midnight, & so, Christmas is here) eighteen hundred & sixty-nine years ago, the stars were shedding a purer lustre above the barren hills of Bethlehem—& possibly flowers were being charmed to life in the dismal plain where the Shepherds watched their flocks—& the hovering angels were singing Peace on earth, good-will to men. For the Saviour was come. Don't you naturally turn, in fancy, now, to that crumbling wall & its venerable olives, & to the mouldy domes & turrets of Bethlehem? And don't you picture it all out in your mind as we saw it many months ago? And don't the picture mellow in the distance & take to itself again the soft, unreal semblance that Poetry & Tradition give to the things they hallow? And now that the greasy monks, & the noisy mob, & the leprous beggars are gone, & all the harsh, cold hardness of *real* stone & unsentimental glare of sunlight are banished from the vision, don't you realize again, as in other years, that Jesus *was* born there, & that the angels *did* sing in the still air above, & that the wondering shepherds *did* hold their breath & listen as the mysterious music floated by? *I* do. It is more real than ever. And I am glad, a hundred times glad, that I saw Bethlehem, though at the time it seemed that that sight had swept away forever, every pleasant fancy & every cherished memory that ever the City of Nativity had stored away in my mind & heart.[37]

It was not in this mood, however, that Mark Twain had his final say about Palestine in *The Innocents Abroad*. The softened mood slipped away after his Christmas Eve letter to Mrs. Fairbanks and the vision melted under memories of "all the harsh, cold hardness of *real* stone and unsentimental glare of sunlight"; he could do no more than describe the Holy Land as he had seen it.

Palestine sits in sackcloth and ashes. Over it broods the spell of a curse that has withered its fields and fettered its energies. Where Sodom and Gomorrah reared their domes and towers, that solemn sea now floods the plain, in whose bitter waters no living thing exists—over whose waveless surface the blistering air hangs motionless and dead—about whose borders nothing grows but weeds, and scattering tufts of cane, and that treacherous fruit that promises refreshment to parching lips, but turns to ashes at the touch. Nazareth is forlorn; about that ford of Jordan where the hosts of Israel entered the Promised Land with songs of rejoicing, one finds only a squalid camp of fantastic Bedouins of the desert; Jericho the accursed, lies a moldering ruin, to-day, even as Joshua's miracle left it more than three thousand years ago; Bethlehem and Bethany, in their poverty and their humiliation, have nothing about them now to remind one that they once knew the high honor of the Saviour's presence; the hallowed spot where the shepherds watched their flocks by night, and where the angels sang Peace on earth, good will to men, is untenanted by any living creature, and unblessed by any feature that is pleasant to the eye. Renowned Jerusalem itself, the stateliest name in history, has lost all its ancient grandeur, and is become a pauper village; the riches of Solomon are no longer there to compell the admiration of visiting Oriental queens; the wonderful temple which was the pride and the glory of Israel, is gone, and the Ottoman crescent is lifted above the spot where, on that most memorable day in the annals of the world, they reared the Holy Cross. The noted Sea of Galilee, where Roman fleets once rode at anchor and the disciples of the Saviour sailed in their ships, was long ago deserted by the devotees of war and commerce, and its borders are a silent wilderness; Capernaum is a shapeless ruin; Magdala is the home of beggared Arabs; Bethsaida and Chorazin have vanished from the earth, and the "desert places" round about them where thousands of men once listened to the Saviour's voice and ate the miraculous bread, sleep in the hush of a solitude that is inhabited only by birds of prey and skulking foxes.[38]

It was not only the wretched condition of Palestine at this period which brought on Mark Twain's diatribes about its terrain, its holy monuments, and its inhabitants. One must not forget that he visited it, strenuously, at the end of a long summer of hectic sightseeing in Europe, accompanied always by the necessity of keeping up his newspaper correspondence. Presumably his illness in Damascus left him in a poor condition to enjoy much his frantic dash through Galilee, Samaria, and Judea; it is not surprising that his irritation often got the better of him. Moreover, he was constantly annoyed by some of the "pilgrims" in his party, whose enthusiasm for what they saw and their insistence on the manifestations of Biblical prophecy, as they interpreted it, made him even more critical of conditions in the Holy Land than he might have been under other circumstances. Much of his account reflects this irritability. And possibly under his raillery teemed a conflict between the homely Christianity he had known as a boy and the disheartening signs of religious bigotry and conflict in this cradle of world faiths. Thus he concluded that the Holy Land no longer existed in this humdrum world. "It is sacred to poetry and tradition—it is a dream land." [39]

Even though Melville found Palestine harsh and desiccated, he probably benefited considerably from his visit. He seems to have been bothered little if at all by the disappointments over the state of Holy Sites, having expected no more than what he found. It is not surprising that he found Mar Saba more stimulating than Jerusalem. Though he noted in his journal: "No country will more quickly dissipate romantic expectations than Palestine—particularly Jerusalem. To some the disappointment is heart sickening," [40] it is clear that he escaped any deep trauma. His visit not only gave him a vacation from routine but helped him to resolve some of the problems that had plagued him when he left home. After his return he seemed reconciled to earning his living and supporting his family with a modest job in the New York Customs Service. He turned his creative talents toward writing short poems and the development of his epic *Clarel* without worrying whether he reached an audience or not. The ultimate success of the visit to the Levant came with the publication of *Clarel*.

In spite of dirt, fleas, and many other forms of discomfort, Ross Browne enjoyed his visit to the Holy Land. True, he found many things he disliked and said so, as when he wrote, "Perhaps upon the whole face of the globe there could not be found a spot less holy than modern Jerusalem." [41] Yet the condition of Jerusalem did not bother him much. Though he was the youngest of the three irreverent pilgrims, he was the most content with his religious convictions and the least disturbed by relic-peddling at holy places. Not often was he as deeply disturbed by the sight of what he considered religious tawdriness as he was during the ceremony on Christmas Eve in Bethlehem, but, after all, he was homesick that night. To the readers of *Yusef* he warned: "It will be seen that I have not felt it my duty to make a desponding pilgrimage through the Holy Land; for upon a careful perusal of the Scriptures I can find nothing said against a cheerful frame of mind." [42] That cheerful frame of mind resulted from the fact that he was a born adventurer, loved traveling, and, though he was unwilling to see the East "through highly-colored spectacles, with bubbles in the center," had a great capacity for enjoying things as they are. Most of all, he liked people. He listened fascinated to the Arab storyteller, though he could not understand a word he said; he made friends with the muleteers and humanized little Tokina; he was delighted with the rebel Sheik; and he grew truly fond of Yusef, with all his faults. He was most in his element when playing "Ezepa Kouna" for the Arabs on his flute, whether at Baalbek or Damascus. Perhaps today some Arab boy hums the catchy ditty as he sets about to excel his fellows in dancing the raas.

Notes and References

CHAPTER ONE

In addition to sources cited in the text, material for this chapter was drawn from reference books and contemporary guidebooks, particularly Fr. Eugene's Hoade's *Guide to the Holy Land* (Jerusalem, 1962), and observations of the author in Lebanon and Israel in 1968. Place name spellings have been regularized by reference to current *National Geographic* maps.

1. Alexander William Kinglake, *Eōthen* (New York, 1898), p. 68. First publication in 1844.

2. Eliot Warburton, *The Crescent and the Cross* (London, 1844), p. 271.

3. J. W. DeForest, *Oriental Acquaintance, or Letters from Syria* (New York, 1856), p. 60.

4. Bayard Taylor, *The Lands of the Saracens* (New York, 1894), pp. 44–45. First publication in 1855.

5. Kinglake, *Eōthen*, p. 180.

6. DeForest, *Oriental Acquaintance*, pp. 65–66.

7. Taylor, *The Lands of the Saracens*, p. 71.

8. John Lloyd Stephens, *Travels in Egypt, Arabia Petraea, and the Holy Land* (London, 1856), p. 131. First publication in 1837.

9. Warburton, *The Crescent and the Cross*, p. 200.

10. John Franklin Swift, *Going to Jericho* (San Francisco, 1868), p. 210.

11. Warburton, *The Crescent and the Cross*, p. 234.

12. Charles Dudley Warner, *In the Levant* (Boston, 1907), p. 180. First publication in 1876.

13. Much of the material dealing with American consuls and missionairies in this section was drawn from David H. Finnie's *Pioneers East* (Cambridge, Mass., 1967).

14. Henry H. Jessup, *Fifty-three Years in Syria* (New York, 1910), I, 134.

15. Finnie, *Pioneers East*, p. 262.

16. Quoted in R. J. Mitchell, *The Spring Voyage* (New York, 1964), p. 94.

17. Ibid., p. 95.

18. *Voyages and Travels of Sir John Mandeville*, ed. A. Layard (New York, 1898), pp. 48–49.

19. Kinglake, *Eōthen*, pp. 119–20.

20. George William Curtis, *The Howadji in Syria* (New York, 1856), pp. 158, 183. First publication in 1852.

21. DeForest, *Oriental Acquaintance*, p. 80.

22. *Overland Monthly*, I (July 1868), 101.

23. Gustave Flaubert, *Notes de Voyages*, I, 290 in *Œuvres Còmplètes de Gustave Flaubert* (Paris, 1910), vol. 9: "We enter through the Jaffa Gate and I let a fart underneath as I cross the threshold, very involuntarily; I was even annoyed, at bottom, by this Voltairianism of my anus."

24. Benjamin Disraeli, *Tancred, or the New Crusade* (London, 1927), p. 56. First publication in 1847.

CHAPTER TWO

General sources: Francis Rock's *J. Ross Browne: A Biography* (Washington, D.C., 1929) is a short biography, accurate but not detailed. Two later studies have drawn on Browne's confidential reports covering his activities as a special agent for the Federal Government: Richard H. Dillon's *J. Ross Browne, Confidential Agent in Old California* (Norman, Oklahoma, 1965) is principally concerned with the role he played in uncovering corruption in federal bureaucracy on the Western frontier; David Michael Goodman's *A Western Panorama, 1849–1875, the Travels, Writings and Influence of J. Ross Browne* (Glendale, California, 1966) puts its main emphasis on the reflection on western history in Browne's records and published writings. It contains an excellent bibliography of Browne's writings. A helpful contemporary biographical sketch appeared in *Harper's Weekly*, VII (21 February 1863), 125.

The writer has drawn on the family papers in the hands of Lina Fergusson Browne of Berkeley, the granddaughter-in-law of J. Ross Browne. These have been supplemented by Mrs. Browne's informative introduction to Ross Browne's *A Dangerous Journey* brought out by the Book Club of California (San Francisco, 1950) and her ably edited and invaluable *J. Ross Browne, His Letters, Journals and Writings* published by the University of New Mexico Press, Albuquerque, in 1969. As a fair amount of the material for my three Browne chapters has been drawn from the latter source, I refer to it in the footnotes under the short title, *Letters*; similarly I have used the short title *Yusef* for J. Ross Browne's *Yusef; or, The Journey of the Frangi: A Crusade in the East* (Harper & Brothers, New York, 1853). All quotations from *Yusef* are from the first edition.

1. Anon., *The Parson's Horn-book, Printed and Sold at the Office of "The Comet,"* (Dublin, 1831) p. 13. Much of this pamphlet material put out by Browne and Sheehan, Printers is to be found in the British Museum.

2. *Letters*, p. 260.

3. *Yusef*, pp. 76–77.

4. J. Ross Browne, *Crusoe's Island* (New York, 1864), pp. 46–47.

5. *Letters*, p. 1.

6. J. Ross Browne, *Etchings of a Whaling Cruise* (New York, 1846), p. 4.

7. *Letters*, pp. 4–5.

8. Preface to *Yusef*, pp. v–vi.

9. J. Ross Browne, *Etchings of a Whaling Cruise*, p. 401.

10. Ibid., p. 401.

11. Ibid., p. 369.

12. Byron Farwell, *Burton* (New York, 1963), p. 139.

13. Quoted in Perry Miller, *The Raven and the Whale* (New York, 1956), pp. 137–38.

14. J. Ross Browne, *Etchings of a Whaling Cruise*, pp. 131–32.

15. Melville's review appeared in *The Literary World* (New York) I, (6 March 1847), pp. 105–6.

16. J. Ross Browne, *Crusoe's Island*, p. 11.

17. *Letters*, pp. 121–22.

18. Ibid., p. 122.

19. *San Francisco Chronicle*, 13 February 1881.

20. See the excellent edition of Bayard Taylor's *El Dorado*, with introduction by Robert G. Cleland (New York, 1949), for detail on Browne's friendship with Taylor.

CHAPTER THREE

General sources: See notes for Chapter Two. As Browne's shorthand journal did not survive, his letters to his wife and the clearly factual passages in *Yusef* provide the details for reconstructing his experiences in the Levant, particularly his trek through the Holy Land. His 1852 correspondence to the Washington *Daily National Intelligencer* (4 March, p. 2; 25 March, p. 4; 6, 13, 29 April, p. 4; 8 May, p. 4; 10, 17 June, p. 4) adds little information, for the sections dealing with the Holy Land were used in *Yusef* with practically no revision.

1. *Letters*, p. 141.
2. *Daily National Intelligencer*, Washington, D.C., 10 June 1852, p. 4.
3. *Letters*, p. 140.
4. Preface to *Yusef*, p. vii.
5. *Letters*, p. 145.
6. *Yusef*, p. 92.
7. Ibid., p. 111.
8. Ibid., p. 129.
9. Ibid., p. 199.
10. Ibid., p. 214.
11. Ibid., p. 249.
12. Ibid., p. 255.
13. Ibid., p. 275. On letter to his wife see f.n. 15 below.
14. Ibid., p. 306.
15. Unpublished letter from Browne to his wife, Jerusalem, 17 December 1851. In Lina Fergusson Browne Papers.
16. *Yusef*, p. 306.
17. Ibid., p. 390.
18. *Letters*, p. 157.

CHAPTER FOUR

General sources: See notes for Chapters Two and Three.
1. Preface to *Yusef*, p. iv.
2. *Yusef*, pp. 396–97.
3. Ibid., pp. 136–37.
4. Ibid., p. 267.
5. Ibid., pp. 357–58.
6. Ibid., p. 316.
7. Ibid., p. 337.
8. Ibid., p. 299.
9. Ibid., p. 305.
10. Ibid., pp. 402–3.
11. Ibid., p. 346.
12. Unpublished letter from Browne to his wife, Constantinople. 30 October 1851. In Lina Fergusson Browne Papers.
13. *Yusef*, pp. 404–05.
14. Ibid., p. 193.
15. Ibid., p. 178.
16. Ibid., p. 228.
17. Ibid., pp. 229–30.

18. Ibid., p. 294.

19. Ibid., p. 416.

20. Ibid., p. 419.

21. *Mark Twain to Mrs. Fairbanks* (San Marino, Calif., 1949), p. 31 and f.n.

22. *Letters*, p. 399.

CHAPTER FIVE

In preparing my two chapters on Melville I have consulted a number of biographies, the most helpful of which for my purposes were those by Lewis Mumford (1929), Newton Arvin (1950), and Leon Howard (1951)—the last was the most nearly definitive. I have consulted a number of special studies such as Natalie Wright's *Melville's Use of the Bible* (1949), Morton M. Sealts's *Melville as a Lecturer* (1957), and Howard P. Vincent's edition of Melville's *Collected Poems* (1947), which confines itself to the shorter poems and does not include *Clarel*. Like all scholars interested in Melville I have found Jay Leyda's *The Melville Log* (2 vols., New York, 1951) very helpful. This remarkable work is made up of a wealth of source material on Melville's life, accurately edited and presented chronologically. I have used the customary short title, *Log*, in referring to it in the footnotes.

In my immediate task in this chapter of exploring Melville's visit to the Levant, and more particularly, the Holy Land, I have depended somewhat on Walter E. Bezanson's introduction and notes to his definitive edition of *Clarel* (New York, 1960) but much more extensively on Melville's journal kept during that visit, which has been most ably edited by Howard C. Horsford for the Princeton University Press. It is titled *Journal of a Visit to Europe and the Levant, Oct. 11, 1856—May 6, 1857, by Herman Melville* (Princeton, 1955). The nature of this journal and my use of it are clearly explained in my text; I have not footnoted the many quotations from the journal because the context makes this unnecessary. I have followed Melville's spelling and punctuation as found in the Horsford edition.

1. *Log* II, 521. Letter from Lemuel Shaw to Samuel Shaw, Boston, 1 September 1856, extracted from the Papers of the Shaw Family. Reprinted by permission of the Massachusetts Historical Society, Boston, Mass.

2. *Log* II, 523. Extract quoted from Evert Duyckinck's diary, 1 October 1856, Papers of the Duyckinck Family. Reprinted by permission of the New York Public Library, New York, N.Y.

3. Detail from facsimile of Melville's passport, *Log* II, 524.

4. The details of Melville's visit to Hawthorne in Liverpool and the short quotations dealing with it are taken from Hawthorne's *The English Notebooks* edited by Randall Stewart (New York, 1941), pp. 433-37.

5. *Journal of a Visit to London and the Continent by Herman Melville*, edited by E. M. Metcalf (Cambridge, Mass., 1948), pp. 9–10.

6. Introduction to *Log* I, p. xvii.

7. Hawthorne, *The English Notebooks*, p. 437.

CHAPTER SIX

General sources: See notes for Chapter Five. All quotations from *Clarel* are taken from the superb Hendricks House edition (New York, 1960), edited by Walter E. Bezanson. Professor Bezanson has collated his text carefully with the original and has supplied more than adequate critical paraphernalia. As the original two volume edition put out in 1876 is extremely rare, the Bezanson edition has made *Clarel* available to today's scholar and general reader. Longer passages of *Clarel* are identified in my text by giving Part, Canto, and verse numbers for the opening of each quotation.

1. *Log* II, 786. Letter from Melville to James Billson, New York, 10 October 1884, Martin Collection of H. Bradley Martin, Jr., New York, N.Y.

2. *Log* II, 567. Letter from Augusta Melville to Peter Gansevoort, 7 April 1857, Papers and Library of the Melville Family. Reprinted by permission of the Harvard College Library.

3. *Log* II, 741. Letter from Elizabeth Melville to her stepmother, 9 March 1875, Papers and Library of the Melville Family. Reprinted by permission of the Harvard College Library.

4. Howard C. Horsford in his introduction to *Journal of a Visit to Europe and the Levant*, p. 40.

5. Lewis Mumford, *Herman Melville* (New York, 1929), p. 308.

6. Walter Bezanson has indicated in his introduction and in his notes on *Clarel* many allusions to works on the Holy Land which Melville used in preparing *Clarel*.

CHAPTER SEVEN

Among the biographies of Mark Twain I have drawn most frequently from those by Albert Bigelow Paine (1912), DeLancey Ferguson (1943), and Justin Kaplan (1966). Among more specialized works I have found Paul Fatout's *Mark Twain on the Lecture Circuit* (Bloomington, Indiana, 1960) helpful in discussing Mark Twain's lectures based on his Holy Land visit. I have used Leon Dickinson's unpublished doctoral thesis "Mark Twain's *Innocents Abroad*: its Origins, Composition, and Popularity" (University of Chicago, 1945) and Dewey Ganzel's *Mark Twain Abroad: the Cruise of the "Quaker City"* (Chicago, 1968) principally in checking my own conclusions concerning Mark Twain's visit to the Holy Land and his use of that experience in writing *The Innocents Abroad*.

I have gone through much material in the Mark Twain Papers at the University of California, Berkeley, giving particular attention to his note-books compiled in the Levant; many omissions from these notebooks were made by A. B. Paine in his *Mark Twain's Notebook* (New York, 1935), and I found some of these entries pertinent to this study. The complete notebooks are now about to be published by the University of California Press under the title *Mark Twain's Notebooks and Journals*, edited by Frederick Anderson, Michael B. Frank and Kenneth M. Anderson. I have referred to the location of the items I have used by giving the page number of the forthcoming work; Mr. Anderson has kindly allowed me to examine the page proofs for this purpose. Such other unpublished material as I have used from the Mark Twain Papers (MTP) is identified in the notes.

Of very great value has been *Traveling with the Innocents Abroad*, edited by Daniel McKeithan, copyright 1958 by the University of Oklahoma Press. In this volume Professor McKeithan has republished all of Mark Twain's correspondence which appeared in the San Francisco *Daily Alta California*, together with the few letters which appeared in the *New York Tribune* and *New York Herald*, which deal with the *Quaker City* excursion. He has also provided an informative introduction and a complete collation of the newspaper letters with *The Innocents Abroad*. Much of the material in this chapter is taken from the *Alta California* correspondence; in footnoting the quotations I have given both the original date of publication of the letter and the page in McKeithan where it can be found. I have used the short title: *Alta* (date), McK, p.—.

1. *Mark Twain's Letters*, ed. A. B. Paine, I (New York, 1917), 126. MT to his mother, New York, 1 June 1867.

2. Inscription by Mark Twain in Griswold's *Sixty Years with the Plymouth Church*. MTP.

3. *Alta, 4 December 1867*. McK, pp. 183–84.

4. *Alta*, 1 December 1867. McK, p. 180.

5. *Alta*, 29 December 1867. McK, p. 205.

6. See Alphonse de Lamartine, *A Pilgrimage to the Holy Land*, I (London, 1835), p. 364.

7. Mark Twain's notebook as quoted in *The Innocents Abroad*, 1869, pp. 454–55.

8. *Alta*, 8 December 1867. McK, pp. 188–89.

9. *New York Tribune*, 9 November 1867. McK, p. 211.

10. Ibid., McK, pp. 211–13.

11. *Mark Twain's Notebooks and Journals* I (Berkeley, 1974), 432. MTP Notebook 9, p. 44.

12. *Journal Letters of Emily A. Severance* (Cleveland, 1938), p. 173.

13. *Alta*, 16 February 1868. McK, p. 252.

14. *Alta*, 26 January 1868. McK, pp. 232–33.

15. *Alta*, 2 February 1868. McK, p. 239.

16. *Alta*, 5 January 1868. McK, p. 217.

17. *Alta*, 9 February 1868. McK, p. 248.

18. *Alta*, 17 May 1868. McK, p. 301.

19. *Mark Twain's Notebooks and Journals*, p. 438. MTP Notebook 9, p. 50.

20. Ibid., p. 368. MTP Notebook 8, p. 40.

21. *Alta*, 15 March 1868. McK, pp. 274–76.

22. *Alta*, 8 March 1868. McK, p. 271. See interesting article by Alexander E. Jones titled "Mark Twain and Freemasonry" in *American Literature* 26 (Nov. 1964), 363 ff. which puts forward the theory that Mark Twain considered Godfrey De Bouillon a fellow Freemason and hence was much interested in his sword and the Cedar of Lebanon he had planted outside the walls of Jerusalem.

23. *Alta*, 15 March 1868. McK, pp. 273–74.

24. *Alta*, 26 April 1868. McK, pp. 291–92.

25. *Mark Twain's Notebooks and Journals*, p. 439. MTP Notebook 9, p. 51.

26. *The Innocents Abroad* (Hartford, Conn., 1869), p. 597.

27. Ibid., p. 599.

28. *Alta*, 17 May 1868. McK, p. 300.

29. *Mark Twain's Notebook*, ed. A. B. Paine (New York, 1935), p. 101. A. E. Jones in "Mark Twain and Freemasonry," says that Mark Twain had his cedar bough made into a gavel and sent it to the Polar Star Lodge, his mother lodge in St. Louis, where it is cherished to this day.

30. Dewey Ganzel lists these relics in his *Mark Twain Abroad* (Chicago, 1968), p. 252.

31. *Mark Twain's Notebooks and Journals*, p. 444. MTP Notebook 9, p. 56.

32. Ibid., p. 451. MTP Notebook 9, p. 60.

CHAPTER EIGHT

General sources: See notes for Chapter Seven. Quotations from *The Innocents Abroad* are taken from the first edition published in Hartford, Connecticut in 1869.

1. The fragments of this play are found in MTP—DV, 134. They have been published in Appendix A of Ganzel's *Mark Twain Abroad*, pp. 310–18.

2. *Alta*, 8 January 1868. McK, p. 311. The *New York Herald* letter appeared on 20 November 1867, (see McK, pp. 313–319) and was included by Mark Twain in *The Innocents Abroad*, pp. 644–47 with a few minor changes.

3. *Mark Twain's Letters,* I, 142–43. MT to his mother and sister, Washington, D.C., 8 January 1868.

4. Ibid., I, 144. MT to his mother and sister, Washington, D.C., 9 January 1868.

5. Quoted in Paul Fatout, *Mark Twain on the Lecture Circuit,* p. 90.

6. *Roughing It* (Hartford, Conn., 1872), pp. 57–59.

7. See *Mark Twain's Letters,* I. MT to family, Constantinople, 1 September 1867.

8. *Alta,* 18 October 1867. McK, p. 105. Also see *Mark Twain, Business Man,* ed. by Samuel C. Webster (Boston, 1946), p. 96 for use of head in family.

9. *Mark Twain's Speeches* (New York, 1923), p. 21.

10. *Mark Twain's Letters to his Publishers* (Berkeley, 1967), p. 12. MT to Elisha Bliss, Washington, 2 December 1867.

11. Ibid., p. 20. MT to Elisha Bliss, Elmira, 20 April 1869.

12. *Mark Twain's Autobiography,* ed. A. B. Paine, I (New York, 1924), pp. 245–46.

13. Passim. This discussion of Mark Twain's revision of the *Alta* letters in writing *The Innocents Abroad* is taken almost verbatim from an unpublished paper which I read to the Pacific Coast Philological Association in 1940. In preparing it I used the University of California, Berkeley, file of the *Alta.* Since then DeLancey Ferguson has treated the subject in much shorter form in his *Mark Twain: Man and Legend* (Indianapolis, 1943), pp. 121–23; and Leon T. Dickinson has published a detailed analysis of the revisions in "Mark Twain's Revisions in writing *The Innocents Abroad,*" *American Literature,* 19 (May 1947), 139–57. D. M. McKeithan in *Traveling with the Innocents Abroad,* has taken up the matter in his introduction and has provided notes of his collation after each newspaper letter so that others could make their own interpretations of Mark Twain's revision methods.

14. *Mark Twain to Mrs. Fairbanks* (San Marino, Calif., 1949), pp. 24. New York, 10 March 1868.

15. Justin Kaplan, *Mr. Clemens and Mark Twain* (New York, 1966), p. 67.

16. For Mark Twain's creation and development of Mr. Brown, see *Mark Twain's Letters from the Sandwich Islands,* ed. by George Ezra Dane (San Francisco, 1937) and *Mark Twain's Travels with Mr. Brown,* ed. by Franklin Walker and George Ezra Dane (New York, 1940).

17. The bathing scene is in *Alta,* 3 November 1867. McK, pp. 139–40.

18. *Overland Monthly* IV (January 1870), 100–1.

19. *Mark Twain's Letters to his Publishers,* p. 28. MT to Elisha Bliss, [Buffalo], 3 September 1869.

20. William C. Prime, *Tent Life in the Holy Land* (New York, 1865), p. 142.

21. *Alta*, 1 March 1868. McK, p. 265.

22. *Mark Twain in Eruption*, ed. by Bernard De Voto, p. 349. Mark Twain has much more to say about Prime in this passage, some of it commendatory.

23. *The Innocents Abroad*, p. 532.

24. Prime, *Tent Life*, p. 60, echoed in *The Innocents Abroad*, p. 567. This thrust at Prime was pointed out by Leon T. Dickinson in his "Mark Twain's Revisions in writing *The Innocents Abroad*," p. 156.

25. Quoted in Justin Kaplan, *Mr. Clemens and Mark Twain*, p. 74.

26. John Franklin Swift, *Going to Jericho* (San Francisco, 1868), passim.

27. *Overland Monthly*, 1 (July 1868), 101.

28. Unpublished fragment on Israelites, MTP, file DV, 134.

29. *Alta*, 16 February 1868. McK, p. 250.

30. The two passages quoted are from unpublished fragment, MTP, file DV, 134.

31. *Mark Twain's Autobiography*, II, 112.

32. Albert Bigelow Paine, *Mark Twain*, I (New York, 1912), pp. 379–80.

33. Quoted by Dixon Wecter in his introduction to *Mark Twain to Mrs. Fairbanks*, pp. xxvi, f.n. 2.

34. *Mark Twain's Letters to his Publishers*, p. 21. MT to Elisha Bliss, Elmira, 29 April 1869.

35. Mark Twain, *Following the Equator* (Hartford, Conn., 1897), p. 578.

36. *Mark Twain to Mrs. Fairbanks*, pp. 59–60. Lansing, Mich., 24 December 1868.

37. *The Innocents Abroad*, pp. 607–8.

38. Ibid., p. 608.

39. Melville's *Journal of a Visit to Europe and the Levant*, p. 154.

40. *Yusef*, p. 360.

41. Introduction to *Yusef*, p. iv.